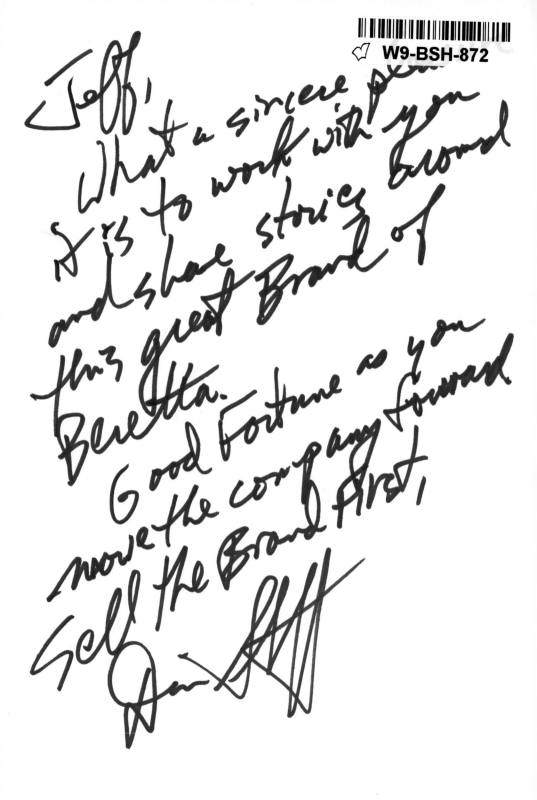

Jeff,
What a sincere pleasure
it is to work with you
and share stories around
this great Brand of
Beretta.
Good Fortune as you
move the company forward.
Sell the Brand first,
Dan [signature]

W9-BSH-872

Praise for *Sell the Brand First*

"*Sell the Brand First* can cure a positioning malady for every salesperson, as it provides an active strategy to clearly differentiate the brand."
—H. C. Zachry, CEO, Zachry Associates, Inc.

"Brand selling is the most difficult challenge for a company and its marketers. In *Sell the Brand First*, Dan Stiff has done a remarkable job of constructing a working model that draws on facts, experiences and creative ideas. Dan's approach outlines a winning blueprint for any business, be it a consumer or industrial brand."
—Paul E. Fulchino, Chairman, President & CEO,
Aviall Services, Inc.

"*Sell the Brand First* hits the bull's-eye for how sales and marketing professionals will have to change in order to excel in the next 20 years. The concept of your 'Brand Pillars' being your lead punch in every customer interaction is powerfully and persuasively delivered by the author. This book should be required reading for every sales, marketing, and C-level executive."
—T. Tracy Bilbrough, President & CEO, Juno Lighting Group,
a division of the Schneider Electric/Square D company

"By using the 'brand staircase' model, it assures you that the entire organization is focused first and foremost on the brand. When we '*Sell the Brand First*' it eliminates the need to sell up, and minimizes chances for objections. It changed our entire sales approach and philosophy to premium brand selling."
—Michael Babula, President & CEO, Franke/Kindred USA

"Dan Stiff has created a very practical and cutting-edge brand staircase that helps improve brand value selling techniques within a sales organization. The ability to reinforce and establish the value of your brand in the marketplace not only reduces SG&A cost, but it builds the overall brand equity in a company."
—Todd P. Barth, Senior Vice President and General Manager,
Paint Sundry Brands, a business unit of the Sherwin-Williams company

"Brands are the synthesis of a company's value proposition. Millions of dollars and years are invested building brands. Yet the full return on brand investment is not realized unless everyone in the organization, starting with sales, understands how to create value using 'brand' in every transaction. Brand Selling unleashes your most valuable asset, creating a powerful competitive advantage that increases sales and profits, expands market share, improves negotiations and enhances customer loyalty. When you consider ROI, *Sell the Brand First* should be at the top of your reading list."
—Jim Paterson, Senior Vice President of Sales & Marketing,
D&D Technologies, USA

"Dan Stiff's book provides smaller businesses with access to the kind of strategic sales thinking and training that is typically beyond their reach. The lessons learned can provide a competitive advantage that offsets increasing pressure on margins that could haunt any company."
—Richard C. Faint, Jr., serial entrepreneur & President, ARRRK Properties

"*Sell the Brand First* is a new street smart approach to presenting your product. This mindset keeps your best asset in the forefront, the brand. I wish this book had been around in 1980 when I started my company—who knows where our Brand and franchises would be today!"
— J. Douglas Scheidt, Jr., Founder/President, Shepherd's Guide USA, Inc.

"Dan Stiff's *Sell the Brand First* is destined to create a paradigm shift in the burgeoning literature of sales training. This is a powerful message for anyone in the sales and marketing business, and I encourage sales leaders of all experience levels to read and apply the lessons learned."
— James T. Quinn, Senior Vice President, Sales and Marketing, Aviall Services, Inc.

"In *Sell the Brand First*, Dan Stiff brings the 'power of the brand' to the forefront of the selling process. By reorienting the salesperson's approach with the Brand Staircase, it creates a new way to think and sell value producing very positive results."
— Mary Distl, Director of Sales, Globe Union Services

"Dan's model of selling your brand as an *experience* has gone beyond the traditional selling methods of features, benefits and price. His approach leads all of us into selling the entire value of your company and what you stand for, not just selling product anymore. Anyone who considers themselves in sales as a profession would benefit from *Sell the Brand First*."
— G. Patrick McDonald, Vice President, Sales & Marketing, Beretta USA Corp.

"Knowing how to move from Intuitive to Intentional in terms of selling your brand is critical in today's Business to Business setting. Dan Stiff captures this in his book *Sell the Brand First* and gives us the tools to make this important transition."
— John Allenbach, President, Danaher Tool Group, Professional Tool Division/Delta Consolidated

"WOW! This book is not what you might perceive. A wake up call for the experienced sales person! If you think your company participates in a commodity market, think again! Reverse the way you approach a sales call utilizing the Brand staircase method and watch your sales climb!"
— Keith G. Steuer, Vice President of Sales, RSI Home Products

"To have the concept of selling framed in a way that is less focused on conquering was one of the most important elements of the book. We should sell what people really need and this book helps us do that."
— Lily M. Kelly-Radford, Ph.D., Executive Vice President, Global Leadership Development, The Center for Creative Leadership

SELL THE BRAND FIRST

HOW TO SELL YOUR BRAND AND CREATE LASTING CUSTOMER LOYALTY

DAN STIFF

McGraw-Hill

New York   Chicago   San Francisco   Lisbon   London
Madrid   Mexico City   Milan   New Delhi   San Juan
Seoul   Singapore   Sydney   Toronto

The McGraw·Hill Companies

Copyright © 2006 by Dan Stiff. All rights reserved. Printed in the United States of America. Except as permitted under the United States Copyright Act of 1976, no part of this publication may be reproduced or distributed in any form or by any means, or stored in a database or retrieval system, without the prior written permission of the publisher.

1 2 3 4 5 6 7 8 9 0 DOC/DOC 0 9 8 7 6

ISBN 0-07-147042-5

This publication is designed to provide accurate and authoritative information in regard to the subject matter covered. It is sold with the understanding that the publisher is not engaged in rendering legal, accounting, or other professional service. If legal advice or other expert assistance is required, the services of a competent professional person should be sought.

> —*From a declaration of principles jointly adopted by a committee of the American Bar Association and a committee of publishers.*

McGraw-Hill books are available at special quantity discounts to use as premiums and sales promotions, or for use in corporate training programs. For more information, please write to the Director of Special Sales, McGraw-Hill Professional, Two Penn Plaza, New York, NY 10121-2298. Or contact your local bookstore.

 This book is printed on recycled acid-free paper containing a minimum of 50% recycled, de-inked fiber.

Library of Congress Cataloging-in-Publication Data

Stiff, Dan.
    Sell the brand first : how to sell your brand and create lasting customer loyalty / by Dan Stiff.
        p.   cm.
    ISBN 0-07-147042-5 (alk. paper)
    1. Brand name products—Marketing.   2. Customer relations.   3. Consumer satisfaction.   4. Customer loyalty.   5. Brand name products—Social aspects.
I. Title.

HD69.B7S75 2006
658.8'27—dc22   2006000695

To my parents, Al and Vivian Stiff

Dad, thanks for your living example of courage.
You taught me dedication, honesty, and hard work—
all from a wheelchair. I know you're smiling now.

Mom, you thrived through 10 kids.
You showed me how to love unconditionally,
forgive and move on, and laugh with life.

Thank you both for beating the odds
and leading us by example.

CONTENTS

ACKNOWLEDGMENTS

You cannot write from experience unless you have been fortunate enough to have had good experiences. You can share what you know only when your past environments have allowed you to learn invaluable lessons. Surely, you can have the confidence to write only when countless people have encouraged you to do so. Many people have contributed greatly to *Sell the Brand First*—whether they know it or not. I am grateful and blessed by your time, efforts, examples, thoughts, and prayers. To the following teams and colleagues:

Corporate Team

The Black & Decker Corporation and DeWALT—the lessons I learned while waving the company flag were invaluable. When you are able to work, learn, play, and give back freely in a strong leadership, marketing, and sales environment, it is much easier to claim the Brand and sell it first. There are far too many people to thank within the sales and marketing organizations there, but suffice it to say that this book is theirs too.

NCR Corporation, which gave me my first glimpse of excellent sales training and grounded me in the importance of being a professional within the world of sales.

The Ken Blanchard Companies for providing me a great example of training with passion, showing me the importance of culture and the power of simple truths.

The Center for Creative Leadership for showing me the importance of feedback and "give-back" in leadership.

Executive and Sales Teams

Tracy Bilbrough—your uncompromising passion for Brands, insights into the trade business approach, and mentality of overdelivering on promises were great examples to live by. You immediately saw how this idea could affect the marketplace, and you fueled the dream.

Ron Foy—your support and early encouragement of the Brand Staircase and its underlying concepts made it easy not to compromise my beliefs. Your input on the business-to-consumer setting and ideas that impacted selling the Brand first helped the material come alive.

John Schiech—thank you for allowing Black & Decker/DeWALT to be put on public display in terms of its beliefs and Brands. You saw the potential for looking at a new way of selling and marketing the Brand, when it would have been easy to say, "We already have it figured out."

Jim Quinn—your willingness to get creative with the Brand and draw from your past experiences, yet allow me the freedom to drive new ideas and concepts opened unexpected doors. Your commitment to stay the course will always be remembered.

Todd Barth—your persistence, pursuit of excellence and clear understanding of the power behind selling the Brand has given me ideas, provided energy, and challenged my thinking along the way.

Jim Paterson—your belief that we had hit on something big with this concept kept my wheels turning and momentum going forward. You fueled the fire for understanding consumer Brands at retail in light of the invaluable role of the reseller.

Mike Babula—your viewpoints on crossover Brands within traditional channels of distribution created valuable insights to help demystify the most complex sales. Also, your passion for strong Brands within a real-world selling environment was contagious.

Rich Teza, Cris Gross, and Charlie Elkins—your friendships, long-term commitment, and willingness to be creative risk takers around your Brand allowed me to dream beyond what you could imagine. You have also set a standard of excellence in collaboration that other sales and marketing teams will be hard pressed to match.

Rich Stam, Michael Dwyer, and Charlie Stover—your excitement about Brand selling, confirmation of the topics in multiple channels within your real world, and willingness to bring together new reinforcement ideas for the future have made it easy to build a strong infrastructure for the future.

Creative Team

Donya Dickerson at McGraw-Hill—you were able to see the gem that this book could become, with an eye for editing the important things, not the mundane. Thanks for believing in the unique approach and fresh ideas within this book. Your support and encouragement have been instrumental.

Marcia Horowitz—you brought a fresh eye to the book, a clear understanding of the publishing and writing process, and the ability to chide me, challenge me, and congratulate me at the appropriate moments. Your editing left me laughing at myself while maintaining a clear voice.

Danny Flanagan of Zachry Associates—your graphics will be the visual cornerstone of this book. Your patience, persistence, and creativity will long be appreciated and remembered.

Jeff Warr of Zachry Associates—our brainstorming while on "the road to Abilene" feels like it was only yesterday. Your creative insights and cheerleading approach to Brand selling were a valued source of ideas and energy for me along the way.

My Colleagues

Sue Dunlap—you were there to verify and test the trade business model. Thanks for helping to crystallize, debate, and implement the core concepts in the classroom with the early adopters. You have believed when I was down, kept me going through some "brush fires," and helped me dream along the way.

Gary Connor, Greg Forte, and Todd Davisson—you have helped me forge ideas, and trained with me side by side. You listened to me harp on new ways of thinking and encouraged me to pursue this project.

My Local Team

Doug Scheidt—your business sense, insights, entrepreneurial spirit, and thoroughness left me thinking big about this project.

Geoff Miller—your encouragement, positive thinking, and sense of humor allowed me to believe in myself.

Peter Kirby—your curbside chats and business conversations over the years have been a significant "sanity check" for my ideas.

Joel Freeman—your encouragement as an author and your knowledge of publishing greatly reduced my anxiety and learning curves.

To my siblings—Kathy, Sue, Tim, Greg, Becky, Tony, and Penny . . . Robin and Mack. Growing up in the "Stiff Clan" taught me many lessons on life, including the value of belonging and the importance of believing in something bigger than yourself. Thank you all.

Matt and Adam—my boys. You have kept me focused on the importance of family while giving me the freedom to follow this passion.

Kim—my wife. You have put up with the schedule and roller-coaster ride of book writing. You have been dedicated, honest, encouraging, insightful, and tireless. Thanks for your cheerleading, love, and support.

To God—you have opened many unexpected doors. I would not be here without you.

FOREWORD

Whether you are businessperson or a consumer, you never fully appreciate how valuable a strong Brand is unless you have experienced one of lesser value. Dan Stiff and I grew up in a world where we had an outstanding consumer products Brand at Black & Decker. However, because of that consumer image, we struggled as a company to become a relevant Brand choice for the professional contractor. Even when our product was superior, it was tough for us to sell against another strong competitive Brand in the professional marketplace. After all, what self-respecting contractor is going to walk onto a job site with a circular saw that has the same Brand name as his wife's hair dryer? All of the success that we have subsequently achieved with DeWALT started from that simple dilemma.

Intuitively, we can all recognize how important a strong Brand is to an organization's success. Brand gives a company its personality; it becomes the rallying point around which Sales, Marketing, and the entire organization work together. Brand becomes a source of pride for employees and customers by making them members of an elite club that uses the Brand. So, knowing all of this, why don't we push our selling organizations to fully capitalize on that strength? Until now, the answer probably has been that Management assumes that Sales is selling the Brand, while Sales assumes that Management and Marketing are taking care of the Brand. Another possibility is that we don't consciously make the connection between the Brand and sales at all, or that we simply don't know how to sell the Brand. Now, with *Sell the Brand First*, we have a great tool to allow us to bridge this knowledge gap.

Sell the Brand First does an outstanding job of introducing the insightful yet logical notion of leading with your Brand, and then weaving this concept into a tried-and-true selling process that can be quickly understood and implemented by your sales force.

Let's face it, even great companies sometimes make it hard for their sales team to perform well. They unconsciously create self-imposed roadblocks like price increases, product quality problems, and sales personnel changes. Brand, standing as the surrogate for the strong company behind it, can be the long-term stabilizing force that provides continuity through these challenging times and events. Selling your Brand is not something to pull out only when times get tough. Instead, it has to start from day one, constantly reinforcing the idea that a great brand represents a great company, one that may not win every battle, but in the long run has the strategy to win the war.

Dan Stiff is uniquely qualified to be an authority on Brand selling. He began his career as a salesman, selling strong brands and competing against them. He taught other salespeople similar lessons as a manager, and then was promoted to run our training organization, where he led a training effort that drove the concept of cherishing and leveraging the Brand into marketplace success. Since then, he has crystallized these ideas across multiple industries and now has effectively captured the key concepts in this book for other companies to utilize. I believe that if sales professionals and leaders across industries read this and apply it, they will perform at a higher level and with more consistency than they could in the past, thus having a positive impact on their organization's future growth.

John Schiech
President, DeWALT Professional Products
A Division of Black & Decker

INTRODUCTION

All of us come to a moment of truth in our careers, a defining moment when our profession becomes clearer than ever because of what we've experienced in the trenches. You may have experienced this in your career, too—a moment when a stirring event changes your belief system, when a huge success spurs you on to new levels of performance, or when a subtle change in how you sell proves invaluable to your business. We all have at least one epiphany in our career.

My profession is selling, training, operations, and leadership. My moment of truth arrived when I least expected it—one day at lunch with a very good friend and business owner. I was sharing some observations that I had drawn from my experiences with key customers. These particular customers had been asking my sales consulting company for help in selling their Brand creatively. As I described some of the experiences I had encountered with many of these salespeople and their managers, we both noticed the same two themes surfacing:

- Most salespeople are taught how to sell their product or service, but not how to sell their Brand.
- Salespeople don't know how to insert Brand into their sales language to bring it alive for the buyer.

This awareness of these repeated behaviors, within organizations, in selling Brands launched me on a great adventure that has been both rewarding and challenging. I began to learn, document, and practice the fine art of Brand selling—and it is an art. My customers were my inspiration and my teachers. They taught me a great deal about the importance of selling the Brand—through their everyday sales experiences, their challenges, and their searching questions. In fact, over time

I have been able to develop a system of ideas and practices that those very same customers now use and find effective in their organizations. They are now Brand sellers.

As I look back at my past selling and leadership experiences, it has become increasingly clear that salespeople need to *sell* the Brand, and that they need to be taught how to do it. While I was conducting some of the initial workshops on Brand selling, numerous participants approached me saying that these ideas should be written down. Over time, I resolved to share in a book what I had learned about this new and successful practice of Brand selling. My intent here is to help you, whether you are a salesperson in a retail store, a salesperson calling on a wholesale distributor, or a sales manager leading the charge, to understand the power and satisfaction of selling the Brand first.

How This Book Is Different

As I was sharing with my friend the discovery of the simple reality that salespeople are not encouraged to sell the Brand, it struck both of us that there is actually little, if anything, out there in print on how to sell a Brand. Why not? Probably for the same reasons that salespeople don't sell the Brand—because they believe that the Brand is in Marketing's territory, and, frankly, it just doesn't hit their "sales radar." However, it seemed obvious to us that knowing the value of the Brand and using it as a sales lever can actually have long-term positive effects on a company's reputation and marketplace position. Sure there are many books out there on how to market a Brand or how to create a catchy slogan to be the rallying cry for a product or ad campaign. There are books on how to

- Build Brand strategy.
- Build Brand allegiance.
- Take advantage of Brand touchpoints.
- Add or assess Brand value.
- Create Brand power.
- Launch a Brand into the marketplace.
- Operationalize the Brand.
- Develop a Brand metrics system.
- Spend the Brand advertising budget.
- Develop a media plan for the biggest Brand impact.

These are all valid and important topics. Nevertheless, I would argue that they are looking at Brands from other perspectives: inside the company boardroom, battles within the marketing "war room," or through the eyes of the advertising agency. But the best set of eyes on this topic has been largely ignored—that of the salesperson. In other words, there was nothing on how to *sell* a Brand and keep it simple, and also nothing on how to build on the marketer's efforts to leverage a Brand's identity or a Brand's positioning in the marketplace at the point where the "Brand message" really matters the most—during conversations with the customer. What's more, because there is nothing on how to sell the Brand, there is also nothing on how to build the company's culture around a Brand, with all employees becoming stakeholders in the process.

This book fixes that problem. It is directed to the salesperson and his issues, challenges, and rewards when selling the Brand. It is straight talk from me to you on Brand selling. It delivers concepts and tools that will serve the entire sales profession. I introduce here a simple Brand selling model called the *Brand Staircase* that explains how to sell the Brand where all of us routinely buy the Brand—at the consumer level. Later on, the book expands and broadens this concept by outlining implications for selling to the professional buyer in a business-to-business setting.

The Core Premises of This Book

In this book, you will find the expression of these simple beliefs:

- Salespeople need to discover Brand as a foundational sales tool and sell it first.
- Salespeople need to put the Brand into their sales language in order to leverage their Brand's strength in the marketplace.
- Brands are very personal in nature, and we experience them daily. Our Brand preferences and selections (as buyers) are affected by personal interactions with salespeople.
- Every Brand has some inherent value. The key is to find that value and sell from it.

After watching many companies spend millions building powerful consumer Brands and business-to-business Brands, one big problem became obvious: they failed to maximize their investment and educate their employees, customers, and, most importantly, salespeople on the power of their Brand and how to sell the Brand first.

Many experienced salespeople simply adopt the marketing department's version of their Brand and do not make it their own and leverage it as part of their sales language. In fact, salespeople often sell everything but the Brand. They will sell on price, delivery, product quality, features, benefits, and warranty, but seldom do they speak to what the Brand means to the buyer in terms of her lifestyle, her experiences, and even her emotional connection to the Brand. At best, they seem to take their Brand for granted, and could not tell you why people buy the Brand even if you doubled their bonus payout. (Now, for most salespeople, that's some serious neglect!)

When salespeople can't sell something, they may revert to complaints like, "The price isn't right," "We don't have the right products to sell," or "The warranty isn't good enough" (to name a few). They act as *Brand imposters* because of their neglect of the Brand. Instead, they should be *Brand ambassadors*, so aligned with the Brand that it might as well be "Branded" on their foreheads to signify their allegiance. They should be so committed to the Brand that when competitive salespeople are crying the wrong price or wrong product woes, they are busy selling the experience of their Brand, the connection to their Brand, or the affiliation with their Brand.

The myopic view of Brand in most sales organizations needs to change. Companies, leaders, and salespeople are seriously underselling their Brands.

In this book, I attempt to change that view. The book provides a system of ideas and a set of actions that will help the individual salesperson in the business-to-consumer setting and the corporate salesperson in the business-to-business setting.

In Part 1, we address the importance of Brands. How many of us, consciously or unconsciously, make major purchasing decisions based on Brand? It is hard to fully grasp the scope and impact of current Brand messages in our daily lives. We also discuss the importance of developing what I call *Brand language*. As if he were in a foreign country, the salesperson has to learn another language to be able to communicate effectively.

Part 2 speaks of a model called the *Buyer Stair-Step*, which highlights the key components buyers consider when purchasing products. The focus then turns to the Brand, and you are introduced to the *Brand Staircase*. These chapters provide tools for the salesperson, examples from real life, and lots of good advice from experienced Brand sellers.

Part 3 discusses the very important areas of the internal landscape of both buyers and sellers during a sales interaction. Mindset and motives are introduced, and we discuss why people buy and the importance of migrating the buyer from his current mindset to a Brand mindset.

Part 4 focuses on the business-to-consumer setting. It identifies the importance of the buyers' lifestyle choices and the emotional receptors of buyers that could connect them with the Brand. We also discuss the *Brand Rules of Engagement* and the need to ask questions. We walk through proven methods, exercises, and action steps on how to migrate the buyer toward Brand.

In Part 5, we build on the foundation developed in the business-to-consumer section, and provide additional ways to move buyers toward Brand in a business-to-business context. Here we focus on the differences in selling to a professional buyer in the trades by identifying your company's *Brand pillars*. Again, proven tools are provided.

Finally, Part 6 contains a discussion that is relevant to organizations: How can Brand selling become part of the culture? What do they need to do to help their salespeople become familiar with the concept and the language?

Who Should Read This Book and Why

This book is by an experienced salesperson for experienced salespeople. Yet, to the astute student of the Brand in any organization, it will quickly become obvious that this book has widespread application beyond the sales and marketing teams. It is useful to senior management and those in operations, manufacturing, distribution, customer service, logistics, and supply-chain management. It is useful for any major decision maker within an organization. As a matter of fact, if the sales organization embraces Brand selling and the rest of the organization does not, then the effort will have less of an impact. Accordingly, this concept is a practical approach to selling the Brand and building a companywide Brand culture.

The book is written in a pragmatic, hard-hitting fashion that salespeople, business owners, and senior executives alike can easily absorb. It illustrates key teaching points through numerous case studies, proven personal selling experiences, anecdotes, and common Brand examples in the marketplace. Through corporate examples and other practices, the chapters will also illustrate how organizations can effectively build a Brand culture.

The practical, hands-on approach carried throughout the book comes from nearly 30 years of corporate experience selling with NCR Corporation, Black & Decker, DeWALT, and LPD Inc. to consumers and professional buyers. I have represented great Brands and competed against great Brands. I have sold on the street, am a practitioner, and understand the issues and problems facing salespeople and their leaders today.

Training, coaching, and developing salespeople was my focus while I was running the training organization at Black & Decker / DeWALT. In addition, I have mentored and counseled sales leaders and executives throughout my career. In the last six years, while delivering custom workshops to LPD Inc. clients, I have seen these sales mindsets and skill sets come alive. LPD Inc., founded in 1999, develops and delivers customized workshops to thousands of participants on the topics of leadership, sales performance, and development of people. We engage the customer with a specialized approach to its issues and how the Brand affects the culture. In particular, the customers who have taken the Brand selling workshop have confirmed that the topic is on target, hard-hitting, practical, unique, and transferable across industries. This book supports and adds value to what has been learned in customer workshops and from selling experiences in the field. Should you desire more information on these business applications, refer to the section About the Author at the back of this book.

Lastly, this book will supplement the good skill sets that you have learned from sales processes, training workshops, and good sales coaches. It may even change the way you look at selling, operations, or your culture for the better, and permanently. My hope and dream for this book is that it will help people sell the Brand first and benefit personally, professionally, and financially from what they learn.

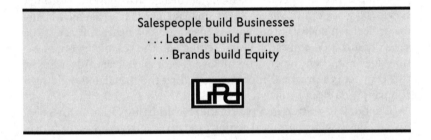

Salespeople build Businesses
. . . Leaders build Futures
. . . Brands build Equity

SELL THE BRAND FIRST

PART 1

IT'S ALL ABOUT
THE BRAND

CHAPTER 1

THE IMPORTANCE OF BRANDS

T wo simple statements describe the foundation of this book:

1. Brands are more prominent than ever for the buyer.
2. Because Brands are so prominent in the sales interaction, salespeople must learn how to speak *Brand language* and sell the Brand first.

There has been a revolution in the way in which buyers perceive and use Brands in their buying decisions. Chapter 1 describes this phenomenon and speaks to the reasons that it has occurred. The premise here is that you will understand the importance of developing Brand language if you understand the fundamentals of Brand. In addition, this chapter introduces an important concept that is interwoven throughout this book: the emotional components of Brand sensitivity. I also highlight what the typical salesperson is missing by not recognizing the importance of addressing Brand awareness.

The Branded Society

We live in a Branded society. What does this mean? It means that our families, our jobs, our careers, and even the larger society we live in are all affected by the Brands we buy, sell, and experience. We are in love with Brands. Look around your house. Walk into any room. Chances are you will quickly identify more than a dozen Brands. Brands have invaded every part of our lives—from the minute we arise until the end of the day, we live in and through Brands. They enter by way of the coffee we drink, the soft drinks we consume, the cereals we eat, the photos we take, the clothing we wear, the computers we use, the toys our kids play with, the music we listen to, the windows we peer through, the doors we walk through, and the cars or trucks we drive every day.

In fact, over the last 25 years or so, we have become ever more conscious of Brands. We are literally swimming in a Brand-sensitive culture where people's buying decisions are much more likely to be influenced by Brands than ever before. It's not that buyers suddenly "woke up" to Brands. Our parents knew about Brands, and they often would save their money to buy an RCA TV set or all-wood Hitchcock kitchen furniture. But what I am talking about here is the huge rise in the buying public's awareness of Brands and the impact that Brands have on buyers' behavior. As I said earlier, we are surrounded by them.

In their book *Trading Up*, authors Michael J. Silverstein and Neil Fiske from Boston Consulting Group discuss the demographics and changes that are having a critical impact on Brand awareness. According to them, "These shifts in our society have given American consumers greater purchasing power, consumer knowledge, and a broader range of goods to buy. They feel excited by the possibilities and want to experience as much of life as they can. They aspire to live well and enjoy themselves, be healthy, and achieve prosperity for themselves and their families" (p. 43).

Several factors have contributed to this recent upsurge in Brand sensitivity, and it's important to examine each of them.

Globalization

Many people worldwide are aware of and make daily use of products that once were known only in North America and other parts of the Western world. For instance, Nike made millions on its footwear campaign by initially using the image of Michael Jordan and connecting that image to an already familiar product—athletic shoes. Now, people from Saudi Arabia to Iceland respond to appeals to buy athletic gear endorsed by Michael Jordan. Nike continues to choose athletes to drive its Brand globally with this endorsement strategy. As Silverstein and Fiske say,

> The middle-market consumer of today is better educated, more sophisticated, better traveled, more adventurous, and more discerning than ever before. . . . In 1970, three million Americans visited Europe; eleven million visited in 2000. And their travels have exposed them to styles and tastes of other countries, particularly those of Europe. Well-traveled consumers seek out the tastes and styles they

discovered in foreign places in goods they can buy and enjoy at home (pp. 11–12).

The global traveler is inundated by Brands that have crossed over onto foreign soil—from Lipton Iced Tea adorning tabletops on the Seine River in Paris to Evian bottled water or Coca-Cola at the ruins of Pompeii in Italy. You need look no further than first graders in the United States playing with Legos from Denmark; or the backs of youngsters in Singapore, who sport the Colors of Benetton; or kids buying CDs at a Virgin records store on Oxford Street in London or at Times Square in New York.

People are looking for brands with an international flavor—brands that can span the globe. Paul Stobart from Interbrand Group PLC, who edited *Brand Power*, speaks to this global approach:

> *Brand power is a quality possessed only by the strongest international brands. A power brand is characterized by the distinctive nature of its brand personality, by the appeal and relevance of its image, by the consistency of its communication, by the integrity of its identity and by the fact that it has stood the test of time (p. 19).*

Companies are now able to trade more effectively on a global scale. Silverstein and Fiske say,

> *The easing of international trade barriers, the improving capabilities of global supply-chain-services providers, and the reduced cost of international shipping have enabled companies of almost every size to take advantage of foreign labor markets and put together and manage complex global networks for sourcing, manufacturing, assembling and distributing their goods (p. 13).*

We live in a branded society, it has gone global, and it's not going back.

Brands Now Often Trump Quality in Terms of Importance

Quality used to be a major factor for the buyer. Many of us remember shopping with our Dad, who would look for a "good-quality piece of wood furniture." His method would be to knock on the wood and listen for density, feel for sturdiness, and proclaim the item worthy or unworthy based on his quality test. Back then, the ultimate test of quality could be seen in the durability that the shopper for antiques looked for in furniture. Quality meant that a product would stand the test of time. In those days, people would buy a wood product rather than a plastic product because of its image of durability.

Of course, quality is still paramount, but over the past 25 years, many other factors have entered the buying decision, some of which relate to lifestyle and its relationship to Brand. Now, depending on their lifestyle, some people might choose a coffee table made out of marble by the world-renowned furniture designer Brancusi, a traditional solid wood table by Ethan Allen, or an end table made out of space-age plastic by IKEA.

Fortune magazine did two interesting studies in 2002 that were highlighted in the book *Building the Brand-Driven Business* by Scott M. Davis and Michael Dunn from Prophet, a management consulting company based in San Francisco. One study was a ranking of the "Best Companies to Work For." Another was the magazine's annual list of "Most Admired Companies." A number of familiar names made both lists: Southwest Airlines, Intel, Microsoft, Wal-Mart, FedEx, Charles Schwab, American Express, Goldman Sachs, and Harley-Davidson. According to the article's authors, the

> *Ranking is a function of eight key attributes that are directly tied to the way they conduct business internally and the overall performance of their business externally: In short, they are admired as a leader in innovation, in their financial soundness, for having strong employee talent, their use of corporate assets, the long-term investment value they provide, the level of social responsibility they embrace, the quality of management they have, and the level of quality their products and services provide. To make both lists means only one thing: These companies understand the power of their brands, both internally and externally (pp. 1–2).*

The interesting idea presented here was simple: quality has become just one good ingredient of a great Brand.

No matter what the product category, the point here is that Brand has increasingly become a factor above and beyond the quality of the products and services for many buyers.

Culture

Over the past few decades or so, people have become more prone to identify the products they buy with the values they espouse. For instance, those who are interested in environmental issues will be more likely to purchase a Toyota Prius for oil conservation; recyclable diapers from an environmentally friendly manufacturer like Procter & Gamble; or organic food from a grocer like Whole Foods, an organization that is sensitive to environmental and health concerns.

Our culture also promotes the Brand image of products and how they represent our lifestyles on an ongoing basis, through the clothes we wear and even the actors we admire (who often become a brand in and of themselves). The police character in the movie *Minority Report*, John Atherton, comes across many instances of Brand images as he navigates through the future in his quest toward crime prevention. We see a superhighway with Aquafina billboards. Atherton is then shown in a retail mall, where advertisements read the retinas of his eyes and pop up all over him to engage him personally. A road converges in the desert, which looks like a nod to the luxury car Lexus. Century 21 pitches homes. Atherton is then personally asked about having a Guinness. How about a needed vacation on American Express or going to a favorite store to purchase his favorite clothes? Sound far out? Probably not. This short movie example shows not only that Brands are in favor today as broad influencers of our buying decisions, but also that if the momentum of Brands continues, they will have an even more dramatic impact on us in the future. The bottom line is that our modern culture loves Brands and what they represent.

Disposable Income

There are many more two-income families today, resulting in more dollars available to spend. Higher-level Brands are more attractive when the household income level is in the upper ranges. In *Trading Up*, an excellent case is made for the growing trend of American consumers to "trade up" because, simply put, they have more disposable income to do so.

In *Trading Up*, authors Silverstein and Fiske deeply examine the changing trends in consumer spending and demographics that are allowing many middle-income consumers to spend discretionary money on luxury brands. They assert that

> *American households simply have more discretionary wealth available to be spent on premium goods than ever before. Real household income has risen for all Americans over the last thirty years, and it has risen fastest for the highest earners . . . as a result, those twenty-one million affluent households control nearly 60% of the nation's discretionary purchasing power. Home ownership has also contributed to consumers' increased wealth (p. 10).*

The book also discusses the new company leaders in Brands and what they are "doing right" from a marketing perspective to attract and keep these new "luxury buyers" who are choosing to trade up. It high-

lights a diverse group of industries and products focused on consumers. Examples are Kendall Jackson, BMW, Panera Bread, Calloway,
Victoria's Secret, and Sam Adams.

Do-It-Yourself

With the advent of home improvement stores like Home Depot and
Lowe's, many more buyers have become "do it yourselfers," who do
their own home-repair and building projects. Such hands-on customers make more purchases of home-related products and engage in self-
education. They are now more confident buyers of materials and are
more aware of the characteristics of the products they need to use.
This subsequently leads to a higher awareness of Brand. Interestingly,
even the stores that began the do-it-yourself (DIY) craze have bene-
fited from their own Brand expansion—and they have made their
stores the "destination location" for picking up any DIY need. To be
more specific, their store names have essentially become the Brand—
Home Depot and Lowe's are two great examples of the "store Brand
trend."

In addition, this do-it-yourself trend has migrated to other venues
beyond home improvement, such as photography (online photo shops
and photo Web sites), travel (expedia.com, hotels to go, online reserva-
tions), car shopping (Carmax, autotrader.com), and even the book
series addressed to dummies (*Accounting for Dummies, Cooking for
Dummies*). This list could go on and on. Obviously, because DIY shoppers are more educated about home repairs and capable of making buying decisions, their perception of the Brand becomes even more
significant in their decision process.

Communication

The Internet, with its search engines like Google and Yahoo, has
greatly enhanced people's access to products and information and has
provided a forum for making more informed buying decisions. eBay
has created a nearly cultlike following for allowing people to find
products and services on their own timetable and at their own
leisure, while at the same time legally gambling as they race to a purchasing deadline. I, and many others I have spoken with, find eBay a
virtual treasure trove for searching out Brands. When I want to
search for quality kitchen faucets, I punch in Kohler, an American
Brand, or Grohe, a European Brand, or Franke, a Swiss Brand, and
receive listings on these products in all price ranges and styles. Of
course, the trick here is that I have already been educated as to the
desirability of these Brands. Also, online bookstores have become a

virtual shopper's paradise for products. This easy access to information, education, and Brands has increased the likelihood that the buyer will consider a certain Brand as a primary focus in the buying decision.

All of these trends lead us to believe that Brands will increase in importance in the future. Indeed, we are in the midst of a Brand revolution—one that has tremendous momentum and potential. During any revolution, Brand or otherwise, there will be change. Change is inevitable; growth is optional. As salespeople, we must change and grow to have future success in the marketplace.

The Emotions of Brands

Even amidst these changes in a mass market with a vast amount of information available to us, our choices are still very personal, usually emotional, and often subliminal. The Brand pioneer Walter Landor of the Brand research company Landor St. James argued that, "Products are made in the factory, but Brands are created in the Mind."

Yet, as buyers, we still seem to be blind to the impact that Brands have on our daily lives and to the emotional connections we make with them. Even worse, salespeople are not sufficiently aware of the emotions of Brands. I've observed through my consulting that understanding this emotional component of Brand selling can be critical to a successful sale. To fully understand the impact of Brands, it is important to have an awareness of the emotions that go with them. That is why I introduce this concept early in this book and refer to it often in subsequent chapters.

Let me illustrate the impact of emotions by relating an interesting Brand awareness exercise from one of LPD Inc.'s workshops. Teams are handed a packet of information. The activity is designed to get participants to make decisions based on their own perspective and life experiences. Their instructions are to match images of cars and trucks to the labels that best represent each image. The labels are words like *innovation, safety, quality, built to last,* and so on.

When each team has completed its sorting and matching process, it presents its findings and explains why it chose the labels it did. Often teams are quite passionate about their choices—for example, "Volvo means safety to me," or "Jaguar means prestige." The fascinating thing is that in a group of 20 people, the five teams have always had some different labels (language) associated with the same vehicles. Why? We have found that we all experience Brands differently. We have different emotional ties to Brands. We connect to them for our own reasons. We also affiliate with the Brands that we choose to affiliate with. Again, the choices are very personal and emotional.

You will probably heartily agree that we live in a Branded society. You are also likely to agree that we all experience Brands in a very personal way. Right? So why should understanding the emotional component of Brands be hard? Well, I have found that what sounds simple is not always easy for salespeople to grasp.

The first time that I realized how emotional the attachment to the Brand can get for buyers was during my first sales role. I was selling minicomputers to commercial and industrial businesses. The mini-computer was a descendant of the first real interactive computers, originally built by IBM. It predated personal computers, including desktops, laptops, and personal digital assistants (PDAs). It also preceded menu-driven software like Windows, Lotus Notes, and any other version of user-friendly software. In those days, the computers were all trade brands and were used only for business applications. They were the size of modern-day desks. There was also an extensive training period required, and the sales cycle was long. It was not uncommon to call on a prospect for a year before you secured the deal.

I was working for a major computer manufacturer that was selling against IBM on a regular basis. In one instance, I was competing head to head on a $50,000 deal with an electrical wholesale distributor. The firm was currently an IBM user, and to my good fortune, IBM was back-ordered two years on the newer replacement model System 36—the very model that the customer would need to order. I had been working incredibly hard on this order, and I was convinced that the customer was ready to buy my product. Here's how I knew:

- We had a better product. It had more storage, it had a removable disk (a 10-MB disk that was as big as an extreme Frisbee), and it was $10,000 less expensive.
- The aesthetics were better—the styling and the look were better; the size was more compact—in short, the physical appearance was better.
- The quality was unbeatable and proven. The warranty was excellent, and the service support was proven and local.
- To top it off, the buyer had told me that he didn't even like the IBM salesman! I knew then that we had a better solution to meet the firm's needs.

The day came when I was to close the deal and reap the benefits of all of my hard work. So, when the closing moment came, I asked the question: "I believe we've covered everything, Bill. Can we go ahead and get this new system on order?" There was a hesitation on his end. I thought maybe he hadn't heard me. I was about ready to rephrase the question, when Bill answered, "I think I'm going to wait for the IBM System 36." I sat in stunned silence. All I could say was, "I'm sorry?" It was an invitation to him to repeat his statement. He did so, and, in mild shock, I went back and summarized the benefits of my system once again, hoping to convince him that his decision was a mistake, *especially if he had to wait two years for his new IBM system.*

He agreed with my summary, yet he stopped me halfway through. He then said something I would remember for the rest of my career: "Dan, I can't get fired for buying IBM." Wow! I can't get fired for buying IBM! He had made a totally emotional response to a logical decision. He was basing his decision on the trust and job security of buying a known commodity (IBM), and I was dead in the water. His decision was all *emotional.*

As a sales professional or a leader, can you relate to that story? Have you been beaten by a great Brand because of an emotional allegiance? Have you sold your heart out and lost in the end game because you didn't recognize the power of the Brand and the buyer's emotional connection to it? Most of us have been beaten under similar circumstances and could tell similar stories. The main reason for these defeats is our lack of ability to speak Brand language. We'll talk about that in the next chapter.

Key Points

Brands have achieved primary focus in the minds of buyers. Marketing has been so successful in conveying the idea of Brand strength that we now see Brands as an integrated part of our everyday lives. Many people cannot live without their Starbucks coffee or Nike athletic shoes. There are several reasons for the current prominence of Brands in our buying decisions:

1. Globalization of products has exposed more people worldwide to Brands.
2. Brands now often trump quality in terms of importance in the buying decision.
3. Culture or lifestyle has become a primary force in buying decisions.
4. More people have more disposable income, which leads to greater recognition and purchasing of Brands.
5. More people are involved in do-it-yourself projects, which raise awareness of many home-related Brands.

6. The Internet has exploded, bringing with it tremendous opportunity to identify and research Brands.

It is now essential for the salesperson to know the emotional components associated with Brands. In any buying interaction, it helps if the salesperson observes and knows how to use the knowledge about what emotions particular Brands evoke in the buyer and how emotions can often outweigh intellectual factors (logic) in making a buying decision.

SPEAKING BRAND LANGUAGE

What do I mean by "speaking Brand language?" Is this a new dialect that salespeople need to go back to school to learn? Is it a set of technical terms that go along with the profession? Is it a secret code? Not exactly. In fact, it's none of these. It is more of a mental process, in which the salesperson adapts his mindset to his knowledge of the buyer. The salesperson needs to discover what will make the buyer purchase a certain Brand, and in what circumstances. Once that knowledge is acquired, the salesperson adapts selling techniques to address it.

An analogy is helpful here. Have you ever traveled to another country on business or vacation? Did you find yourself struggling with the new language? How do you order food? How do you ask for directions? How do you find the bathroom? How do you exchange money? How do you know if you're being ripped off? Life quickly comes down to the basics, doesn't it, when the communication gets that tough?

Yes, we all feel the immediate language barrier. You also might feel some level of frustration as a result of your inability to communicate. That frustration can quickly lead to *distrust*. So, when you travel abroad, you quickly understand the need to communicate in order to survive.

What's interesting to me is watching other foreigners try to communicate across the language barrier. Usually one of three things happens:

- They make no attempt to communicate at all because they quickly get frustrated; instead, they resort to pointing their finger at entrees and grunting if they feel they are close. Their other reaction is to quit trying because it is too hard. Usually their lack of attempts leads to a similar response from their hosts.

- They make no attempt to learn the language prior to the trip, yet they act as if they know the language upon arrival on foreign soil. This foolishly gives them the right to make a futile language attempt, much like Chevy Chase did in the movie *European Vacation*, where he was so terrible at the language that he was ridiculed.
- They buy the little "Speedy French (or other language)" pamphlet that has the basic requests in the language phonetically displayed and at their fingertips. Before they arrive, they attempt to practice saying common phrases with their friends, relatives, and anyone who wants a good laugh. The good news about this attempt is that it seems to be the one that is most respected by people in the host country. The people you come in contact with relish the fact that you have made some kind of attempt to learn their language, get in their world, and honor their customs and traditions.

Now, there is a simple lesson in this for us as salespeople or sales managers. Salespeople currently find themselves "on foreign soil" when it comes to speaking Brand language. Too often, we make no attempt to connect with the buyers on their own soil with Brand language, instead giving up too soon because it's too hard. Too often, we act as if we have figured out what the buyers want by bludgeoning them with product knowledge—only to have them laugh at our futile attempts to get at their emotions and speak Brand language. Seldom have I encountered salespeople who have attempted to learn what Marketing is putting into the Brand, then practice what they've learned. They may have learned "Speedy Brand Language" well enough to speak that language with their buyers, which, though not enough, is a positive step forward.

This chapter points out that salespeople were not intentionally taught this Brand language as they grew up in sales. They were taught a different language, one that emphasized verbs and action words that facilitated efficient communication about products and their features and benefits. They need to get comfortable with a Brand language that speaks to emotions and uses adjectives like *prestige, aspiring, classy, timeless, craftsmanship, heritage, distinctive, peace of mind, exclusive, security*, and *discriminating*.

I remember when it hit me that Brand language was becoming more important in the sales equation. I was telling a current customer about this dilemma with speaking Brand language. I was sharing my experiences when he stopped me in the middle of a sentence, looked at me, and said, "You don't realize what you know." I was puzzled. He went on to explain that I had been around this type of thinking so long that it was already "in my bloodstream, in my language set." At the time, I kind of blew off the comment. Yet six months later, in a Brand selling workshop, it came back like a flood. As we were reviewing the need for salespeople to speak a new Brand language, I figuratively saw lightbulbs going off in salespeople's heads. Something that I had taken for granted in my language set, in my bloodstream, was a revelation for the salespeople in the group.

In the book *Emotional Branding* by Marc Gobé, CEO of D/G Worldwide, this thought is captured equally well from a buyer's perspective: "People's deepest emotions, aspirations, and dreams always need a new language that crystallizes their mind-set and sends their message to the world" (p. 136).

So as you enter this discussion on Brand language, you need to realize, as we saw in Chapter 1, that Brands have achieved primary focus in the mind of the buyer. Also, as a salesperson, ask yourself these questions:

- Am I adequately meeting the needs of a buyer who is now more than ever interested in looking at the attributes of Brand in considering a product?
- Am I typically emphasizing concepts that relate to Brand in my presentation to the buyer?
- Do I even have the words in my vocabulary to express the importance of Brands?

The simple answer to all of these questions is most often an emphatic no. There are reasons for this—I call them *language barriers*.

The Four Brand Language Barriers

In the nearly 30 years that I have been a salesperson and have coached and taught salespeople, I have heard four key reasons that salespeople struggle with speaking Brand language. (We will later label these as sales mindsets, but for now, let's look at them as *language barriers for salespeople*.)

1. "It's Marketing's job."
2. "Just give us the product or service to sell and let us go."
3. "We don't have a $XXX million dollar budget to 'build the Brand.'"
4. "We are taught to sell logically, not emotionally."

1. "It's Marketing's Job"

Most salespeople believe that controlling the product, the Brand, and its message in the marketplace is Marketing's role. Anyone who attended a Marketing 101 class in college has heard about the "Four

Ps" of Marketing—*product, price, placement (distribution),* and *promotion.* We are historically taught that

   a. The *product* or *product mix* is researched and established by Marketing.
   b. *Pricing* is generally set by Marketing in order to hit the correct "contribution margin" and marketplace price points.
   c. *Placement* is based on the channels that the company has chosen to sell in and the types of customers that are targeted by the product or service.
   d. *Promotion* is made up of the "promotional mix," which includes
   • *Advertising.* Spending money to promote a product or service in a mass appeal kind of way—through television, radio, newspaper, periodicals, and so on.
   • *Publicity.* Promoting the product or services through a department within the company whose main goal is public relations with the society at large.
   • *Direct marketing.* Mass mailings directly to potential end users of the products and services based on demographics, prior purchasing habits, and mailing lists.
   • *Internet.* A large variety of bundled vehicles that have a huge mass appeal with instant accessibility over worldwide computer networks on the Web.
   • *Sales promotion.* The ability to promote a product on a specific, targeted, and usually local basis.
   • *Personal selling.* The salesperson's interaction, relationship, and targeted sales efforts with individual customers on a daily and ongoing basis.

   Now, professional salespeople, before your eyes glaze over due to bad memories of marketing classes gone by, let me bring you forward to what your street smarts tell you about the four Ps today. The best way to get at this is to pose a question for you: How many of the four Ps do salespeople really have an impact on? Go ahead, review real quickly. That's right, maybe two: *placement* and *promotion.*

   Placement starts in Marketing's hands by way of the product-development process and the user groups it decides to market to (consumer, residential, retail, light industrial, commercial, heavy industrial, and so on) and ends up in the sales division's hands to "place into the marketplace."

   Promotion involves salespeople mainly in two of the six promotional mix ingredients: sales promotion and personal selling. That is to say, salespeople traditionally participate in promoting the products or services in two significant ways:

   • Through the local marketplace, which promotes the products or services (local ads, promotions, events, and so on)

- Through their personal selling efforts, which directly influence the customers who are buying their products and services

To sum up, as salespeople, we have not been taught to think about the four Ps at all; that has always been Marketing's job. Now, add the power of the Brand to the marketers' four Ps, and we are really like fish out of water! The reality is that salespeople have been on the receiving end of the product machines that marketers turn out. So when you add the Brand to the four Ps, we feel even further removed from the Brand's positioning and message in the marketplace.

Interestingly enough, studies have shown that the salesperson is the most vital link to the customer. Prophet Company, management consultants based in San Francisco, conducted a study, highlighted in the book *Building the Brand-Driven Business*, which stated that best practices noted by companies "ranked the salesforce as their most effective brand building tool, ahead of traditional tools such as advertising and marketing." It went on to say, "It is clear what drives customer perceptions during the purchase cycle is traditionally managed by other parts of the company, outside [of] marketing. Whether it is field sales, store operations, the customer contact center, the Internet team, or various channel partners, these people in effect became the brand at purchase" (pp. 119, 129).

2. "Just Give Us the Product or Service to Sell and Let Us Go"

Most of us who have been around selling for a while have earned our stripes by becoming product experts. We grew up in the business, and we learned to sell by practicing certain behaviors:

- Knowing and memorizing the features and benefits of our products
- Selling the benefits of the products, that is, "What's in it for the buyer/user?"
- Making competitive comparisons of our products and why they were better than the competition
- Demonstrating the products in a superior fashion

This belief system has been influenced not only by all of the product knowledge courses we have taken over the years, but also by the product launches at sales meetings, the information and competitive comparisons on marketing bulletins, and the rewards our companies bestow on us because of our expertise in a particular product knowledge category.

So prevalent is this love for product expertise that most companies that are known for the marketing and selling of high-quality products have established special "clubs" that product experts strive to belong to, associate with, or be voted into. For instance, when I worked at Black & Decker, we had a product expert club called "The Dirty Dozen." The club consisted of the very best product gurus with field sales territories, who were chosen by a vote of their peers and managers to join an esteemed club. This privilege carried with it a responsibility: to train the organization, test participants for "product certification," pass along their product expertise, and eventually identify their future replacements—the young talent who would become the future Dirty Dozen. These people were a highly respected and select group. As a company, we were rewarding behavior—working to become a product expert. The interesting side note for me was that the product experts were not always the best salespeople that we had in the field. As a matter of fact, the strength of their product expertise at times became a weakness, and it probably held them back from selling the Brand.

You see, we have habits, behaviors, and reward systems in place to solidify our product expertise. We are used to selling the tangible things that we can touch, see, and feel. However, when it comes to the Brand, we are not familiar with selling the intangible asset that the Brand represents to the company or how it feels to the user or buyer who buys the product.

> In short, we have been taught to be product experts, at the expense of the Brand.

3. "We Don't Have a $XXX Million Dollar Budget to 'Build the Brand' "

One of the best arguments for not selling the Brand that I have heard from salespeople is that the company's advertising budget is not big enough to spend millions of dollars on TV or mass media to build the Brand image and its message. In other words, "Get real, Dan; we are not Procter & Gamble, GE, IBM, Intel, Guinness, Ralph Lauren, Ferrari, Evian, Coca-Cola [you name the company], with 15 Brand managers, a huge marketing department, years of experience in Branding, and a nearly inexhaustible budget to fight the 'Brand street wars.' " You know what? I agree.

These arguments are good for a couple of reasons:

- Not every company is big enough to play in the consumer Brand channels.
- Not every company could or should try to advertise its Brand in mass media.

- Not every company should view Branding as simply internal "budgeting wars" for advertising dollars.
- No company should try to build a Brand different from the way the marketplace and customers see the Brand.

So after I have agreed with the people offering this argument, I consistently ask them a simple question: "Where do you think the average company invests the most amount of money in building its Brand?" (Most of the answers I get go back to the four Ps of marketing, with a high amount of focus on marketing promotion.) My answer to them is simple: "No, the biggest Brand-building investment the company makes is [pause for effect]—you!" There is usually a stunned silence, a pregnant pause, a slowly developing smile, a futile argument, and the inevitable discourse that I build throughout this book.

The book *Brand Babble,* by Don and Heidi Schultz, again lends credence to the salesperson's worth: "Brands today are indelibly shaped by the people employed to interact with customers. It's this 'people thing' that many brand babblers don't recognize or account for in their charts, graphs, consumer projections, and conceptual hocus-pocus." They continue, "It's those 'non-brand-trained' marketers, aka employees, who drive brand sales and profits. Their commitment and the experiences they deliver to customers shape and deliver the brand, and it's only through that commitment and those experiences that success occurs" (pp. 25–26).

The bottom line is

> Salespeople are the biggest investment a company makes in its Brand . . . they are a "walking billboard" for the Brand.

4. "We Are Taught to Sell Logically, Not Emotionally"

Because we are product experts, we tend to sell from a logical standpoint. As buyers, we think: "I'll buy this product because it's on sale," or "It has a great rebate," or "I'm getting a better price." So, logically, as salespeople we think: "This product is better because it has a longer warranty, or more horsepower, or a longer shelf life, or more run time."

Both lists could be endless. Here's the point: as salespeople, we are mired down in

- What the product will do, rather than how the buyer experiences the product
- How the product will work, versus how the buyer will feel when using it, wearing it, or driving it

We had a saying at Black & Decker that makes the distinction quite well:

You don't sell the drill, you sell the hole.

In other words, the end users don't buy the drill—how it looks, its rpm, its battery pack life, and so forth. What they really buy is the end result of using the product—a cabinet that is fashionably installed, or draperies that finish a window treatment, or a dollhouse for their granddaughter. If they're end users, what they are really buying is a battery pack that runs a cordless drill for four hours without the hassle of stopping work and wasting time to recharge the battery (in essence, saving them time, money, and hassles). Now, as buyers, we can all relate to those examples, but when we become sellers, we somehow become brain-dead to the emotion and sell to the logic by comparing features and benefits of the drill.

Another quick example: MasterCard had a well-orchestrated TV ad campaign that got to the emotional connection quickly. It would show real-life examples of the prices paid for certain products and services— for example, an ice cream cone for $2, a pair of shoes for $100, a sport jacket for $200, getting your son ready for his senior prom—*priceless*. Someone at MasterCard "gets it," that is, gets the emotional connection to life and selling to that connection.

Dale Carnegie, the great motivational speaker, understood it, too. He once said, "When dealing with people, you must realize that you are dealing with creatures of emotion over logic." I will make an argument in this book that salespeople should become more wired to speak to emotions, not just logic. That is the essence of speaking Brand language.

The Four Brand Language Breakthroughs: Reasons That Salespeople Should *Speak the Brand Language* in the Marketplace

Let me begin this section with a little anecdote from my direct-selling experience that helps to illustrate the importance of speaking Brand language. I was making a sales call to the vice president of sales at a new prospect. We had just met, and I was introducing my company to him. My goal was to build the need for a consistent sales process in the field and leadership training for all of his managers. We had built rapport and shared common ground in terms of our sales histories and backgrounds. I was beginning the questioning and listening process that I teach to salespeople, trying to practice what I preach, when suddenly he pulled out a brochure from a competing company, laid it in front of me, and asked, "What do you think of their training services?"

Now, I have come to appreciate a thinly disguised objection when I see one. But I still found myself mildly surprised (even though I knew that objections can happen at any time during a sales call and that they tell you immediately where a customer stands). Recovering quickly, I professionally applauded the competitor's company and told the vice president that I'd like to ask him a few questions about his company and what he wanted to accomplish by investing in training and developing his salespeople and leaders. I also said that I'd like to come back to address that flyer later on. He smiled slightly and nodded approval, and we moved forward. As he explained his objectives, I learned that he wanted to

- Build the team.
- Create leaders for the future growth of the company.
- Make sure that his people were communicating better on sales calls.
- Build a common language among his salespeople and leaders.

I'd heard all of those goals before, and I knew that my company could help. So, I started sharing my solutions with him. At one point, we were discussing the professional sales process that my company, LPD Inc., teaches. The specific topic was how to handle objections. I pulled the competitive flyer back out and simply said, "If your goal is to build the team, create future leaders, have salespeople communicate better, and build a common language, then you shouldn't invest in 'flavor-of-the-month' training. You see, there are dozens of companies that offer training solutions—some better than others. But if you allow Pat in Atlanta, Scott in Los Angeles, and John in Chicago to sign up for any local training class that sounds good, then you will all be speaking different languages. Yes, you may pay less for those various training solutions, but you will never know what your people have learned, and you will not accomplish any of the goals you have been talking about for the last hour. My solution will be to get all of your people on the same page and speaking the same language. Yes, it will be a bigger investment, but it will be worth it."

He looked at me, and a broad smile began to crease his face. I'll never forget his response: "I guess you really *do* use this stuff!" My response was, "You shouldn't hire me if I don't use it. I need to practice what I preach when it comes to handling objections." He put the competitor's brochure aside, and we never saw it again.

To this day, that customer is a very good client. I'm convinced that there are two simple reasons why: we got clear about speaking the same language, and I differentiated my Brand from the competition in a practical way.

As I reflect on that sales call, I realize that the goals of effective Brand selling were the same: Be intentional about the Brand, and speak the same Brand language when dealing with customers. Represent the Brands you sell, and differentiate them from the competition.

You can see that speaking Brand language is not just a good idea, but an intentional effort on the part of salespeople that yields real results. Now, if you're a senior leader reading this book, or a key sales leader looking to grow your team in selling the Brand, or a high-flying salesperson looking to get better at your profession or further your career, then read on. Since we've already discussed the reasons people struggle in selling the Brand, I will now briefly discuss the best reasons *to* sell the Brand. (Please note that many of these arguments for selling the Brand first will resurface when I address the topic of building the Branded culture in Chapter 13.) Here are the four reasons why you should speak Brand language.

1. Brand Language Is the Best Defense against "Transactional Buying" and "Commoditizing of the Category"

As the manufacturing arena has developed into a global marketplace, products are continually being manufactured overseas with cheaper labor and remarketed in other countries. This global change has made it harder to compete with foreign products marketed at lower prices. This has fed two trends in the marketplace:

1. *Trend 1: the transactional buyer.* This type of buyer generally wants to buy generic products at the lowest possible prices. The buyer has usually devalued the quality of the product and the Brand by making decisions on purchasing largely on the basis of price. Thus, those companies that value and sell the Brand can defend against the transactional buyer by creating value through differentiation of their products and services.

2. *Trend 2: commoditizing the category.* The more your category moves to transactional buying, the more it will logically move toward selling and marketing in a "commoditized category." In other words, the category that will be treated like a commodity, where price is the major buyer consideration, and where it is negotiated most heavily because there is no need for product or Brand differentiation.

To avoid this situation, as salespeople, we need to think and sell differently.

2. Brand Language Is the Best Defense against Price Objections/Imports

Through my years of selling, training, and leading, I have found that the most common and usually the biggest objection is price: "Your price is too high." It is universal, it is misunderstood, and it is often a false objection. But, importantly, it cannot be ignored. The impact of the price objection has continued to grow as a result of the expansion of imports from overseas. Why? Mostly because imports normally enter the marketplace with lower labor costs, and consequently with the intention of selling at a lower price.

You will see in the models built within this book, that the Brand is the furthest thing from the price in the buyer's consideration of your product or services. Thus I assert here that a strong Brand is the best defense against the price objection and the infiltration of imports into the marketplace.

3. Brand Language Is the Best Offense for Negotiating Key Account Programming/Incentives

When selling to larger customers or repeat buyers, salespeople often are embroiled in negotiating the best deals for their company. They are usually faced with buyers who believe that they have extra leverage because of their sales volume, their size, their business model, their impact in the channel or marketplace, and so on. To combat this, the salesperson needs to use the Brand as a leverage point for negotiating contracts, rebates, promotional buy-ins, and incentive programs. If this is done well, I would argue that the Brand is the best offense for positioning your company in repeat buyer situations, in key customer relationships, and in important negotiations.

4. Brand Language Is the Best Offense against Competitors Telling Your Brand Story

Lastly, every Brand is the accumulation of the company's attention to it, the identity it has obtained in the marketplace, and the user's experiences with and perceptions of it. As companies and salespeople, we are not good at telling our Brand stories. Why? Largely because we haven't been taught to tell them, so it's not a positive sales habit for us.

Some of you might argue: "I've survived so far without selling the Brand; why should I change now?" I had a manager who once told me, "Unless you have 100 percent market share, then you have room to grow." His message was twofold:

1. *Increase your market share.* Don't rest on your laurels, because that is when you risk market share erosion. Instead, always look to increase your market share and customer loyalty as a sales professional.
2. *Don't be vulnerable to competition.* Never get mentally lazy and give the competition an edge, because that's when your customer base becomes most vulnerable to being displaced.

Remember, if you have a decent Brand (not even a great Brand, just a decent one), your competitors probably don't like your story. As a matter of fact, if they could, they would like to tell your story for you, but they would tell it as their version of your story. Now, I can guarantee you that your competition will not tell your Brand story in a way that will benefit you or put your product or company in a good light.

I was recently in a workshop talking about the power of the Brand story. I had just made the following point:

> Everyone has a Brand story.
> The question is . . .
> Who is telling it?
> You, or the competition?

The vice president of sales looked over at the table where the CEO and the vice president of marketing were sitting and commented, "You know, that is so true. We just introduced our new Brand at the sales meeting in February with no real sales story behind the logo and its Brand meaning. Then, I noticed at our industry conference two weeks ago [four months after the Brand launch] that we got more questions on our Brand strategy and what it meant than on any other one issue. One buyer looked at my card and said, 'Do you know what your competition is saying about this new logo and the Brand change you are going through?'" He went on to describe the conversation and his surprise at how the customers' perception of the new Brand was being colored by what they had heard from the competition.

The bottom line is that you cannot afford to leave this to chance. You need to go on the offensive with your Brand story. My point here is simple: if you're not telling your own Brand story with consistency within your sales organization and to your customers in the field, then surely your competition will be telling it, and it won't be pretty.

The Brand Sales Language

Let's end this discussion with some definitions that will give the right context to where we sell Brands, what channels we sell them in, and how to approach Brand selling based on that knowledge. I identify and define all four of the most important Brand channels here so that you can see them in relation to one another. But keep in mind that Consumer Brands, our first category, are the focus of most of this book. In other words, we are addressing needs that occur in a sales transaction between business and consumer. Later in this book, in Part 5, which is about business-to-business transactions, I will talk more about the remaining three categories: Trade Brands, Service Brands, and Crossover Brands.

- *Consumer Brands* are found in day-to-day living and are purchased by the average consumer. They are part of everyday society, are in the public eye, and are talked about in consumer channels. They are bought, used, and consumed by people in their own personal lives. Consumer Brands have a mass appeal and are often advertised in the mass media.
- *Trade Brands* are Brands specific to a trade, industry, or specialty channel. They are well understood by the customers and sellers within that business, but they are not widely known to the "average Joe consumer" on the street. Essentially they are hidden from consumers, yet they are understood, relied upon, and important to professionals within that specific trade.
- *Service Brands* are also specific to different trades. They can be defined exactly like Trade Brands, with one big exception: instead of selling products, these companies are selling services. Examples are professional services like accounting, tax preparation, engineering, legal services, financial services, operations, audit work, recruiting, and so forth.
- *Crossover Brands* are brands that can be sold as both Consumer Brands and Trade Brands. Many are sold from the manufacturer to the supplier to the eventual end user or consumer. This can be quite complex for salespeople, as they must deal with the Brand in multiple channels and selling situations.

Key Points

Brand is crucial in the mind and behavior of the buyer of today. It permeates almost every level of a person's life, whether that person is aware of it or not. It is obvious that the buyer usually has preferences and ideas about Brand choices in mind. But does the salesperson come to the buying transaction ready to speak Brand language and sell a product that targets the desire for Brand? In many cases, the answer is no, because of the four Brand language barriers:

- "It's marketing's job."
- "Just give us the product/service to sell and let us go."
- "We don't have a $XXX million dollar budget to 'build the Brand.'"
- "We are taught to sell logically, not emotionally."

These barriers create a disconnect between the desires of the buyer and the technique of the salesperson. In very simple terms, the salesperson often is not selling to the right need of the buyer, and the buyer is not always getting what she wants. This situation can be corrected if the salesperson knows how to speak Brand language.

There are some very good reasons for speaking Brand language. I call them *Brand language breakthroughs:*

- It is the best defense against transactional buying and commoditizing of the category.
- It is the best defense against price objections/imports.
- It is the best offense for negotiating key account programming/ incentives.
- It is the best offense against competitors telling your Brand story.

Salespeople need to be aware of the traditional Brand language barriers and must also be equipped with a Brand language "breakthrough" to be effective sellers of Brand.

PART 2

THE CORE COMPONENTS OF BRAND SELLING

CHAPTER 3

THE BUYER STAIR-STEP

If you are like most salespeople, you probably grew up selling a certain way. I know I did. Sales was fundamentally about two things: selling skills and product knowledge. In the selling skills arena, it was all about creating a need, understanding "What's in it for the buyer?," handling objections, and pulling it all together for the proper solution at the proper price. In the product knowledge arena, it included knowing features and benefits, memorizing facts that I could call out at the proper moments, surveying the products or services that the buyer was currently using, and demonstrating the product better than my competition.

The first professional sales-training course that I attended was at NCR. It was the first company to develop sales training for professionals, and the course was held in Dayton, Ohio. The initial training was a three-week lock-in and immersion into computers: the language, the specs, the pricing, the demonstrations, the survey/discovery of buyer needs. It started and ended with the product and the services that would keep the product running.

My next job was at Black & Decker, then on to the new industrial division—DeWALT. The initial training was a two-week class: again, the traditional immersion. We had just been included in the book by Harkavy entitled *The 100 Best Companies to Sell For*, and our training program got a perfect 10. I remember that initial "boot camp." We stayed up late at night, laboring over catalogs to memorize catalog numbers, specifications, and features that turned into buyer benefits. We were quizzed and tested on all of those facts. Then I returned to the field with an assignment: go through the catalog and learn one product category each week. We were instructed to learn at night and sell that category during the day. At week's end, I was quizzed on the category by my manager. It was all to achieve one goal—to be product certified as an expert and earn THE JACKET (an award synonymous with the "green jacket" given to the winner of the Masters golf tournament). We would nearly kill ourselves to be good on the product.

Looking back on it, I don't begrudge one minute of that time. It did two key things for me: it established great work habits, and it emphasized the undeniable importance of the product to the buyer. It made a lot of sense back then, and it still does. But this kind of sales and product training is not enough anymore. As salespeople, we certainly need to understand all of that, but we also need to understand a whole lot more, given the prominence of Brands.

The Buyer Stair-Step Method, which I cover in this chapter, embodies a solid understanding of the buyer's motivations coupled with good salesmanship. This method is based on my experiences with buyers and my observations of many salespeople over the years. Using the metaphor of a stair-step, this method represents the set of steps that many salespeople intuitively use in their relationships with buyers, primarily in the order that they are laid out in the following discussion. Most sales veterans will also be familiar with the terminology, as the average sales-training course includes parts of this language. The difference in my discussion is that I have put these steps together to create a sales model that sequences the steps to match the buyer's mindset when the buyer enters a transaction. The model then coaches the salesperson on how to understand that mindset and how to track with the buyer's needs at each step. It's important to review these steps here because we need to understand where we have been in order to know where we are going in regard to the Brand. In the next chapter, I will take the Buyer's Stair-Step Method one step further and introduce you to my Brand Staircase Method, which is a more effective approach to reach your customers and close your sale.

Again, an analogy is useful here. One of the best pieces of advice my Dad gave me was to look in the rearview mirror to see where I'd been, before looking through the front windshield to see where I was going. In other words, learn the lessons from your victories, defeats, choices, and experiences before you trudge on blindly to the next chapter of life. What I'm about to share with you comes from looking in the rearview mirror and applying that information and knowledge to see more clearly through the front windshield. I hope it serves you well on your journey as a salesperson and a leader.

The Buyer Stair-Step is formulated from experience and reflection into the rearview mirror. It puts together three key components that every buyer considers as steps in the purchasing process, and it reconfirms what the average salesperson has intuitively learned about selling, except that it goes a couple of steps further by:

1. Pulling three major components together at one time with a clear focus on the buyer's perspective (which I will later call *buyer mindset*).
2. Getting into the buyer's head in terms of how the buyer thinks, evaluates, and reacts to these components within a sales interaction.
3. Challenging the seller to understand the Buyer Stair-Step and highlighting the inherent problems with continuing to sell this way.

Three Components of a Product Purchase

When the buyer or end user of the product is making a buying decision, historically this person has been considering three things: *Price*, *Style*, and *Quality* (see Figure 3.1). (*Note:* It wasn't until recently that Brand was added to the buyer's consideration, which is why Brand is not included in this model.)

- *Price* is the amount the buyer is willing to spend on the purchase.
- *Style* is how the product functions, its fashion, or its finish.
- *Quality* is the workmanship, materials, or warranty the buyer gets with the product.

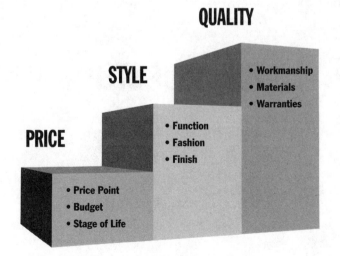

THE BUYER STAIR-STEP

FIGURE 3.1

The Buyer Stair-Step best illustrates not only the sequence, but also the interrelationships of these components. Each component has several defining characteristics (for example, Style has function, fashion, and finish), and each component also has a "level of mental engagement" (or mindset) for the buyer, where the buyer unlocks the key to his own thoughts and feelings about the product. That is, what does the buyer "think," "evaluate," or "react to"? Let's examine each of these more closely.

Price Is Usually the First Component

When buyers enter the transaction to buy a product, they generally have a price in mind. And as part of the Price component, they are typically thinking of three things: the price point of the product, their budget, and their stage of life (see Figure 3.2).

Price point can be subdivided further into three categories. The first is OPP, which means *opening price point*. It is the least expensive entry point for a product. Commodity items and generic "knockoffs" are in this pricing category. The second is MPP, which means *mid-price point*. Price points in the middle have more features and product benefits. The third is HPP, which means *high price point*. This refers to higher-end items with good quality and value. They are usually the most expensive products. Salespeople probably recognize these terms because they are used extensively in sales lingo. Many companies follow the marketing strategy of pricing products in these three categories to give the buyer a "good, better, or best" choice when buying their products.

THE PRICE STEP

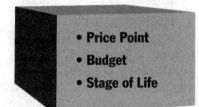

- Price Point
- Budget
- Stage of Life

FIGURE 3.2

The second important factor in the price component is budget. That is essentially what the buyer expects to spend on the product. How much has the buyer allocated for that product or purchase? Is it even in the buyer's current budget? If so, how much does the buyer enter the transaction willing to spend?

The third factor is stage of life. Is the buyer retired? Married? With children? An empty nester? Double income—no kids? Saving for college? Buying a first home? Paying alimony? Where is the buyer in her life in terms of responsibilities? Understanding that helps the salesperson properly position the products.

Budget and stage of life work together to a considerable degree to determine what buyers are willing to spend on a product. Obviously, the more discretionary or disposable income a person earns, the more that person can afford to pay. However, people will overspend on certain items that they value greatly. In *Trading Up*, Silverstein and Fiske say,

> *Every consumer has a different idea of what is necessary for him to survive in his own world and what he is willing to spend to do so. As one consumer put it, 'Necessity is one of those relative terms that depends on who you are or where you are in life. When things become important to you, they become necessities (p. 30).*

The key questions buyers are asking at the Price step are: "How much is it?" "Can I afford it?" and "Is it in the budget?" Also, they are often thinking of financial choices or trade-offs. For instance, a young couple might ask, "Should we buy this luxury car, make a down payment on a house, or save money to start a family?" A middle-aged couple might be asking, "Should we save for college, invest for the future, trade up for luxury goods, or build a vacation home?" A couple headed toward retirement might ask, "Will we travel, invest in our grandchildren, or treat ourselves to our dream home, car, vacation, and so on?" Regardless of where they are in terms of stage of life, when they enter the sales situation at the *Price step*, they are mentally asking questions primarily based on the Price—or in other words, they have a Price mindset.

Style Is the Second Component

At the style step, the buyer evaluates the product according to its function, fashion, and finish (see Figure 3.3).

- *Function.* This is how the product works, operates, or performs the functions it was meant to do. Whether it's a copier making copies, a dishwasher washing dishes, a computer playing games or running

THE STYLE STEP

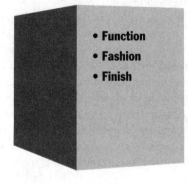

- Function
- Fashion
- Finish

FIGURE 3.3

Microsoft Office or Lotus Notes, a cordless drill driving screws, a lockset on your front door, an outdoor cooking grill, or a snow blower moving the white stuff, all products have functional parts that buyers evaluate in the decision process, and these are usually related to the features and benefits that salespeople speak to during product presentations.

- *Fashion.* This is how the product looks—how you look "in it," how it looks "on you," or how you look "with it." Do those clothes look good on me? Do I look good in that car? Is this piece of artwork pleasing to look at? Fashion, of course, is a significant player in many buying decisions.
- *Finish.* This is how the product feels—how you feel "in it," how it feels "on you," how you feel when "others see you with it." It feels good that I received flowers for Valentine's Day. I like that paint color or finish better. I like the feel of leather seats in this car. This feels good when I wear it, or I'm comfortable in this sweater.

The key questions that the buyer is asking at the Style step are: "How does this work, anyway?" "What does this feature do?" "How does this feel (when it gets hot out)?" "What is the finish on this product?" "How long will it last?" "How does this look on me?" "How does it taste?" "Can I try it on to get a feel for it?" "Do you like the way it looks?"

These three evaluation factors of function, fashion, and finish can be independent of one another or can work together for a buyer. The Style component typically takes different paths as a result of the independent characteristics of the three factors and also the emotional nature of fashion and finish. However, function can also have a direct connection to fashion and finish. Interestingly, most often the average salesperson gets caught up in the function of the product (how it works) and sells the features aspect of it too strongly. At the same time, salespeople can easily forget about how the product feels to the customer or how it could look aesthetically. When buyers enter the sales situation at the *Style step* of the staircase, they are primarily interested in asking questions about style and not about price or quality. In this case they have a Style mindset.

It is helpful to illustrate how these three Style components interact by going back to the car analogy. Let's suppose you are shopping for a car and looking at the myriad of accessory choices available. You are primarily interested in three extra features: heated seats, a DVD player for the kid's entertainment, and a sunroof.

The function of the heated seats is to keep you warm in the winter. Finish comes in when you consider how it feels when you start your day off in a better mood because you're not chilled to the bone (thanks to your warm bottom), especially on those brutally cold winter mornings. It also may be fashionable for you to have leather seats that you can brag about to your friends. In this example of heated seats, function and finish play a bigger role in the Style component of the product.

With a DVD player, fashion and finish would play a larger role than function. Since most people know how DVD players work, the fashion elements of its size, where it sits in the vehicle, how accessible it is, and how it looks with the rest of the interior design would be natural points for you to evaluate. The finish could be black or silver; it could be made out of indestructible materials with a space-age look and feel; it could have an antiglare screen and the ability to fold up into the ceiling to get out of the way when you invite another couple out on a double date.

Regarding the sunroof, function may be the most important point here—how the thing works, how you can retract it completely or slightly, how you can make it tilt for a small amount of air or open it wide on a bright, sunny day. Now, a good salesperson could also sell this accessory by helping the person dream about the sunny days when the roof can be thrown wide open, the windows rolled down, and the music turned up. Of course, that would be playing directly into how it feels to enjoy a nice day in your vehicle—the finish.

So, it is instructive to note the interplay of function, fashion, and finish when a buyer is evaluating the style of a product. Unfortunately, too many salespeople sell mostly on actual features here (a strategy based on logic) and miss a huge opportunity to get to the emotions of the fashion and finish.

Quality Is the Third Component.

Here the buyer reacts to the quality of the product with regard to its workmanship, its materials, and the warranties associated with it (see Figure 3.4).

- *Workmanship.* Is the item hand-made or exclusive? Is it custom-produced or mass-produced? What value does the buyer place on the workmanship?
- *Materials.* Are the ingredients, parts, or materials unique, antique, or rare, or are they everyday, run-of-the-mill, or mass-produced and widely available?
- *Warranties.* What does the manufacturer's warranty state—how long does it cover the product for, how comprehensive is it, how credible is it? How much does the manufacturer back up its products?

Buyers now consider product warranties to be a main part of the up-front selling transaction, not just an after-sale service/maintenance agreement.

THE QUALITY STEP

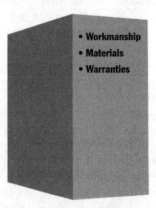

FIGURE 3.4

Key questions the buyer is asking at the Quality step are: "How does your product hold up?" "How well does the manufacturer back up the product?" "What is the warranty?" "Is there an extended warranty?" "What is this made of (materials)?" "Where or how does the manufacturer build this product?" Quality has become a key component of many sales transactions in three key ways: it has impenetrable advantages because it deals with innate characteristics that are immutable or unbeatable; you can compare the value of a product with that of other products in the same category through quality criteria; and buyers often are willing to consider "trading up" because of quality issues. Quality has become a key and expected ingredient that buyers react to during buying decisions. The smart salesperson finds out the buyer's viewpoint on quality and sells accordingly. When buyers enter the sales situation at the *Quality step* (or Quality mindset) of the staircase, they are primarily asking questions about the product's durability and long-term quality. To illustrate the differences in what the buyer thinks is important to ask about these three steps, I have put the three sets of questions in table form (see Table 3.1).

Now, consider this example that shows the interrelationship of Price, Style, and Quality. Say you paid $275 to $350 for a Montblanc fine writing instrument. Do you think it was worth it? After all, there are other pens out there that cost far less and probably write just as well. You could have bought a Cross pen for $50 to $80. But the Montblanc pen is classy; after all, it represents "the Art of Writing." It feels

TABLE 3.1   The Buyer's Key Questions

Price	Style	Quality
How much is it?	How does this work?	How does it hold up?
Can I afford it?	What does this feature do?	Does the manufacturer back it up?
Is it in the budget?	How does it feel?	What are the warranties?
Does it fit into our stage of life?	What is the finish?	What is it made of?
How will I pay for this? (cash, credit, and so on)	How long will it last?	Where is it made?
What promotional offers come with it? (cash back, rebates, and so on)	How does it look, taste, or feel?	What is their reputation for quality?
Is the price point what I was expecting to spend?	Can I try it on?	What workmanship goes into the products?

great in your hand, and it probably writes like no other pen you have ever owned. Also, customers probably notice the quality and craftsmanship that went into this fine writing instrument when you are using it. In short, this pen functions better for you, looks good on you, and makes you feel good about yourself and your status within your peer group. All three of those characteristics contributed to your decision to pay up to $200 more to have it in your possession. In this case Price, Style, and Quality worked together to influence your purchasing decision.

So, the rearview mirror has taught us as salespeople that there are three steps to the Buyer Stair-Step: Price, Style, and Quality. We have also established that there is an interplay among the three steps around the buyer's perception of these steps. Our experience (as a buyer and seller of products) also intuitively tells us that

1. Buyers enter the transaction looking for these three components.
2. Buyers may value one step more than the others, depending on what kind of goods they are purchasing.
3. Buyers may focus on certain steps, for example, the price and whether it's in the budget or not, or the warranty and whether the product will last, or the style and the fact that it "just looks great!"

Could we go on? Sure, and you could come up with examples from every industry or goods category imaginable, couldn't you? So to the sales professionals, the people in the trenches, it all makes sense, doesn't it?

The Missing Link: Brand

But wait, lest we be naïve! There is something missing. The astute practitioner of the sales transaction is often aware of a fourth step that may be more subtle and sometimes doesn't get included at all, but is critical. It is the almost invisible ingredient that should be added to Price, Style, and Quality—the Brand. This point was made painfully clear in a workshop I was running. We had just built the Buyer Stair-Step, and we were discussing the issues and challenges with it, when a puzzled look came over the face of a 20-year sales veteran I had gotten to know a bit. He stood up and said, "Wait a minute, what about the Brand? I thought we were here to learn about selling the Brand, and by the way, I think I sell our Brand pretty well!"

I stopped short, and the pause was brutal. The crowd thought that the experienced salesperson had again stumped the inept facilitator. My response, I believe, floored him. I said, "I'll bet you do sell the Brand. So why are you even here, anyway?"

He looked around at his classmates as if to say, "Yeah, why am I here anyway?" He stammered something like "to learn what I'm doing wrong?" I reassured him that I had not seen him sell enough to know what he even might be doing wrong, but I guessed that he clearly knew how to *buy* a Brand, so he probably intuitively knew how to *sell* a Brand.

He gave me that quizzical look that exists somewhere between being doped and being mystified. Of course, his curiosity had gotten the better of him. I had to relieve the pressure. "So, you're wondering how I knew, right?" I walked over to him and pulled the Montblanc pen out of his pocket. I rattled through the analysis of the purchase of a Montblanc compared to the purchase of a Cross pen, and then I took it one step further.

I said, "I'll bet that the biggest part of your purchase decision was an emotional dimension based on the Brand. You would probably passionately defend this purchase decision if challenged. That passion helped you arrive at the feelings that were behind the purchase of this premium pen. The way this makes you feel and look, and also what the Brand represents to buyers like you, often drives people to spend more for products that functionally do the same thing!" I looked at the group. "The lesson here is that salespeople are often missing the boat on tapping into the feeling dimension, and in understanding what the Brand could mean to the buyer. This pen meant something to Dave. That's why I knew he could connect with Brands and maybe even sell them. He intuitively gets this, and many of the rest of you might also. The question is, can you sell the Brand intentionally?" Dave's chest was puffing up with pride. He turned to sit.

I tapped Dave's shoulder before he could sit and said, "Let me illustrate this. Sell me this Montblanc pen!" He went ashen white. "You're kidding, right?" "Actually, no, I'm serious." He then stuttered, stammered, and mentioned a few pen features. I stopped his pain after about a minute, apologized for putting him on the spot, and simply said to the group. "So, how do you represent a brand like Montblanc?" The company's CEO, Norbert Platt, once exclaimed, "Montblanc is about passion and soul. . . . As the world keeps winding up, we unwind. . . . Consumers crave things that preserve a moment." How, then, do you sell a Brand? You get intentional with your Brand sales language.

We need to move from
intuitive to intentional.

Why Be Intentional?

There are some of you out there who can relate closely with Dave. You can feel it. You've sold the Brand before, and you can even give a few examples of when you did it. My questions to you are these: how did it work, could you repeat it, would you know what to look for, could you teach it, and could you do it under pressure in front of a workshop if you were Dave? When asked those questions, you lose a bit of confidence, don't you? Because you realize that there is a certain amount of pressure with selling. It is a competitive environment. Oh, and by the way, you do have a number to hit. But, no pressure!

You see, we revert to habits under pressure, and your habits are only as good as your sales mindsets and the selling that you practice every day. Lou Holtz, the Hall of Fame college football coach, tells a short story about a placekicker on his Notre Dame team. The kicker, it seems, became unnerved whenever Lou was watching him practice kicking field goals. Of course, his nerves were making him miss badly. So one day, the kicker got up the nerve to approach Coach Holtz and said, "Coach, you make me nervous when you watch me taking kicking practice."

Without missing a beat, Lou retorted, "Well, I plan on being at every game." The implication was simple: there will be more pressure in the game than there is at practice, so get used to it! Sales is the same way. There is pressure, so we need to build better habits under pressure because someone is watching, even if it's just our buyer.

Incidentally, I grew up selling around some very good salespeople who did sell the Brand intuitively, but they were the exception, not the rule. I give you all the credit, intuitive salespeople, because you are further along than most, and you are halfway there if you even have the Brand on your "selling radar." My job in this book is to help you sell the Brand more intentionally.

The Invisible Step

The Brand step of the traditional Buyer's Stair-Step is what I've come to call *the invisible step*. It is invisible for most salespeople because they are

1. *Blind or indifferent.* This is a common stance. Allow me to illustrate. In workshops, I often ask salespeople to think of a time when they were beaten by another Brand in a competitive situation. People in the group usually struggle to come up with examples; either they can't come up with one, or it takes them a long time. Why? It's because selling the Brand isn't a top priority for most salespeople. They are literally blind at best or indifferent at worst to its impact on them.

It's like the Indiana Jones movie where Indiana is facing a wide crevasse with a 1,000-foot drop to sure death. His enemies are chasing him from behind, and he can see the other side and the opening to freedom some 500 feet across the canyon. His choices are to take a step of faith with no visible path over to safety or to succumb to the enemy pursuing from behind. Thank God for his fans worldwide, because we see him take a deep breath and a step of faith, only to have his foot land on a rock-solid "invisible bridge." Having found his answer, he throws dirt onto the invisible bridge to "show the way" to the other side.

2. *Unsure or unconvinced.* Salespeople seem unsure of the next step or unconvinced that it will lead them to better sales. It's like a classic horror film where the evil creature is chasing the hero (or heroine). Of course, all of them are in a haunted mansion, walking up a dilapidated winding stairway, and (you guessed it) the hero is unsure of his footing, and his foot falls through the rickety step just as he is being pursued by the evil creature and needs that step to hold his weight.

Much like Indiana Jones, you will need to see the invisible step, to take your blinders off. Once you do, you will get more comfortable with how Brand fits into your sales process. You also may need to test the step to see that it is sturdy. You may need to be convinced that it will take the weight of the buyer's objections or the competitor's claims. Either way you look at this, it may take a leap of faith. But, if you can learn to sell this way, it will be worth the faith and the effort.

Brand: The Last Component

Now, we have established that Brands are more important than ever and that salespeople often do not recognize that simple fact. We have also established that the Buyer Stair-Step is where buyers have traditionally engaged the salesperson around the Price, Style, and Quality of the products they are purchasing. Some of the difficulty for salespeople lies in their almost total immersion in the traditional ways of selling, and also the barriers to developing a language to express Brand that we discussed in Chapter 2. Many salespeople are stuck there and have not yet adapted to new trends, such as the importance of Brands and speaking Brand language. So Brand is usually considered last, if it is considered at all.

We're traveling on this journey together to discover the power of Brand. So now, let's briefly discuss how Brand fits into the Buyer Stair-Step.

Brand is what the brand means to the buyer on a very personal and emotional level (see Figure 3.5).

It is usually the *last* step to be dealt with when selling to the buyer. Here a buyer associates particular *experiences, connections,* and *affiliations* with the brand. The easiest way to get at the emotional and personal connection to the Brand is to use short (usually one- or two-word) descriptors that people can envision—words or phrases like *peace of mind, security, craftsmanship, heritage, distinctive, aspiring, discriminating, exclusive,* and *prestige.* These descriptors convey a certain mental image of what life is like or would be like if the buyer had an association or experience with this Brand.

The key questions the buyer is asking at the Brand step are "What Brands do you carry?" "Do you carry XXX Brand?" or "I've heard good things about XXX Brand." Salespeople often hear statements or notice visible actions that the buyer makes while shopping for Brand, such as "I'm used to buying 'the top end' and not bashful about telling you so," "I live in Beverly Hills," or "I have a big house worth far more than $500K." In some cases, price may never come up. Also, the Brand

THE BRAND STEP

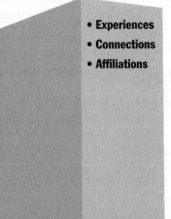

- Experiences
- Connections
- Affiliations

FIGURE 3.5

mentality customer can and will drop other Brand names during the conversation (Kohler, Corian, and JennAir, for example, when shopping for Whirlpool ovens or bathroom fixtures). When buyers happen to enter the sales situation at the *Brand step*, they are primarily asking questions about the Brand or indirectly talking about other high-end brands (a Brand mindset). The next chapter will dive deeply into the Brand and its impact on the rest of the Buyer Stair-Step.

What's Wrong with the Buyer Stair-Step Model?

There is a fundamental problem with the Buyer Stair-Step Model. But it's not in the components of the stair-step, it's in the sequence. When you start with price and move toward Brand, several things in the sales transaction begin to fall apart. If the salesperson allows price or even style to be the starting point in the conversation, then the quality of the product may never be examined, and surely a connection to the Brand is unlikely to be made. So, I have found four key reasons why salespeople and leaders historically have struggled with the Buyer Stair-Step:

1. *It is time-sensitive.* Think of how little time most people have to spend when buying a product or service. We all have places to go, people to see, and things to do. Our time has become our most valuable commodity and our most wasted resource. Yet, with customers having so little buying time, the big mistake so many salespeople continue to make is to spend the majority of their selling time on Price or Style. Because of time constraints, they get little time to talk the Quality story, and they seldom, if ever, address the emotional connection to the Brand. In effect, they run out of time.

2. *It is energy draining.* Buying takes energy, and selling takes energy. People have only so much energy to give to the process. So, why would good salespeople spend most of their energy and effort on the Price and Style, when the real story should be the Quality and Brand? They wouldn't. The fact of the matter is that a great salesperson would invest her energy and effort where she would get a bigger payoff—on the Quality and, in an additional step, the Brand.

3. *It lacks momentum.* Sales is about momentum. It's analogous to sports. It is competitive, goal-oriented, results-driven, and emotional in nature. In sports, the momentum ebbs and flows with great plays, penalties, matching of strategies, the head-to-head competition, and the rush against time. In sales, the momentum ebbs and flows with the seller's level of enthusiasm, product knowledge, engagement of the customer, and ability to carry on a conversation. The momentum also changes with the buyer's interest level,

product questions, interplay with the salesperson, and tension in the decision-making process. Thus, when selling up the stair-step, a salesperson has a harder time building and sustaining momentum. He spends his time and energy in the lower steps, and frankly, he may run out of gas—and, more importantly, the buyer may as well. The buyer also may get more impatient with the salesperson because she feels that the conversation is droning on, taking too much time and energy, and not getting to the point quickly enough.

4. *It's like pushing water uphill.* The laws of gravity work in selling, too. If you continually start at the Price step and attempt to go up the stair-steps toward the Brand step, you will find yourself figuratively pushing water uphill. You are less able to engage the customers; they become impatient, and they feel that this is like pulling teeth. In essence, they have become time-sensitive and drained of energy, and they lack any sort of momentum to reach into their wallets and buy.

So, we have a dilemma. We have four perfectly good components of a successful sale, but they are often approached in the wrong order, and often one of them is missing—the invisible step, the Brand. It takes all of our skill and knowledge as salespeople to pull off a sale with the components in the order that they are in now—with Price first. Does this dilemma require a complete reordering of what we know about selling? No, but it does require a reordering of the stair-step to produce a new mental model. In the next chapter, we'll talk about the solution to the stair-step dilemma.

Key Points

Most salespeople grow up in the industry learning a particular way of approaching the selling interaction. They typically use the elements of what I call the *Buyer's Stair-Step*. It is based on core elements that the buyer usually is concerned with when considering the product. The steps, in sequence, are Price, Style, Quality, and, distantly, and sometimes not at all, Brand.

- Price *is the amount the buyer is willing to spend on the purchase.*
- *Style* is how the product functions, its fashion, or its finish.
- Quality *is the workmanship, materials, or warranty that the buyer gets with the product.*
- *Brand,* the often invisible step, is what the brand means to the buyer on a very personal and emotional level. In short, it is how the buyer experiences the product or service.

But, although these steps are usually part of a typical sales transaction, there are problems with this sequence if you are operating on the assumption that Brand should have greater prominence. These problems are

- Sellers often waste too much time on Price or Style.
- The process is energy draining because the salesperson's effort may be spent on the earlier steps.
- The process lacks momentum because the buyer wearies of the pitch and becomes impatient before the important points are made.
- It's like pushing water uphill.

The solution lies in the next chapter.

CHAPTER 4

THE BRAND STAIRCASE

The term *missing link* may be a cliché, but it is a perfect phrase for what is left out or simply ignored in the Buyer's Stair-Step. In the previous chapter, I reviewed the typical steps that salespeople take with buyers in the course of a transaction—that is, talking about Price, Style, and Quality. But what is missing? Brand, of course. Even if it is part of the equation for the salesperson, it is often either ignored as an important factor in the sales transaction or placed dead last. In this chapter, I want to convey an important message: Brand is essential and should come first in the buying transaction.

This missing-link idea became more evident as I witnessed failed sales transactions that didn't include sufficient attention to Brand. This became especially clear while I was working with a top prospect. We were pulling together the elements of the Buyer Stair-Step, and we had reviewed the four components: Price, Style, Quality, and Brand. We had discussed many of the issues with the Price, Style, and Quality steps, and we were just starting on the Brand step.

I was explaining the connection that Brands have with people's lifestyle. When purchasing products and services:

> People are not just purchasing a product,
> but rather supporting a chosen lifestyle.

This lifestyle choice is based on

- *Past experiences* with the Brand: "I've tried it, and I like it."
- *Present connections* to the Brand: "I've heard good things about it and would like to try it today."
- *Future affiliations* with the Brand: "That will be the next brand I buy."

THE BRAND STEP

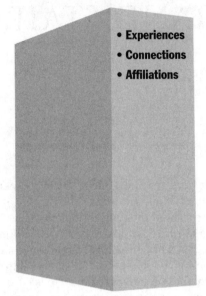

FIGURE 4.1

At the end of the day, people buy brands that they have experienced, want to connect to, or want to affiliate with in the future (see Figure 4.1). People buy Brands that they can trust.

As I gave this explanation, I could tell that my client was not getting it. The client had a strong sales and marketing background, so to support my point about lifestyle choices, I decided to share some everyday examples of good marketing companies that have made their Brands come alive for the buying public. I went on to share the following examples:

- *Think about Polo shirts for a minute.* That name has become generic for a Ralph Lauren casual or dress shirt. It's a symbol of status, and it's not the least expensive Brand on the market. But it makes a statement that you have arrived as a young businessperson. It's a connection.
- *Harley-Davidson.* It's a high-end premium motorcycle with an expensive price tag. But it makes a statement about your freedom, your sense of adventure, and even your lifestyle. It's become so

popular as a brand that there are now Harley-Davidson restaurants, clothing stores, and even "lifestyle festivals" that travel the country in the summer and attract Harley owners from miles around. There's also a Harley-Davidson rally in Sturgis, South Dakota, every year where over 1 million devout Harley fans drive their bikes from all over the country just to basically hang out and enjoy their lifestyle. It's an affiliation.

- *Nike athletic shoes.* They have become a fashion statement. Every young kid who aspires to play sports was told to "be like Mike"; they wanted to associate with Michael Jordan's personality, his mastery of the game of basketball, and his charisma under pressure during competition. Kids so connect with the Nike brand and what it represents to them that I have personally witnessed a line of over 200 kids at 8 a.m. on a Saturday morning clamoring to enter the Foot Locker store to willingly spend $150 to $200 on the newest pair of Air Jordan or T. (Tracy) McGrady shoes and simultaneously forgo many other creature comforts, including a hot meal. Now, Nike has expanded its legion of personal endorsements to include Pete Sampras, Tiger Woods, Lebron James and many other sports superstars. By the way, this has allowed it to support its Brand mania with clothing, equipment, and other offerings. It's a connection.

- *Coke.* Better known now as Classic Coke. Flashback. Who would have expected that an unbranded "blind test taste" in the mid-1980s would have convinced Coca-Cola to jettison its tried-and-true Coke formula and introduce a new Coke? Result: the loyal Coke drinkers created a public outcry, with Coke receiving 40,000 letters of complaint and over 6,000 calls a day to the company's 800 phone number. After only 87 days, the company responded to the loyalists' demands and reintroduced the old formula under a new name— Classic Coke. What went wrong?

1. The company focused on the product (its formula), not the Brand.
2. It neglected the emotional attachment and value of "Coke" to the loyal American public.
3. It forgot that Coke lovers associated flavor with the Brand. It's an experience.

You see, people who buy these Brands uniquely experience them. The Brands are part of their lifestyle—and in some cases their life story. When I had finished my sales "sermonette," the client looked at me and said simply, "I see that you are passionate about Brands and believe in this, and it does make so much sense to pay attention to the Brand, but if Brand is so important, then why

- "Can't I get my salespeople to talk about the Brand?
- "Do my salespeople get stuck on the lower steps and never get to the Brand?
- "Don't they just *sell Brand first?*"

His reply that day validated what I had been thinking all along and brought my perspective on the Buyer Stair-Step into clearer focus. Up to that time, I had formatted the four elements of the model as a staircase because it is illustrative of the uphill, and nonproductive, climb that many salespeople are making today. As pointed out at the end of Chapter 3, it is like climbing up a steep flight of stairs—you can take only one step at a time, and you're exhausted when you finally reach the top (see Figure 4.2).

FIGURE 4.2

Originally I had formulated the model starting with Price, based on observations of what is important in the typical sales transaction. But after a while, I observed that even though the elements were solid, there was something wrong with the order. The pattern I noticed was that when salespeople allowed the transaction to begin with Price and work toward Brand, the interaction was not as successful as it was when approached the other way around. The participants in the early sales workshops agreed, coming back to me with the observations that selling from Price first takes too much time, drains their energy and the buyer's energy, doesn't produce the proper buying momentum, and is like "pushing water uphill." But they kept doing it because they didn't know any other way to sell, or what to do about this counterproductive use of energy, or how to produce better results.

What I realized was that salespeople needed new beliefs, habits, and behaviors in order to pull together the intuitive selling that they use daily on the job. But I didn't abandon the Buyer Stair-Step. I recognized that all of the steps were significant and thus should be an essential part of the salesperson's daily selling tools. That day, when the top prospect asked, "Why don't they just sell Brand first?" I realized that I was on to something and that others also appreciated the need for Brand first, but just didn't have the language or skills for it yet. The big insight was that there should be a more intentional focus on Brand because of its importance. I thought about it, and then went to work to develop a way to express the importance of Brand first. It took three major changes to the Buyer Stair-Step Model to make all of the difference:

1. Rename it.
2. Reverse it.
3. Sell it.

Changes That Launched the Brand Staircase

1. Rename It from the Buyer Stair-Step to the Brand Staircase

The logic was simple—the focus needed to be moved from the buyer to the Brand. If the buyer can experience, connect with, or affiliate with the Brand, then Brand is a *natural entry point* for the salesperson to meet the buyer at and sell from the strength of the Brand (see Figure 4.3). This is especially true if the Brand represents a lifestyle choice by the buyer. It also is a very strong place to begin or continue the relationship with the buyer.

In the book *Brand Babble*, the Schultzes support this relationship and lifestyle approach to Brands. They assert that "Brands in all of their

THE REVERSED BRAND STAIRCASE

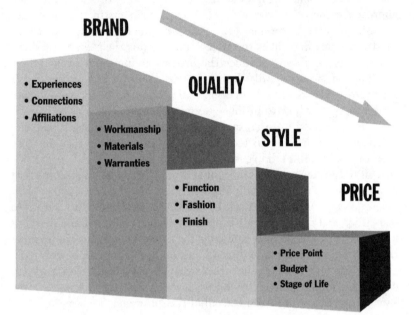

FIGURE 4.3

intangible glory, really represent relationships. They connect the organization to the customer and vice versa." They continue with,

> *Brands survive because customers buy into them. Simply put, that means they live in the hearts and minds of customers. They are part of those people's life experiences. They aren't easily displaced or replaced. They are long-term, high value products and services for the people who have internalized them (pp. 20, 32).*

There is also a far less scientific method to my madness here. Think of a stair-step for a moment. What images emerge for you? Now, hold that thought and think of a staircase. What images emerge there? Now compare. If your imagination kicked in, you probably described the stair-step as basic, narrow, possibly steep, maybe with guardrails—but maybe not. However, when you think of a staircase, the image changes, doesn't it? A staircase is grand; it is inviting; it has a sweeping banister, is flowing and gradual in its descent, and is wide to accommodate many guests. A staircase is also sturdy and stable; thus, it is anchored well within the house. The steps on the staircase support one another and need one another. You get the picture. Isn't it also easy to associate the staircase with a lifestyle, a party with many invited guests?

You see, it sometimes seems that salespeople view their buyers as people to conquer, as competitive adversaries, rather than as invited guests. We need to change our sales imagery and our sales mindset to a new mental model in order to be successful; we need a word picture to anchor our thinking. Instead of seeing ourselves looking uphill, ready to climb a steep flight of stairs, huffing and puffing if and when we arrive at the Brand, and all the while dragging our buyer along; we need to instead see ourselves standing at the top looking down the Brand Staircase.

We should be talking about the cornerstone step, which is offering Brand first and being able to walk our prospect down the staircase. Then we could stop on the steps that need attention, as if we were taking our guest on a gallery tour of our fine artwork. We need to allow the transaction to unfold in front of us by taking a more natural path on the Brand Staircase.

There is one more reason for changing the name from Buyer Stair-Step to Brand Staircase. When you name something, you give it meaning. For instance, many couples spend countless hours deciding on a name for their newborns. They read through the book of names, ponder who this little one will be in terms of personality, and discuss with relatives their best and most laughable options.

When you rename something, you go one step further—you often change its meaning. Marriage is a great example. When people "tie the knot," in our society the female has traditionally adopted the husband's last name as a sign of commitment and change in life. We now see that person with a new identity. Two families have now been blended into one.

You see, Brands need a new identity for salespeople. They need a new spot of prominence in our thinking. They need to be our first thought when selling, not an afterthought. Put another way:

> If we have viewed the "Product as King" in the past,
> we now need to view the "Brand as the Crown Jewel."

And we need to treat it that way. *Rename it.*

2. Reverse the Brand Staircase

Please understand that when I first started teaching the Brand Staircase, it went uphill. I had renamed it, Brand was a component, but it still went uphill. The problem was that the salespeople were still struggling with how to put Brand into focus, to give it the prime attention in their selling. It was still seen as the last step. Something wasn't quite right, yet.

It all came together one day in a workshop. I was teaching a group of veteran salespeople. We had built the Stair-Step, and I had just renamed it the Brand Staircase. They were into an exercise on how buyers associate with their Brand, trying to come up with examples of how they connect with, affiliate with, or experience it. I hate to admit it, but the exercise was going nowhere. People were confused, they were giving me dazed looks, and their questions were asking for clarification. So, somewhat frustrated, I tried to change their focus and simplify the discussion.

Intuitively I asked what I considered to be a smart question. Figuring that salespeople love to tell stories, I said, "Think of a time when you were beaten by another Brand and, more importantly, why." Their additional instructions were to share their story with someone else at their table. I expected the room to get very noisy very quickly. Instead, there was silence. I waited and waited and waited. No response. Reasoning that none of the participants wanted to admit in front of their peers that they had been beaten, I changed the scope of the question to adapt to their comfort zone and asked about their own Brand.

"OK, let's focus on your Brand. Think of a time when you sold the Brand and you beat a competitor. Again, why did you win? Share with a partner." Again, the room went silent. A few people started to tell product stories that were thinly disguised as Brand stories. I was shocked, then it hit me: if it was this hard for salespeople to come up with a story about Brand, then Brand was simply not on their radar. It certainly was not

- *Their first thought*—it was an afterthought.
- *On the front burner*—it was on the back burner.
- *Top of mind*—it was out of sight, out of mind.

They were not even considering it as a major part of their selling arsenal. That very day in that workshop, the Brand Staircase was reversed; it started flowing downhill, and people started getting it.

Think about the benefits of reversing the staircase for just a moment. If our solution to emphasizing Brand is to reverse the staircase, then Brand, not Price, will be the first and most important step on the staircase. This will figuratively allow you to be selling downhill instead of selling uphill. This downward motion is like a waterfall that builds cascading momentum (as represented by the downward arrow in Figure 4.3). If you think of it as being like the way gravity works, it takes less energy to go downhill than to push uphill. Again the climbing stairs analogy: when you go down a flight of steep stairs, it is much easier, quicker, and takes half of the time and energy required to ascend the same staircase and arrive at your destination.

This mental adjustment for the salesperson puts the staircase in the correct order, and it also makes Brand the most prominent step. When you reverse the staircase, then it is much easier to talk about the other steps of Quality, Style, and Price. The reason is that the Brand becomes the support or pillar that in most cases upholds and justifies the other steps.

Reversing the staircase will reorient the salesperson's approach to the buying interaction and broaden the organization's paradigms for selling its products and services. After all, the salesperson is on the front line, the one who can effectively challenge the thinking and buying habits of the buyer, and, as emphasized in Chapter 2, the salesperson has to develop a Brand language to get that across.

Reverse it.

3. Sell the Brand First

That makes the biggest step, the Brand, the first and most important step. If the Brand is indeed where buyers connect the most with your products or services, it is then the smartest place for the salesperson to start. Importantly, when you start with the Brand, it is easier to talk the Quality story and justify the Brand's reputation. If you are doing a good job moving down the Brand Staircase, then by the time you get to the Style step, the buyer understands the differences in Quality and the Brand and is ready to finish the sale here. In other words, the final decision can be made at that step, with Price having become almost irrelevant or a nondetermining factor. Finally, if Price is still a big consideration in the decision process, the buyer is more focused on the "value for the money I'm spending," instead of thinking, "Can I afford it?" or "Does it fit my budget?"

There are other good reasons for putting Brand first, both from the perspective of the buyer and from the perspective of the seller. Not only does it alleviate the conditions that make selling uphill such a challenge, but in doing so it also plays into the natural mindset of the buyer, who is probably already thinking in "Brand mode" but is not encouraged to expose that thinking within most current sales transactions. By making this simple switch of priorities in the sales sequence, the salesperson can create a much more hospitable environment for the buyer to break out, so to speak, and to converse with the seller in Brand language.

Finally it is important to build a concrete model and process that represents this new belief system that will allow salespeople to move beyond the intuitive selling that comes from years of on-the-job selling experience and intentionally sell the Brand. *Sell it first.*

Benefits of Reversing the Brand Staircase for You and Your Company

Once salespeople understand the staircase and how it can be made to work for them, they will be more effective in honing in on the mindset of buyers as they enter the buying transaction. You, as the salesperson within a culture, will gain a new, fresh, and effective way to approach buyers by using the Brand Staircase as a key sales and cultural tool. Additionally, the organization can support this effort and gradually integrate a system that promotes Brand first into its culture.

The three most important benefits of reversing the staircase and talking about Brand first reside in the areas of Brand loyalty, Brand leverage, and becoming Brand ambassadors. All three will help you build, maintain, or grow your Brand and its market position. However, each impacts a significant element in your approach to the Brand.

- Brand loyalty is largely a buyer element.
- Brand leverage is mostly a company element.
- Brand ambassadors are a seller element.

Brand Loyalty

Build excellent and unforgettable experiences for your customers, and they will be increasingly loyal to your brand. At DeWALT, we had a contractor appreciation program that worked like this: buy five tools, and we'll give you the sixth one free. We had people clamoring to see which tool they could buy so that they could qualify for the free tool, which had up to a $150 value. Some users even bought an extra tool in order to qualify for the free tool more quickly. We also were the first company in our industry to bring the product to the users at their job site or their favorite NASCAR event, speedboat race, or rodeo. We called it "end-user marketing," but it had a very personal touch—salesperson to buyer. It also created tremendous Brand loyalty because the contractors had an unforgettable experience with our company—one that extended beyond their "day job" and met them where they lived, worked, and played.

Build a Branded culture, where employees would rather come to work than be anywhere else, and you build Brand loyalty. The long-term goal of selling from Brand strength is to create a Branded culture in which everyone, from the janitor to the president of the company, believes wholeheartedly in the message of your Brand, its emotional statement to its buyers, and the collective voice it wields within your organization and within the marketplace. Most companies miss the mark here, because they believe that it's "marketing's job" to produce, roll out, and attend to the Brand. The reality is that it's *everyone's* job to articulate the Brand, and sometimes your buyers are the most Brand loyal of anyone.

Brand Leveraging Is the Company

Many companies are seeing today's marketplace as a Brand leveraging opportunity, where proper execution of the Brand strategy within their competitive marketplace will greatly benefit the company's market position and resulting culture. Too often, however, companies leave the Brand leveraging up to the marketing team and expect it to come up with logical line extensions. The top executives of the company need to be the champions here, driving the culture to be creative and look for logical Brand extensions and places where the company can benefit from its Brand offerings.

I was recently in a meeting with a top customer—Aviall, the world's largest distributor of aviation parts and services. The meeting was hosted by Zachry Associates, a marketing and advertising consulting firm. The presenter, Jeff Warr, vice president of marketing, was describing where the Brand merged with marketing strategy. He had just shown a slide and explained, "You have a Brand whether you intend to or not. . . . Better to shape your Brand than simply let it happen." There was an immediate and passionate reaction to this statement. The chief operating officer, Dan Komnenovich, stated openly, "We already have a good Brand. Yet, the more you think about the Brand, the more you realize it's about the culture. Your people represent your Brand every day in every customer interaction. Your people are your Brand." Jeff and I both agreed; it couldn't have been said any better.

Brand Ambassadors Are the Sellers

Probably the biggest place you can have an immediate impact with your Brand is with the sellers (and resellers) of your Brand. Of course, the salesperson's readiness is important here. Unfortunately, many of the people I share this with are not ready.

Let me illustrate. Some salespeople are like the great Pacific salmon that swim upstream to spawn. By the time the salmon have reached the spawning grounds, they have spent so much time and energy fighting the water flow that they are exhausted; they lay their eggs and die. In the same way, many veteran salespeople are exhausted from pushing water uphill for so long; they are tired and caught in a rut by the time they reach the Brand story and what it means to the buyer. In effect, they die in their sales efforts just when the Brand needs them the most. So, they become *Brand imposters* instead of *Brand ambassadors*.

Now, what do Brand ambassadors do better than Brand imposters?

First off, they understand the meaning of being an ambassador. In short, an ambassador is a representative of a cause, a people, or an organization (including a company) that has its best interests in mind. Second, *Webster's American Family Dictionary* says that a Brand is "a stamp, trademark or the like; or a mark made by burning to indicate kind, grade, make or ownership." In other words, Brand ambassadors become Branded, to the point where they believe that

1. They fully represent the Brand.
2. A user would be compromising to buy anything less than their Brand.

Could you imagine any company in America, or anywhere in the world for that matter, that would not want every salesperson it has in the field to be that committed, to be that sold on the company's Brand? You probably can't. A company with that focus on Brand would be very hard to compete against, wouldn't it?

I know that to be true, because I sold for, led, and trained people for 18 years at some of the best trade or consumer Brand companies in the world: NCR, Black & Decker, and DeWALT. We did many things well in the sales and marketing arena. Most of what we did well, we did intuitively and not intentionally. I am challenging you right now to take a lesson from my learning curve—to take an intentional approach to building Brand ambassadors.

My current customer base has challenged me to take this intentional approach over the last six years, to get beyond my own comfort zone and think about the lessons I'd learned about selling the Brand in order to create the Brand Staircase so that salespeople would immediately understand.

Company Examples of the Reversed Brand Staircase

Allow me to illustrate the impact of the reversed Brand Staircase with some company case studies. You will see interwoven here how it has helped build Brand loyalty, Brand leverage, and Brand ambassadors in a selling environment. These examples come from the industries I have been serving and working with on Brand selling, and each contains a Brand problem and a Brand solution.

Brand Leverage and Expansion
Following an Acquisition

Purdy, based in Portland, Oregon, is a paint applicator company that manufactures and sells paintbrushes, rollers, and accessories; it is primarily known for its high-end, professional-quality paintbrushes. It is a crossover Brand that touches both the professional painter and the do-it-yourself consumer and sells through distribution in multiple channels. Its end users are as Brand loyal as any you will ever find. They literally will sell other painting contractors on changing to Purdy by promoting the high-quality, long-lasting, easy-to-clean, and hassle-free brushes they have owned for years. Over time, Purdy has catered to the professional trades and helped educate upcoming painters by putting Purdy brushes in the hands of the educators, thus creating the next generation of professional users of Purdy products. It has created Brand ambassadors.

Purdy is now at a point where it can further leverage its strong Brand name by expanding beyond the professional into the do-it-yourself channels and extending its Brand allegiance to other product categories like paint rollers. Sherwin-Williams recently acquired Purdy and now has it well positioned for future growth. Purdy now has a long-term strategic owner, and is aligned with other strong Brand names that will help to expand its impact in the marketplace as a full-service painting project company. Brand leverage.

PROBLEM: You might say, "Gee, it seems that Purdy has everything going for it; what's the problem?" Remember that Purdy originally built its Brand loyalty with the professional end user in the trades—professional painters, remodelers, and educators. Now Purdy's Brand is finding opportunities in the retail store environment. Specifically, store consolidation within consumer channels has opened up doors with larger accounts that carry paint and sundry products serving both consumers and professionals. Thus, many of the Purdy salespeople need to learn how to intentionally sell the value of the Purdy Brand to the retail buyer. Those skill sets are different from selling to the trade user, as you will see in Chapter 11.

Also, the Sherwin-Williams team now has access to the Purdy Brand to complete its lineup within the Sherwin-Williams stores. So, the real issue here is, what happens when you engage large numbers of staff in expanding their Brand-selling skills?

SOLUTION: The senior management team at Purdy and Sherwin-Williams decided not to rest on its laurels with the company's Brands. Instead, Purdy is advancing its organization with Brand-selling workshops to anchor everyone in its sales teams on the importance of selling the Purdy Brand first in multiple settings and channels. As a company, it is driving its culture and its future around two core beliefs:

1. The company wants a radical "love" relationship with the end user (emotional connection—Brand loyalty).
2. The company wants any associate involved with the Purdy Brand to feel extremely proud of this association (Brand ambassadors).

Getting Brand Language to the Street

One of the early requests I had for Brand selling came from the aviation business. I had been working with Jim Quinn, the senior vice president of sales and marketing at Aviall Services Inc. in Dallas, Texas, the world's largest independent distributor of aviation parts and services. Now, because Aviall is in distribution sales, it most often is selling the same products that its competitors sell. Whether it is Michelin or Goodyear tires, GE lamps, Champion ignition components, or Lycoming engines, it is generally selling a similar product where Style and Quality are equivalent. So, in reality, Aviall has three things to sell that will differentiate it from its competition: its Brand, its reputation, and the excellent service it provides.

PROBLEM: The problem was that Aviall was not conveying those benefits to the buyers as a part of its everyday sales language. We had provided two years of sales and leadership training, and the resulting culture change was very positive. Yet, when I met with Jim, he was concerned about a number of bad habits that his salespeople were developing:

*   They were getting beaten on price.
*   They weren't selling creatively.
*   They needed to listen better for opportunities.
*   They had no idea what their Brand meant to the buyer and how to leverage and sell it every day.

Jim's request to me was to build an easy understanding of the Brand for his salespeople. We needed to create a new way to think about the Brand and help them remember it, and sell value as opposed to price in the field. I told him that there was no model out there on how to sell a Brand and its value, but I had been doing a lot of work on developing one.

I shared with him a word picture that I was using in the beginning to develop my model for selling a Brand. In short, most people (in this case, salespeople) change habits in a three-step process. I call it *the triangle: the head to heart to mouth transfer* (see Figure 4.4).

HEAD – HEART – MOUTH TRANSFER

FIGURE 4.4

It starts at the head, where information is processed and logic is utilized. It then moves to the heart, where your belief system exists and emotions are encountered. It then travels to the mouth, where our language kicks in and we put our beliefs into action. I told him that most people will stop at the logic part and play a "head game" with themselves. They seldom get to the heart, much less the mouth. So, in order to effect change, we need to move from attitudes (head) to beliefs (heart) to behavior (mouth). We needed to create the right Brand sales language for his people and find a way to get it to their lips.

SOLUTION: Over a series of 10 workshops, we ran some Brand and creativity exercises. We brainstormed what Brand meant to the buyers, internal customers, and competitors of Aviall. We essentially identified all of the top reasons that buyers did business with Aviall. We came up with 43, and then we combined, summarized, and whittled these down to the top four reasons for doing business with Aviall that would represent the Brand on the street.

Then we talked about intentionally telling the Aviall story on the street, thus making the Brand come alive. The salespeople now have something to talk about that differentiates Aviall from the competition, and that backs up the company's excellent service and great reputation in the trade. They have become proud to sell their Brand and take credit for the value of their brand.

Today we have built a new belief system and sales process based on Aviall's Brand. We are also into round two of Brand selling, where we will be focusing on the business-to-business model highlighted in Chapters 11 and 12.

Building Brand Ambassadors at Retail

Baldwin Hardware Corporation, based in Reading, Pennsylvania, is a high-end lockset, trim, and hardware manufacturer whose primary business is selling high-end locks in home decor showrooms and dealerships. Company executives came to me to discuss how to better sell the company's Brand against competition from overseas that was undercutting its price by up to 40 percent. I shared with the executive team the Brand Staircase model and its implications, and received their approval to see where it could help their sales team. Prior to implementing the Brand Staircase, I then went out to the field to observe how the salespeople were currently selling.

PROBLEM: To understand the issues more, I went on sales calls to watch the interactions with buyers. I also sat in on the traditional product-knowledge sessions where the sales reps were educating the store personnel on the product line. The Baldwin reps did all the things I expected them to do; that is, they did a great job of articulating the superior features and benefits of the company's product versus the competition. They were telling a great Quality story. I then watched the store personnel (Baldwin resellers) continue to struggle to make any kind of association with the Brand and the value it brought to the end user/buyer. Upon observation, I came to the conclusion that it was not the product-knowledge session that was broken. Instead, it was their overreliance on the product knowledge to the detriment of the Brand that kept the salespeople from creating Brand ambassadors (passionate resellers of the product) within that retail store environment.

The interesting thing was that no one questioned Baldwin's Quality. What buyers were struggling to understand was *why that quality should be worth 25 to 40 percent more* to the consumer shopping for products. These resellers needed to know how to sell the Brand first and why it was worth it to step up. If that happened, then the Quality story would simply reinforce and justify the value for the dollar and also the Brand.

SOLUTION: We ran a series of Brand selling workshops and equipped the salespeople with the Brand Staircase to return to the field. During the next three customer-training sessions, we asked them to start with the Brand Staircase model and walk the resellers through all four steps. We told them to spend a minimum of 50 percent of the time talking about the Brand, and dedicate the other 50 percent of the time to the product and its features, benefits, and quality.

During those three sessions, it was clear that the store personnel were getting it. You could see it on the salespeople's faces. We had them teach back what they had learned to the Baldwin reps. They were now taking credit for the Baldwin Brand in a number of key ways. One big way was to grab some of Baldwin's rich history and speak to it:

- The invention of the mortise lock—still the highest-quality lock in the marketplace
- The invention and marketing of the "lifetime finish," which means, in short, that the polished brass finish on the lock will never tarnish
- How the solid forged brass means that the highest quality and value are built into every Baldwin product

They then started to talk in Brand terms: *timeless craftsmanship, prestige, aspiring,* and *the ultimate security for your home.* The Brand now had value, and the salespeople could claim that value in the selling situation and the price that went hand in hand with that value. Most importantly, the Baldwin salespeople had transferred their thinking and emotions about the Brand to the store personnel who would be selling the products to everyday buyers.

The store owners at each session approached me afterward and shared the following comments:

- "I wish I had known about this 10 years ago. I would have been teaching them to sell this way from the beginning and using the Brand Staircase system to sell any good-quality Brand in our store!"
- "I now have a better tool to sell not only Baldwin, but Kohler, Jenn-Air, Viking, Franke, [and so on]."
- "My store personnel now have a great reason to sell a more expensive product and never be ashamed of the price, because they are

taking credit for the Brand. This is a great way to ask for more money for a product, to make most sales (tickets) more profitable, and to also build our image as a store."

As I have continued to share this model with other companies, many participants seek me out following workshops, and I repeatedly hear some variation of this comment: "I wish I had known 15 years ago about the importance of putting Brand first. It will be so much easier to get into a conversation about high-level Brands, or, for that matter, a conversation on any Brands with a decent value."

Additionally, manufacturer's reps who own their company and represent a manufacturer's product line on a commission basis have said:

- "We need to get this kind of thinking into our whole agency, so we can represent all of our lines using the Brand Staircase."
- "This really makes me think about our own company's Brand and how it is represented by my people every day in the marketplace."

This understanding of Brand comes after many years of observing sales rituals and often seeing them fail. My ultimate goal is to help you enhance your sales performance, in terms of both quality and quantity. I want you to be successful. In the next chapter, I offer some challenges and warnings about what to look for first when embarking on a sales program that emphasizes Brand first.

Key Points

People buy Brands that they can trust. People associate closely with Brands, and as salespeople and leaders, we need to recognize this and sell accordingly. We can do this by understanding the buyers and their Brand behavior. In short, when purchasing products and services, people are not just purchasing a product, but rather are supporting a chosen lifestyle. These lifestyle choices are based on

- *Past experiences* with the Brand
- *Present connections* to the Brand
- *Future affiliations* with the Brand

In order to be successful in the future, salespeople need new beliefs, habits, and behaviors to pull together the intuitive selling that they use daily on the job, and they need to apply these characteristics to the Brand. We have to find a way to get Brand onto salespeople's radar. It needs to be top of mind, not back of mind. It needs to be on their front burner, not their back burner. It needs to be their first thought, not an afterthought.

To accomplish this, we need some major changes in how we sell. Those changes to the model are to rename the Buyer Stair-Step as the Brand Staircase, then reverse the staircase and sell downhill, and finally to focus on selling Brand first.

Long term, the Brand sustains its momentum in the marketplace if the company, its salespeople, and its leaders can focus on three insights that facilitate the creation and sustenance of the Brand:

- Brand loyalty from its buyers
- Brand leverage from its company
- Brand ambassadors within its sellers and culture

CHAPTER 5

CHALLENGES AND OPPORTUNITIES

A fter spending time with the Brand Staircase model and with customers in real selling situations, I have been challenged by others
and even myself to think through how this new system focused on the
Brand actually plays out in the real world. As a matter of fact, some of
you may be doubters, naysayers, and even critics from the "show me"
state. You are probably looking for more evidence before giving a ver-
dict on this "Brand selling" thing. I get it—frankly, I would be skepti-
cal, too.

You see, over time I have come to realize that Brand selling goes
against conventional thinking in some cases, and even against old, and
presumably tested, selling paradigms in a number of other cases. As
you begin to sell in this new way, let me point out some potential pitfalls to avoid based on your old habits and behaviors. This chapter looks
at the Brand Staircase step by step and identifies the most common
issues I have seen arise for salespeople who want to incorporate this
new way of selling into their arsenal of sales techniques.

*Through it all, the conclusion I have come to is quite simply this: When
you reverse the Brand Staircase and sell Brand first, you lessen and even
avoid many of the selling challenges that can crop up around Brand, Quality, Style, and Price in the typical buyer transaction.* Hopefully, you too
will agree with that conclusion by the time you reach the end of this
chapter. You will have many more insights into why this process works
and whether or not it is worth adopting into your selling style. You will
have rounded up more evidence. Later, in Part 3, the evidence for
Brand selling will continue to grow as we dissect further how to understand the buyer's mindset and apply the right seller's habits.

So, let's discuss these challenges and opportunities in the way that a
sales audience would like to receive the answers—that is, head on,
pragmatic, and real world.

The Reversed Brand Staircase: Top Challenges

Each step of the reversed Brand Staircase has its challenges and opportunities that salespeople need to be aware of as they start using the model and selling Brand first (see Figure 5.1). Each step has its own particular challenge, which arises mostly if salespeople are not selling downhill.

To recap, the definitions of the steps of the Brand Staircase are

- *Brand* is what the brand means to the buyer on a very personal and emotional level. It is grounded in the buyer's experiences, connections, and affiliations.
- *Quality* is the workmanship, materials, or warranty that the buyer gets with the product.
- *Style* is how the product functions, its fashion, or its finish.
- *Price* is the amount the buyer is willing to spend on the purchase, based on his budget and stage of life.

The challenges associated with these steps come in the form of key questions and observations:

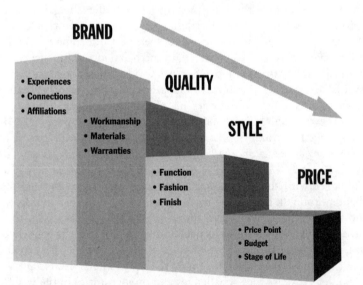

FIGURE 5.1

- At the Brand step: avoiding *hollow Brand promises*
- At the Quality step: recognizing the *competitive assessment*
- At the Style step: understanding *feature and benefit myopia*
- At the Price step: breaking the *glass ceiling of price*

The Brand Step: Avoiding Hollow Brand Promises

How can we focus only on the Brand and forget about the other three steps?

This is one of the questions that I am most frequently asked—in a variety of forms. And the people who ask it are at the highest levels in a company. In the span of a two-week window, I heard the following versions from three top executives:

- "I don't want to forget what got us here, and that is the *quality of our product.*"
- "*The Brand can't stand alone*, or else it becomes an empty promise."
- "*Product is king* around here. We never want to lose sight of it."

What all three of these executives were concerned about was what I call *hollow brand promises* (see Figure 5.2). These are promises that the Brand makes that can't be backed up by the Quality, Style, or Price of the product. Put another way, if buyers associate with Brands based on past experiences and connections or future affiliations, then companies cannot afford to lessen their quality, dramatically change their styling, or price their products and services unrealistically.

If they choose that path, then their Brand will not meet buyers' expectations and the ongoing promises that attracted buyers to it in the first place. The Brand will be seen as making empty promises that ring hollow; that is, they are not believable to the buyer, and in most cases to the seller.

Let me deal with each one in turn:

- *Quality of our product.* If the Energizer Bunny's claim as a Brand is that "it keeps going, and going and going," but the buyer's experience in real life is that it runs out of energy (and battery life) after two hours, then this is an empty promise. If DeWALT claims that its industrial tools are "Guaranteed Tough," then the quality needs to back up this claim. If it doesn't, then it's an empty promise. So the Quality of the product needs to support and back up the statement (and promise) made by the Brand in its advertising and its Brand sales language on the street.
- *The Brand can't stand alone.* I agree completely with that statement! I make this point during my workshops: All four of the steps are important, and they all have value if your Brand is to have a long-

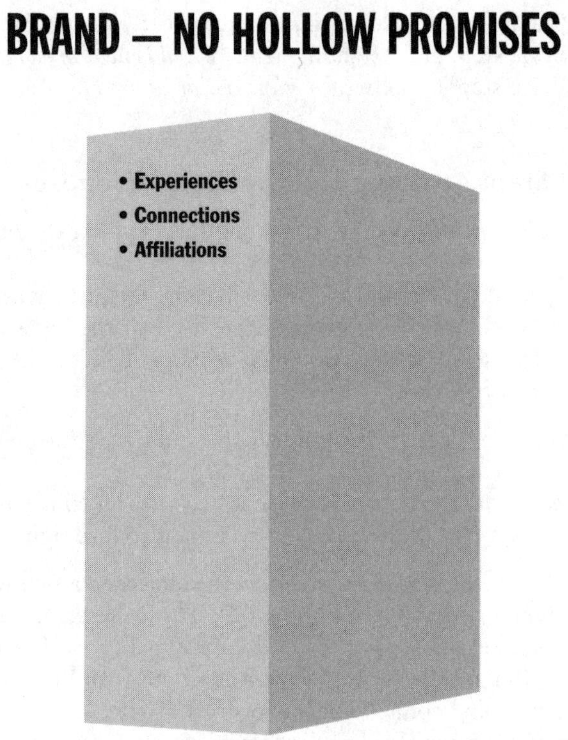

BRAND – NO HOLLOW PROMISES

- Experiences
- Connections
- Affiliations

FIGURE 5.2

term impact. So, you as a salesperson cannot afford to sell from the Brand step alone and forget about the other three steps. If you do, you will have forgotten what made you, your products, and your company successful in the first place. On the other hand, you need to start with the Brand to leverage all of the good things that the Brand supports within the other three steps—good quality, good styling, and a fair price for the value that the buyer receives.

- *Product is king.* Most companies get their start with products. It's how they attract customers: by "building a better mousetrap" with exclusive features or a better price. It is their heritage and their history. Frankly, many companies have great products, with high quality, good styling, and a fair price. I have worked for such companies as a salesperson and leader, and now I am fortunate enough to work with such companies as a consultant and trainer. So, please hear this: I believe that great Brands start with great products. However, I also believe that your competition can duplicate all of the other three steps except the Brand. Think about it. The Brand is the great differentiator. Put another way: the truth is:

- *Product* offerings can become outdated.
- *Price* can often be beaten.
- *Style* can be duplicated or re-created.
- *Quality* can slip in one production run.

The bottom line is:

- *Your competition* can duplicate all of these!

> But the competition can't duplicate
> your people and the power of your Brand.

The Quality Step: Recognizing the Competitive Assessment

How and when do I adequately compare my product to the competition?

You are in your best spot for comparison against your competition when you start at the top of the staircase. Competitive assessment occurs mostly at the Quality step of the Brand Staircase (see Figure 5.3), and we

QUALITY – THE COMPETITIVE ASSESSMENT

- Workmanship
- Materials
- Warranties

FIGURE 5.3

need to recognize that fact and sell accordingly. In other words, the most likely spot for buyers to compare products is when they can look at the warranty, materials, and workmanship associated with the product.

If you are selling a midmarket to upper-level brand, you want the buyer to compare it to the competition starting with the Brand and then move to your Quality story.

Quality is one of those subjects that seem simple but go deep very quickly. Some of that has to do with how we define Quality and its history. *Webster's American Family Dictionary* defines Quality as "character with respect to excellence or fineness," i.e., "materials of fine quality." It goes on to define it as a "superiority, or excellence," i.e., "a reputation of quality." Based on that definition, Quality has probably always been a big part of the purchase decision.

Warranties have fundamentally changed the way we view quality and after-sale service. Now, buyers consider product warranties to be a main part of the up-front selling transaction, not just a service/maintenance transaction. Why? Because some companies have changed the game with respect to warranties. Here are two good examples of recent warranties that changed fundamentally how people market products. DeWALT power tools offered a 30-day money-back guarantee: if you don't like the product for any reason (shape, color, performance, or any other reason), then you can bring it back within 30 days for a no-questions-asked full refund. Second, years ago Chrysler started the car industry's longer-term warranties—for example, 7 years or 70,000 miles and 100,000 miles on the drive train. Both of these warranties represented a commitment to Quality and a lower risk for the buyer.

Additionally, my experience has been that salespeople need to change their view of how to sell the whole Quality step on the Brand Staircase. We simply take the Quality for granted (including the impact of workmanship, materials, and warranties) and don't sell it. Let me put it another way: if you think about it, all of these elements (workmanship, materials, and warranties) are normally provided by the manufacturer of the product. Also, the salesperson cannot transform what has gone into the Quality of the product. Importantly, however, salespeople can change their view of how the buyer reacts to the Quality of the product, and the importance the buyer places on workmanship, materials, and warranties. How? you ask. By changing the way they view Quality prior to the buyer interaction:

- They need to stop taking Quality for granted and start emphasizing it when selling.
- They need to stop ignoring the impenetrable advantages by just assuming that they are a "part of the Quality story."

Salespeople, start asking the buyer to react to the Quality by "comparing value" and looking to "trade up." Good or bad—just to react to it.

To understand this better, a little history is in order. The business archives from 40 to 50 years ago give us a quick perspective on quality. When I was growing up, quality was just finding its name. One company's marketing slogan was, "The quality goes in before the name goes on." American companies were getting the quality connection with consumers. On the other hand, the "Made in Japan" label had an immediate association with "cheap and breakable." Seeing this, visionary leaders in Japan began to realize the reputation of goods made in their country and moved quickly to change that reputation. Today, companies like Sony, Fujitsu, Panasonic, Mitsubishi, Honda, Toyota, and Nissan have done a fabulous job over time of creating some of the highest-quality electronics, computers, televisions, cars, camcorders, entertainment systems, and digital cameras. They have effectively turned around the perception of poor quality and improved the reputation associated with Japanese products. Today, the American consumer/user expects good quality from Japanese manufacturers.

Now, even in America, the term *quality* has taken on greater meaning over the last couple of decades. This is largely in response to the quality initiatives of Japan and other competing global nations. American companies started with W. Edwards Deming's concept of Total Quality Management programs, moved toward the Malcolm Baldrige National Quality Award for companies, and have since made the transition to Six Sigma. Much also has been written about Lean Manufacturing, and the whole subject of Quality will continue to be a big consideration for future products. Candidly, billions of dollars have been spent by companies on increasing the quality of products and services. It's as if the quality of products has taken on a life of its own.

The end result is that Quality has become a key and expected ingredient that buyers react to during buying decisions. The smart salesperson finds out the buyer's viewpoint on Quality and sells accordingly. The smart salesperson who also has a high-quality product offering will make this his number-one spot for comparing the product against the competition, i.e., doing a competitive assessment.

To prove how important Quality has become in comparing products, you could interview buyers on the street and find thousands of examples where Quality was a prime decision driver. You could also come up with your own examples of Quality-based decisions that you made on certain products. However, to illustrate the use of *impenetrable advantages* and *trading up*, I'll just give you two quick examples that I experienced personally.

A few years ago, I bought a high-quality Baldwin lockset for my front door (prior to Baldwin's being my customer). I literally took off my tarnished lockset, which had weathered over five years to the point where I was embarrassed to have people knock on my door. I bought Baldwin based largely on what I call two impenetrable advantages. One was something the company called *solid forged brass*—that is, the foundry process that forges high-quality brass, which means durability and long life to me. The other advantage was something Baldwin called the *lifetime finish guarantee*. The polished brass was guaranteed to never tarnish, no matter what the weather conditions—humid, dry, salty, or anything else. As a buyer, those two impenetrable advantages were what sold me on the quality. There simply was no other manufacturer who could match the advantages that Baldwin put into the quality of its product. The lockset is still working to this day, untarnished and highlighting my front door.

A second example is the replacement of my riding lawnmower with a new John Deere lawn tractor. Again, the decision was mostly based on quality. I co-owned the other mower with another family in the neighborhood, and we had always had problems with the cutting deck. We had replaced pulleys and belts and remachined the spindles. When the lawnmower broke down once again, I finally became totally frustrated with it, and I literally gave it to my neighbor and walked away. Rarely do I walk away from purchases, especially if they are paid for, but in this case I no longer viewed the mower as having any value at all and was willing to trade up to a John Deere. I traded up to a better Kohler engine, a Home Depot guarantee, and a service network and Brand name that I trusted—"Nothing runs like a Deere." The company even speaks quality and long life in its Brand slogan.

The first time I had the new John Deere mower in the shop for routine maintenance and service, I was pleasantly surprised by the company's attention to quality and after-sale service. One week after my mower had been fixed, I received a box in the mail. Inside was a card that said on the cover, "From all of us, thanks for choosing John Deere."

Inside the card was a picture of John Deere employees and a statement, "All 43,000 John Deere employees are honored by your decision to select us. And we're dedicated to making your experience of owning a John Deere as enjoyable as it can possibly be. It's a promise that begins with presenting you with this owner's edition John Deere hat. And never ends."

Inside the box I found a high quality, green John Deere hat with their logo on it. Stitched into the fabric were the words "Owner's Edition" and "Nothing Runs Like a Deere." What a statement of Quality and the Brand promise that comes with owning a John Deere lawn tractor!

So, if you are a salesperson focusing on the Quality step, you need to predetermine the impenetrable advantages that your product has over the competition and then sell from that position. Sell what no one else can duplicate. Don't overlook the high quality that your company builds into your product, or take it for granted that the buyers can simply read the guarantee on the box label or manual. If you do, you will be giving away the number-one opportunity to sell the quality of your product.

Likewise, figure out why it would be to a buyer's benefit to trade up to your product, to spend more to acquire a higher-quality product—especially if you are being compared to a lower-quality product that also carries a lower price tag. Also, find significant and demonstrable differences in the quality of your products versus the competition that make trading up worth the customer's time and money.

For example, when I worked for DeWALT, we had a demonstration to buyers of our industrial-grade power tools that had quite an impact. We would take our tool housing (the casing or "outer skin" that houses all of the moving parts) and put it in a gunnysack. We would then proceed to put similar housings from all of our competitors' tools into the same gunnysack. The next step was to describe the extra quality that we put into our glass-filled nylon reinforced housings compared to the plastic housings that our competition used. Finally, we stopped, put the gunnysack on the ground, picked up a sledgehammer, and whaled the tar out of it. Sometimes we would have buyers join in the fun. When a sufficient beating had been bestowed on the gunnysack and all of our competitors, we simply emptied the sack onto the ground and picked out our slightly dented but never broken housing from the multicolored "housing shrapnel" that now represented our competition. To put it mildly, we sold many tools at these demonstrations, and there was never a question about the quality of our products.

Thus, my challenges to you are simple:

- *Do you know how to identify and sell your impenetrable advantages?* Impenetrable advantages are "super benefits" that can't be matched by any other product on the market. They are considered impenetrable because they can't be touched by the competition. Your product stands alone because of them. They are one of the cornerstones of the successful sale of your product.
- *Do you know how to make a value comparison of your product?* In a value comparison, buyers naturally start to compare the value they get for the money they spend in terms of the quality put into the product. In other words, they are looking for a "distinguishing factor that makes it worthwhile to buy a higher-quality product."
- *Do you know how to help a buyer trade up?* Trading up is the buyer's natural reaction to a good Quality story, and it means that the sales-

person has a good shot at selling a more expensive product. The interesting thing is that many salespeople give up the right to ask for a trade up because they don't even realize that they have earned it with a good Quality story.

Finally, the best anonymous statement that I ever read on quality is re-created here for your benefit:

Buy Quality

When you buy on price alone, you can never be sure. It is unwise, of course, to pay too much. But it is worse to pay too little. When you pay too much, you lose a little money, that's all; but when you pay too little, you sometimes lose everything, because what you bought does not do the thing it was bought to do.

The common law of business transaction prohibits paying a little and getting a lot!!! It can't be done. When you deal with the lowest bidder, it is well to add something for the risk you run, and if you do that, you have enough to "Buy Quality."

Enough said.

The Style Step: Understanding Feature and Benefit Myopia

How do I keep from boring the buyer by droning on about features and benefits?

It is very easy for the average salesperson to get caught up in *feature and benefit myopia*, or "shortsightedness," at the Style step of the Brand Staircase. Instead, salespeople need to refocus on the right things— function, fashion, and finish—to avoid this myopia (see Figure 5.4).

So, before we launch into this discussion of features and benefits, please recall that I have been a "product guy" my entire career. I have been nurtured and groomed on features and benefits language as the solid foundation of good product presentations to the buyer.

Features are typically defined as

- What it is: *The characteristics of the product, program, or promotion*

Benefits are defined as

- What it means to the buyer: *How the features address the needs or priorities of the user/buyer*

We always used to say that "features tell, but benefits sell." This was a good thing for salespeople to remember, because it focused them on the buyers and their needs and got them away from the product and its features. You see, the product doesn't come alive until the buyer

STYLE – FEATURE AND BENEFIT MYOPIA

- Function
- Fashion
- Finish

FIGURE 5.4

engages it. The features matter only if the buyer can translate them into her world. It is the salesperson's job to make that happen.

However, I am just amazed at how often salespeople don't make it happen.

Let me illustrate this in another way. When a group of aspiring salespeople get together in a room, I often ask them to *describe their experiences as a buyer*. I ask them to think of the last big purchase they made, be it a car, TV, stereo, computer, or something else. Once they have that in mind, I ask them to think of the best sales rep they encountered and the worst one. Then I ask them to write down those sales reps' characteristics, habits, and skill sets on a "T-chart," with the best on the left (assets), and the worst on the right (liabilities). I'll bet you can guess what the descriptors on both sides of the ledger are. Table 5.1 shows the most common responses.

You get the drift. What are your observations of these two lists? Most likely, they are something like this:

- We can all relate, because we have all been sold by or bought from one of these salespeople. When we are sold by someone, it is usually by droning on about the features—being "specified to death."
- The best rep list is totally opposite from the worst rep list.
- As a salesperson, I do not want to fall anywhere on the worst rep list.
- Once you get beyond the basic characteristics (honest, trustworthy, and credible), you quickly realize that the rest of the traits or habits can be found in the Brand Staircase: Price, Style, Quality, or Brand.

TABLE 5.1   Best Rep Exercise

Best Rep	Worst Rep
Honest	Dishonest
Trustworthy	Lacked trust
Credible	Lacked credibility
Great Product Knowledge	Lack of Product Knowledge
Listened to "What's in it for Me"	Sold me what they wanted
Listened Well	Didn't listen / talked too much
Made me feel good	"Could care less about me"
Asked good questions	Started selling "Right away"
Competitive Knowledge	Only knew their Products
Easy to talk to	High pressure
Used the time well	Wasted my time
Understood their company / Brand	Sold only on lowest price
Educated me	"I learned very little from him"
High energy / Enthusiasm	Looked bored, or bored me
Sold Benefits of the product	Droned on about Features
Easy and Enjoyable	Laborious, burdensome

- The best reps valued their time, leveraged their energy, and used positive momentum within the transaction. The worst simply didn't. The worst reps fought an uphill battle—*and lost.*

I am not suggesting that you throw away the good skills and product training that you have received. However, I am suggesting that something needs to change here.

- We have got to find a way to engage the buyer more fully at the Style step.
- We have got to find a way to make the features and benefits transfer into the function, fashion, and finish.
- We have got to find a way to get at the emotions that should exist around the style of any good product instead of reciting the specifications and characteristics of the product. (*Note:* We will discuss this further in Part 4.)

Let me close this discussion with a story that illustrates the connection we are looking for here.

Johnny Carson ran the *Tonight Show* for nearly three decades and was arguably one of the most gifted entertainers of our time. He had an ability to make the most humble guest feel right at home, and, on the other hand, he could gracefully put the biggest stars on the spot. Such was the case when his guest was Og Mandino, who was widely touted as the "greatest salesman in the world" at that time and had just written a book with the same title.

Johnny hosted Og on his show one evening just as the book was being released to the public. Following the pleasantries and a quick introduction to the book, Johnny immediately put Og on the spot. Instead of applauding the book, he asked a question on live network television that would have frightened even the most gifted TV personalities.

"Og, if you're the greatest salesman in the world, then sell me this ashtray!" (This was back in the day when smoking was still permitted in public places.) The crowd laughed in surprise, then went quiet, as if to say, "Whoa, I can't believe he just asked him that under all of the lights in front of this crowd and all of America."

Without missing a beat, Og asked, "Why would you even need an ashtray on this show?"

J (stunned a bit): "Well, I entertain some of the world's biggest stars, and some of them smoke."

O: "Can't they smoke offstage in the hallway or waiting room before they come onto the show?"

J (somewhat embarrassed): "No, we couldn't do that. I want to make our guests feel at home, be comfortable, and relax so we can talk freely with them on the show. They need to be themselves, so America can see the real person, the private person behind the star."

O: "OK. So if you were to get an ashtray for your desk, what color would you want?"

J: "Oh, I don't know. Blue is nice because many of our guests wear blue. However, black is nice also, because it goes with about anything."

O: "Well, it comes in either color; which is your preference?"

J: "I guess black."

O: "OK—black. Now if you were to get this black ashtray for the guests on your show, what would be a reasonable price to pay?"

J: "Ahh, 15 dollars?"

O: OK, you can have it for $15."

With that, the crowd spontaneously broke out in laughter and applause. Why? Because they honored Og's creative approach under tough circumstances. Also because they, like you, probably realized that Og could easily have gone into a features and benefits "dump" and droned on and on, doing exactly what they expected him to do—tell, tell, and tell. Instead, he asked, asked, and asked until Johnny had seen the benefits of having a high-quality ashtray to offer his guests.

Og intuitively understood and applied the most important thing at the Style step of the staircase, that is, how to make the features and benefits come alive by linking them directly to the function, fashion, and finish.

- How would guests use the ashtray? On the stage, in front of the cameras.
- How would they feel? Relaxed, comfortable, and real.
- What color would be most appropriate? Blue to match the guests' clothing or black to go with about anything.

Og put the features and benefits on the back burner and instead focused on his buyer by asking questions about his need for the ashtray. He then tied the features into benefits that made sense to Johnny and met his needs. He was as concerned about the Style step in the Brand Staircase as we should be as we move forward.

The Price Step: Breaking the Glass Ceiling of Price

How do I avoid getting stuck on price with buyers who have a preset amount in mind or don't want to go beyond their budget?

One of the key things a salesperson has to do when reversing the Brand Staircase is to move the customer away from considering price initially—to at least consider the other steps that add value. Additionally, I hear salespeople talk about two challenges that often surface right away involving the Price step of the Brand Staircase.

1. The buyer has a price in mind and isn't going to spend even $1 over it.
2. The buyer spends most of the time quibbling over price, then looks at the style of the product—how it functions, how it looks, or how it feels—and frankly we don't have enough time to even get into the Quality story, much less what the Brand means to the buyer.

These two issues help illustrate what gets in the way at the Price step of the staircase. It is what I call the *glass ceiling of price* (see Figure 5.5). The term *glass ceiling* is not new. It was first associated with career women who were struggling to break through into executive positions within companies and was described in the book *Breaking the Glass Ceiling* by Morrison, White, and Van Velsor. This struggle was likened

PRICE – BREAK THE GLASS CEILING

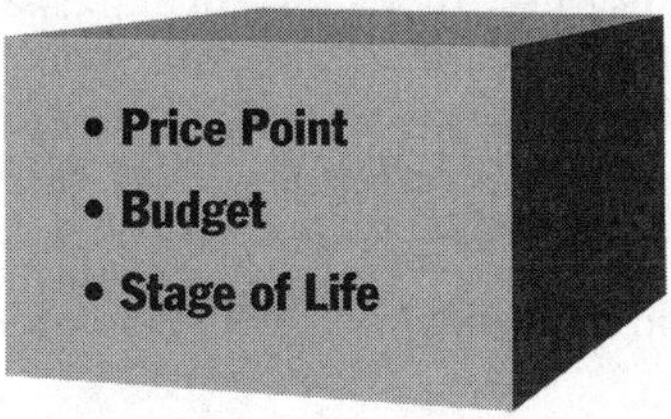

- Price Point
- Budget
- Stage of Life

FIGURE 5.5

to looking through a glass ceiling, where women could see the next position, which they were fully capable of doing, yet they were being held back by an invisible barrier within the culture—a glass ceiling— that would not allow them to attain the next level on their career ladder.

In the same way, an *artificial glass ceiling* can be established around the price the buyer expects to pay for the product. However, in this case it is the salesperson's barrier to overcome, not the buyer's. Remember, the buyer is thinking about three things concerning price: the actual price point of the product, his budget, and his stage of life. In the budget category, the buyer may have an amount in mind that he is willing to spend or expects to spend. If the buyer actually states that amount, then it becomes almost Gospel to him and creates an artificial or glass ceiling on the price that he may not be willing to break through.

So how can salespeople help buyers break through their glass ceiling?

1. By helping them to mentally "reset the bar" on price
2. By not helping them set the glass ceiling of Price in the first place

Let me explain these two approaches by relating a story. I was working with a salesperson at a high-end retail warehouse store. She was selling mid-to-high price-point appliances, furniture, and fixtures with step-up features and good quality. I had seen the salesperson get stumped twice on price when interacting with buyers. So we stepped aside and discussed the glass ceiling of price and reversing the Brand Staircase. By the end of the day, she had sold the lowest-end product twice, had sold a high-quality Brand once, and had made no sale to her fourth buyer. I was working on behalf of the store, so my job was to coach her and give her feedback on how she was doing. Our debriefing conversation went like this (D = Dan, S = Salesperson):

D: "When you approached the customer, did the price of the product come up?"

S: "Yes, it usually came up pretty quickly. The customer said, 'This is what I have budgeted, or what I expected to pay'—$150 in one case, $350 in another. In one instance, I asked what the budget was for this purchase."

D: "I see; so in the first case the buyer set the glass ceiling of price, and in the second case you set it."

S: "What? How did the buyer set it, and, *more importantly*, how did I set it?"

D: "The buyer set it by *stating the price* up front, and you set it *by asking for the price up front*—literally. You see, you sell a higher-end product with better features, quality, and a better Brand. Why would you want the buyer to focus on price?"

S: "I wouldn't, but that's exactly what happened! The buyers focused on price, and I never even got to the quality story."

D: "Exactly. In the case where the buyer stated a price, you couldn't break through the implied glass ceiling and mentally reset the 'price bar' because you didn't anticipate it or have the right sales mindset. In the case where you asked for the price with a 'qualifying question' like 'How much were you looking to spend?' you unknowingly asked a 'disqualifying question' because you helped the buyer set an artificial glass ceiling of price—of what he was willing to pay."

This story is prophetic in two ways:

1. We allow buyers to get stuck on the Price step when they state their price or their budget openly. Instead, we should be reversing the Brand Staircase, taking them to the top, and selling downhill. In that way, even if they still spend only the stated amount of money, we have at least shown them their options, and in many cases we can open their eyes to the other product possibilities and their value for the dollar. More often than not, I have seen buyers break through the glass ceiling of price if we give them the chance.

2. Many salespeople have been taught to ask a "qualifying question" to understand the buyer's ability to afford the product. Questions like "What is your budget?" or "What were you looking to spend?" are common examples of questions that salespeople use to see if buyers can afford the product. However, by asking these questions,

many salespeople over the years have unknowingly been asking a "disqualifying question" instead. They have actually disqualified their prospects from buying their products because they have them focus on Price rather than the story of Quality or Brand. It's time, I believe, for us to teach our salespeople a little differently, so that we quit figuratively deciding for the buyers what they can afford to spend. We will discuss the "migration process" for helping buyers move off of the Price step in detail in Part 3.

I am always amazed by the number of salespeople who are surprised by a price objection. It has become, over time, the biggest objection salespeople have to handle, and we still don't anticipate it well. Let me illustrate how we should be thinking about price by taking a look back at my sporting days and using a baseball metaphor.

When I was taking batting practice, it was always easier to hit during batting practice than to hit against a real pitcher. Why? During batting practice, I was usually facing a pitching machine, or possibly a pitching coach who was telling me which pitch was coming next. So I knew when the fastball was coming, or, for that matter, when the curveball was coming. In other words, I could *anticipate* better during practice. My pitching coach had taught me how to look for the curveballs.

Then when I faced a real pitcher during a game, I was also in the *mindset* of looking for a certain pitch—fastball, curveball, or slider—given a certain hitting situation. I also had the scouting report on the pitcher's best pitches. In baseball, hitters need coaching to become better. Importantly, they need anticipation and mindset.

Salespeople also need both anticipation and mindset to hit the curveballs that are thrown by the buyer. We need to anticipate that many buyers will focus on price and have a mindset to hit that curveball of price when it comes. Also, once you are aware of the Brand Staircase model, you can anticipate what the buyer is thinking about, what step of the staircase she may be entering on, and what her focus could be. You also have a different mindset on how to sell the buyer and what to look for. At the end of the day, you need to know how to hit the curveball of price. Be prepared to handle the unexpected. Anticipate the glass ceiling of price.

Key Points

The Brand Staircase is not without its challenges and opportunities. We have tried to address the common ones that arise from experience with the individual steps, probably when the salesperson is selling uphill. In some cases we are challenging old paradigms. It would be naïve to not address these, as most salespeople have found these old ways of thinking about sales to have been major stumbling blocks in their selling efforts.

The conclusion is simple: when you reverse the Brand Staircase and sell Brand first, you lessen and even avoid many of the selling challenges that could crop up around Brand, Quality, Style, and Price in the typical buyer transaction. The following top challenges were identified:

- At the Brand step: avoiding hollow brand promises
- At the Quality step: recognizing the competitive assessment
- At the Style step: understanding feature and benefit myopia
- At the Price step: breaking the glass ceiling of Price

As with any new sales process, sales practitioners need to reflect on these challenges and reverse their thinking to create sales opportunities within the reversed Brand Staircase. This comes about only through debating the logic the model puts forward; proving its strength by practicing it daily; and breaking old paradigms, habits, and sales behaviors. It also happens by understanding mindsets—yours and the buyers—as you put this process into motion. We'll deal with that challenge in the next section.

PART 3

UNDERSTANDING THE BUYER AND SELLER

CHAPTER 6

MINDSETS

M ost teaching of sales professionals focuses on skill building for the salesperson and tends to lightly brush over the motivations and desires of the buyer. You have probably experienced this in much of your sales training. Sales courses may include some focus on the buying process itself, such as fact finding, discovery, comparison or evaluation of options, resolution of concerns, decision making, and implementation. However, little attention is paid to the buyers' mindset: what the buyers are thinking and feeling in the midst of the sales interaction and the real reasons that they buy.

Why am I bringing this up now? Because in the previous section, I outlined the importance of presenting Brand first in the buying interaction. But in order to do that successfully, you as salespeople need to first understand the buyers' mindset and motives—how they think and feel before and during the transaction—not just what they do. In fact, this entire chapter is about mindset—yours and the buyer's. Not only do I go into what is important to understand about the buyer, but I also cover what is important to know about yourself. What is your mindset now, and what should it be?

So, what I am asking you to do here is absorb this information about mindsets—the buyer's and yours—in order to be a more successful Brand seller. I will lay out the connections to Brand selling as we go along. In subsequent chapters, you will find important knowledge and helpful ways to approach the buyer in the Brand selling interaction.

Buyers' Mindsets

There are three important buyers' mindsets that go a long way toward driving purchasing behavior. You should become familiar with these mindsets so that you can sell effectively in any situation, especially when selling the Brand. Experience tells me that if you acquaint yourself with the principles of buyer mindset, you will be far better prepared when you go into the sales interaction. But first, a note about the meaning of mindsets.

The Reality of Mindsets

As a general rule, salespeople don't give enough thought to understanding the psyche of buyers and how they enter transactions with a certain *mindset*—a mental attitude, fixed state of mind, or inclination. This definition implies that the buyer enters with past experiences, preconceived notions, opinions, information, knowledge, and often beliefs about a certain product, service, or company. These inclinations have been formed from the buyer's past decisions and history with salespeople, products, and companies. They are not necessarily good or bad, and they may or may not have credence. But they are very real and often deeply embedded within the buyer's psyche. They have a powerful influence on where the buyer is leaning, what the buyer is focusing on, and ultimately on the buyer's purchasing preferences. All of that is to say that as salespeople, we would be foolhardy not to consider these buyer mindsets (fixed states of mind or inclinations) before we enter the sales interaction.

In the case of Brand selling, and in the context of what you learned in Parts 1 and 2, buyers will also enter mentally at a certain step or "place" on the Brand Staircase. For instance, during the transaction they may be looking mostly for the best Price, or the most Style, or top Quality, or a great Brand. Sometimes they are willing to move off of that step, and sometimes they may not be willing to move unless we, as salespeople, help to influence or change their mindset. That is why it is important to understand how buyers enter the transaction, so that we can appeal to their logic (how they think) and emotion (what they feel) in order to influence them, educate them, and provide evidence to help change their perceptions of your Brand.

This is exactly where motives come into play. Motives directly affect buyers' decisions. They are the reasons that will influence a choice or prompt an action; simply put, they are buyers' *intention*. Common motives surrounding the product or service would include saving them time, money, or hassles; making them look good; making their job easier; or making them money. In essence, the motive is the real reason they buy. I'll discuss motives in more detail in Chapter 7. Now let's look at the buyer mindsets.

Buyer Mindset 1: The Buyer's Wallet

One of my favorite sayings is, "Mindset precedes skill set" when selling to buyers. Let me illustrate. During workshops that I conduct with groups of salespeople, I run a simple exercise. I ask people to pull out their wallet and hold it over their head. Then, I ask them, "What is the most important thing in your wallet?" Most people say money, credit cards, or pictures of their family. Many survey the room and knowingly laugh at each other. I continue by asking, "Do you have the right to spend it where you want?" "Do you have the right to open it when you want?" (Of course, by this time, all heads are nodding yes, and quizzical looks are appearing on faces, as if to say, "Where is this guy going with this?") Then comes the clincher: "Does anyone else have the right to open your wallet?" Most people react with a resounding no, but then laugh and concede that their "better half has the right and often exercises it." I then ask why no one else has the right. The response is generally, "Because I earned it, and only I can spend it as I please."

My teaching point then rolls out. "You're right. As buyers or consumers, we have the right to spend our money where we want, when we want, and with whom we want. So now, thinking as a salesperson, why would we ever be surprised by a buyer's hesitating to open his wallet for us? After all, it's his money, he earned it, and no one can open it without his permission." Yet I'm always amazed by salespeople who seem almost offended if a buyer doesn't want to spend that much in money on her product or spend that much time on her sales presentation. (You see, buyers do have a mindset when they enter the sales transaction.)

BUYER MINDSET 1
Buyers today increasingly guard their time and money;
they make choices about where they invest these resources
and to whom they give permission to open their wallet!

As salespeople, we should try to put ourselves in the buyer's shoes. In order to sell buyers our brand, we need to identify with this mindset. This buyer, or any buyer, has worked hard for his money. He is going to keep it close to the vest until he is real sure he wants to part with it. You don't want to manipulate him, but you do want to understand the seriousness of his relationship with his own money, so that you will be better prepared to deploy your skills as a salesperson.

Buyer Mindset 2: The Main Reasons Buyers Don't Buy

To get at the second important mindset, let's dig deeper into the emotional landscape of buyers. Remember the exercise in Chapter 5 where

TABLE 6.1   Best Rep Exercise

Best Rep	Worst Rep
Honest	Dishonest
Trustworthy	Lacked trust
Credible	Lacked credibility
Great Product Knowledge	Lack of Product Knowledge
Listened to "What's in it for Me"	Sold me what they wanted
Listened Well	Didn't listen / talked too much
Made me feel good	"Could care less about me"
Asked good questions	Started selling "Right away"
Competitive Knowledge	Only knew their Products
Easy to talk to	High pressure
Used the time well	Wasted my time
Understood their company / Brand	Sold only on lowest price
Educated me	"I learned very little from him"
High energy / Enthusiasm	Looked bored, or bored me
Sold Benefits of the product	Droned on about Features
Easy and Enjoyable	Laborious, burdensome

I asked salespeople to describe their experiences as a buyer: to identify the last big purchase they made, and to write down the characteristics of the best salespeople and the worst? The T chart of common characteristics, habits, and skill sets is given in Table 6.1.

Review it closely again, but this time with a keen eye on the worst side.

What do you notice? Yes, this is certainly a negative list. But worse yet, it's an *emotional* negative list. I believe it's been said before that people make decisions more on emotion than on logic. Now, do you believe that the worst reps could rebound and recover this sale if that's truly how the buyer felt about them? It's very doubtful. As a matter of fact, when I ask most salespeople that very question, their answer is an emphatic no. To take it a step further, I have found that the 16 common characteristics and habits listed in Table 6.1 can be boiled down to three key reasons buyers don't buy:

> ## BUYER MINDSET 2
> Buyers don't buy from salespeople because they
> don't trust, don't care about, or don't know
> the sellers themselves, the sellers' company,
> and/or the sellers' products and services.

Whoa . . . that's a wake-up call! Guess what—two of those three reasons are emotional: *trust* and *care*. Of course, *know* tends to get at knowledge of the competition, industry, channels, products, and services. As salespeople, if we can't effectively answer these don't care, don't trust, and don't know questions for the buyer, then we cannot expect to be successful, especially when selling the Brand. To understand these three reasons better, let's again put ourselves in the buyer's shoes by viewing some common purchases.

- *Home buying.* When you are buying a home, you are routinely asking yourselves questions about the salesperson, such as: Does this person know my family and its needs [care]? Has he taken the time to ask any questions about our family [know]? Is he working on our behalf [trust, care]? Is he trying to sell us more home than we need in order to make more commission [trust]? Has he sold this type of house in this area of town before [know]? Does he know what floor plan, neighborhood, tax base, and amenities would suit us best, or is he trying to put us in any house that meets our criteria of four bedrooms, two baths, and 1/2 acre [know, care]?
- *Car shopping.* As a buyer, you may be asking these questions: Does she look trustworthy [trust]? Does the dealership have a good reputation [trust]? Does the salesperson know the features well enough to educate me [know]? Is she listening to my desires and accessory needs [trust, care]? Is she working on my behalf when it comes to the final deal [trust]? Is she up-front and honest about warranties, service, and so on [trust, know]?
- *Buying insurance:* These questions may arise: How long has the salesperson been selling insurance, and does he have a good background within the industry [know, trust]? Does he have satisfied customers who can provide references that he is willing to share with me [care, trust]? Is he fairly representing all of the options available to me, such as term, whole life, and universal life [know, trust]? How good will his service be after the sale [care]? How will he treat my teenage drivers if they get tickets or get into accidents [care]?

- *Retail shopping:* You may contemplate these questions: Does the salesperson start selling me before asking any questions [trust]? Has she tried to get to know me before trying to sell me [trust, care]? Is she able to compare products and make a solid recommendation [know]? Does she know what she is talking about [know]? Is she up on consumer reports and trends within the industry [know]? Does she try to sell you a product because of the current sale price or because you really need it [care, trust]? Will her company back up what it says in warranty or service [trust, care]? Will it be a hassle if I have to return the product for any reason [trust, care]?

Buyer Mindset 3: The Buyer's Entry Point on the Staircase

At this point, it's important for you to step into the buyer's shoes. Think about the interaction from the buyer's standpoint first, not your own. To be successful in the face-to-face interaction with the buyer, you need to get into the buyer's shoes and stay there. No cheating and no trying to jump out—this is important.

> When it comes to Brand selling,
> it's not all about you (the salesperson),
> it's about him (the buyer).

Understanding this third buyer mindset is crucial because, while it may be the hardest for you to achieve, it will bring big rewards. You have to step over into buyer territory—"it's all about him"—in order to discern where he is entering the staircase. Why does that matter?

Remember the definition of mindset—a mental attitude, a fixed state of mind, or an inclination. As buyers, we are predisposed to our attitudes toward products and services. This is largely based on our past experiences with products, services, and salespeople. So buyers are likely to have already formed an opinion or inclination about what they are going to consider first in the sales transaction—Price, Style, Quality, or Brand.

When you first encounter the buyer face to face, that inclination will be the buyer's primary entry point on the staircase. You may know that buyer well and be able to place her on a step of the staircase easily, or this may be your first meeting with the buyer—she may not even be a customer yet. Obviously, you have an advantage with the repeat buyer because of your past history and various interactions and are at a disadvantage with the "noncustomer" because of your lack of the same. Either way, buyers will give you *evidence* of their entry-point preferences for a certain step of the staircase.

BUYER MINDSET 3
Buyers will already have decided on what step of the staircase
they enter at—Price, Style, Quality, or Brand.

Here are some common forms of evidence of the buyer's entry point that are based on examples like home buying, car shopping, and retail shopping. (Please note that if you are selling in a business-to-business setting with a trade Brand, we will deal with that situation more directly in Chapters 11 and 12. For now, it is instructive to see the basics clearly by thinking like a consumer.)

HOME BUYING

- *Price.* Buyers want to see the low-end houses and bring up a price range or a monthly payment amount in the conversation. They want to stretch their dollars with a variable-rate mortgage.
- *Style.* Buyers are more concerned with house layout, square footage, or number of bedrooms and baths. They may like a particular style: Cape Cod, Ranch, Early American, Southwestern Stucco, or Modern.
- *Quality.* Buyers may be looking to upgrade many of the finishing touches beyond the builder's allowance—for instance, granite or Corian countertops instead of Formica; longer-lasting paint coverings or finishes; upgraded light fixtures, locksets, or ceramic tile; or upgraded 2 × 6 construction instead of standard 2 × 4 walls.
- *Brand.* Buyers may be interested in dealing only with a high-end custom-home builder rather than a tract-home builder. They may want an exclusive or gated community location, or a certain address that connects them to a location or community.

CAR SHOPPING

- *Price.* Buyers may shop exclusively at locations where there is a lowest-price guarantee, such as CarMax, or where there is no haggling, such as Saturn. They may be overly focused on cash rebates or monthly payment amounts at a car dealership.
- *Style.* Buyers may place a heavy emphasis on accessories—DVD player, sunroof, heated seats—or look only at cars with a certain add-on package—the power drive train package, for example.

- *Quality.* Buyers may be extremely attracted to the extended warranty, after-sale service of the dealership, or upgraded features that reek of quality: leather seats, GPS (Global Positioning System), or safety rating in consumer reports.
- *Brand.* Buyers show up at your dealership with one Brand in mind—a luxury sedan like Cadillac, Jaguar, Corvette, Lexus, BMW, or Mercedes, to name a few. They drop that Brand name in their conversation, are repeat customers, or have always wanted to purchase a particular automobile as their dream car.

RETAIL SHOPPING

Of course, there are many examples here that we could use, but let us focus on buying a camera. The same ideas are transferable to other retail shopping experiences.

- *Price.* Buyers come in with an amount they are willing to spend. They are looking at sale items. They want a low-priced camera—a "throwaway" or even a disposable camera.
- *Style.* Buyers like the way a camera looks or are mainly interested in certain colors or finishes. They spend a lot of time reading up on features or how the cameras function: zoom lenses, number of pixels in the picture, or the ability to connect directly to your TV set.
- *Quality.* Is the camera at the highest level of technology and built with the newest materials? These buyers focus on manufacturer's warranty or even an extended store warranty.
- *Brand.* Buyers come in predisposed to a couple of high-end Brands and say so. They gravitate to and generally stay with those Brands. They already own one of those Brands.

Now, transfer this thinking to the buyers and customers that you interact with on a daily basis. Think of the products and services you are selling. I'm sure you are starting to see which step your buyers are on. Can you feel the need to help them move off that step and toward the Brand?

Of course, there are many more examples we could cite from the buyer's standpoint. It is important for us as salespeople to understand and properly offset these buyer mindsets if we are to be successful when selling in general, and when selling the Brand in particular.

The Seller's Mindset

We've talked about buyers and what affects their purchasing decisions. Now let's talk about you. Think about your history in sales—the buyers you've interacted with and sold to, the relationships you've built, the products you've sold, and the objections you've handled. If you've been around selling for any length of time, you've probably seen it all. You may even be tired of talking about the buyer and yearn for some tips on selling—little mental pointers, for instance, that could help you improve your sales game incrementally beyond where it is right now.

So let's talk about you and where you are in this Brand selling "journey."

- Where do you find yourself on the *road map* mentally?
- What is your understanding (and, frankly, buy-in) concerning the Brand selling process?
- How can I help you have a better sales mindset as we move forward?

Remember the triangle concept from Chapter 4, where I said that salespeople build habits in a three-step process called the triangle?

- *Step 1.* They start with their head, by using the attitudes and knowledge that come from experience.
- *Step 2.* They then move 18 inches down to their *heart*, where their feelings and belief system start to become affected.
- *Step 3.* Finally, they transfer their learning 12 inches back up to their mouth, where their habits and behaviors can be acted upon. They have adopted a sales language, or, in this case, more specifically a Brand language, as described in Chapter 2. This is where behavior change occurs and where people see you acting differently from the way you acted before. Importantly for salespeople, this is where Brand selling can have the largest impact by helping to put words on the lips of the salesperson.

So far in this Brand selling journey, we have operated mostly in Step 1, looking at the attitudes, knowledge, and past experiences of you, the reader. You see, most of the people I have shared the reversed Brand Staircase with (whether in a workshop, on a sales call, or in casual conversation) understand the head concept very quickly—the logic of trying to sell this way.

Where salespeople struggle the most is in transferring the concept to their hearts, where their belief system kicks in. We now need to travel to and through Step 2. Somewhere between your head and your mouth, you need to make a big U-turn that passes through your heart. That is the transition that we will make in this chapter.

Breaking Down and Rebuilding the Sales Mindset

One of the first good managers I worked for believed that selling started in your head with your existing mindset. He once said that salespeople often lose the sale before they ever meet the customer because they have negative sound bites and narratives running through their heads as they prepare for the meeting. These are thoughts like

- The competition has better products.
- The price is too high for the marketplace.
- There will be some tough objections with this new product. Can I handle them?
- I haven't sold this in the past. What makes me think I can do it now?

Now, I'm sure that if you're honest, you've had some of these thoughts in the past or heard them from disgruntled salespeople. I know I have had these thoughts. Unfortunately, these negative sound bites and preconceived notions lead us to a faulty set of premises that we are making everyday sales calls based on, and they certainly are not going to work for Brand selling. The salesperson has to work to eliminate the wrong mindsets and engage the right mindsets. For effective Brand selling, there are three "right" mindsets, which we'll discuss next.

Sales Mindset 1: Selling Starts before We See the Buyer

I remember one day early in my career when my sales mindset was off base. I was selling computers, and I had just finished a tough week. I was meeting with my manager. In a desperate and frustrated moment, I remember verbalizing in a forlorn way, "I haven't sold this in the past. What makes me think I can do it now?"

Whoa. Sales mistake! He looked at me with fire in his eyes and said: "If you believe it in here [pointing to his head, then his heart], then it will come true out there [pointing to the outside]." He went on to say something worth remembering:

SALES MINDSET I
Selling starts long before you first engage the buyer.

Selling starts in your head before you ever meet and greet the buyer. It starts with your attitude, your narratives, your "thought tracks," and even your outlook on the day. You see, I believe that many salespeople would sell better and differently if they used what I call *mental bridges*, or positive thoughts that can mentally bring them to the proper mindset as they enter the interaction and greet the buyer.

One of my favorite mental bridges is to build a positive picture of the *profession of selling*. Have you ever thought of yourself as a professional? Think of other occupations, like accountants, doctors, lawyers, or professors. Note the use of the word *professional*. From *Webster's American Family Dictionary*, a professional is "a person who earns a living in a sport or other occupation frequently engaged in by amateurs. A person who is an 'expert' at his or her work." Wow! I don't know about you, but I like the sound of *professional salesperson* just a tad bit better than the sound of *amateur salesperson*. In sales, as in many professions, the major difference between a professional and an amateur is ability and attitude.

Ability = knowledge, skills, and experience
Attitude = willingness and confidence

Like a professional athlete, who envisions the competition, the plays, the crowd, and her success before going onto the field, as *professional salespeople* we should envision the sales environment, the impact of the brand, the conversation, and the close well before they happen!

- We should be proud of the profession we are in and represent it accordingly.
- We should know our company and its Brands and represent them as an expert.
- We should build positive mental soundtracks and narratives about our Brand in order to connect it to buyers.

OK, if that's the case, then let's carry over that thinking to selling the Brand, not just selling in general. Let's start with the top negative narratives or sound bites that our sales breeding has woven into our sales fabric. (By the way, in the words of humorist Dave Berry, "I am not making this up." I have actually heard these from salespeople in one form or another—implied or explicit.)

- "This is a long-time buyer and I know exactly what he needs from this product/in this situation."
- "The Brand isn't important to sales; it's Marketing's job."
- "Most of my customers buy the best quality, and as long as the price is decent, the Brand doesn't matter."
- "The last time he bought this product, it was from us, so he'll do it again."
- "The Brand thing is all smoke and mirrors."
- "My buyers make all their decisions based on logic; they don't buy into the 'magic dust' of the Brand."
- "The Brand is just a slogan, I'm not really sure what it means."

Now, I take no offense at these narratives or sound bites, for they are reality. I also realize that, like buyers, we are human beings, and we all have "our stuff." We all have our reasons for believing these state-ments: our past experiences, opinions, history, preconceived notions, baggage and belief systems. However, let me repeat the words of my manager that day: "If you believe it in here, then it will come true out there. Selling starts long before you first engage the buyer."

It is our job as company leaders, as sales leaders, and as sales profes-sionals to find a way to reverse these negative sales mindsets by record-ing over those negative sound bites and teaching salespeople new narratives so that they can think differently about the Brand by using the Brand Staircase. We need to teach salespeople

- What the Brand means
- How to talk about the Brand
- How to put Brand into their sales language
- To believe that they represent the Brand daily
- How to communicate their unique Brand story
- To become the biggest Brand ambassadors in the company
- That the Brand should be co-owned by them and by Marketing.

You see, we need to change the salesperson's mindset to that of a Brand ambassador prior to the interaction. Then, we need to help him develop stronger sales confidence during the sales interaction. This requires a U-turn at the heart and leads us to Sales Mindset 2.

Sales Mindset 2: The Heart Is the Wellspring of Sales Confidence

Of course, by now you recognize the shameless appeal to the heart analogy. For the heart of the salesperson is her heartbeat, the well-spring of her confidence. The very issues that keep buyers from trust-ing us as salespeople are not logic-based, they are emotion-based. They are not head issues; they are heart issues.

SALES MINDSET 2
Salespeople don't need a lobotomy;
they need a heart transplant.

Let's actually think about the human heart for a moment—what a miracle! It is the world's best-engineered pump. It allows us to live and breathe, and it feeds our whole body with nutrients carried in the bloodstream. It is the spark plug for our neurological, digestive, pulmonary, and reproductive systems. It works while we are sleeping and increases speed when we are exercising. It literally keeps us going.

It is also metaphorically where we store our emotions, our feelings, and our heartstrings. For the salesperson, it is the energy source, the place that will pace her and act as the wellspring of life when it comes to interacting with the buyer in a confident manner. An important factor that gets in the way of salespeople's making this transfer from head to heart is their past sales history and the level of confidence they bring to the sales interaction. Let's explore this further.

BUILDING CONFIDENCE

I believe our confidence issues as salespeople started when we were very young in experience, in life or in the profession. We experienced or were given distorted images of salespeople—pushy, aggressive, loud, and so on. These images were largely the result of bad encounters that others told us about or that we personally had as buyers. The images built for us a reputation as a profession that was anything but strong. Not one that you would be proud to work in. As a matter of fact, the profession has helped us develop a bit of an inferiority complex.

One analogy I use that depicts this viewpoint comes from our youth. Remember the teeter-totter or seesaw on the playground when you were a kid? (See Figure 6.1.) You used to spend time with friends and family seesawing up and down, having a blast, laughing along the way. However, the fun would stop when a big kid arrived and took over the teeter-totter. He weighed twice as much as you did, and he would pick you to be his adversary. Once on board, he could use his weight advantage to hold you in the air for a long time, laughing, enjoying your plight, and ready to drop you with a thud if he "felt like it." That big bully had all the weight and power and was ready to exercise it on the spur of the moment.

For many of us, the sales transaction is like the teeter-totter when you were a youngster. The buyer is the "big bully," and we're the "little guy." As salespeople, we usually think that the buyers have all the power. In some ways, of course, they do have the power because they have the right to open their wallet (Buyer Mindset 1) and they are asking those three basic questions (Buyer Mindset 2) of the seller:

1. Can I *trust* you?
2. Do you *care* about me, my family, or my company?
3. Do you *know* what you're doing?

What I've found over the years is that most salespeople have a dilemma, too. There are three things that keep them from balancing their power with that of the buyer:

THE SALES "TEETER-TOTTER"

FIGURE 6.1

1. They don't know when and how to close.
2. They haven't earned the right to do business.
3. They lack confidence.

Now, if you examine these issues for a moment, you quickly realize that only one of the three is mostly skill-set-related—knowing *when and how to close a sale*. Frankly, that comes with training, time, and experience. The other two are far more linked to mindsets than to skill sets. *Earning the right to do business* is directly linked to the customer's allowing you the right to open his wallet and ask for his business. It is affected by the customer's trusting you, knowing that you care about him, and so forth. At the end of the day, earning the right to do business comes from proving oneself, building trust, and building the relationship, and it often takes time.

But how does one gain confidence? How does one walk into a sales transaction feeling a high level of confidence, but not crossing the line into arrogance? How does a leader effectively build into her sales team the confidence to sell the Brand when the chips are down? Well, it starts at the heart, not the head. Sales Mindset 3 explains what I mean.

Sales Mindset 3: The Salesperson's Confidence = E^2KG

Let's start with a simple formula that I use in my workshops to remember the important elements of building sales confidence:

> **SALES MINDSET 3**
> E^2KG
> E^2 = enthusiasm and experience
> K = knowledge
> G = growth

The first E in E^2 stands for *enthusiasm*. Good salespeople are enthusiastic about their products, service, and company. Enthusiasm and passion go a long way toward convincing the buyer that you believe in your product. Buyers are basically asking themselves, "If it were your money, would you be spending it on your product?"

I enjoy being around young people in sales. They are usually energetic, enthusiastic, and ready to go out and conquer the world. However, they are like the Tasmanian Devil of Bugs Bunny fame: they are running around in all directions, not always knowing what they are doing and sometimes making mistakes. What they need is to be channelled in the right direction, to put that energy to use so that they can gain experience to go along with their enthusiasm.

The other great thing about young people in sales is that they are moldable. Like a lump of clay in the hands of a skilled potter, they can be molded into an exquisite pot. The good news is that they don't have a lot of bad habits, or cracks in the clay pot. The bad news is that if they get into the hands of the wrong potter, then they will learn things like "We don't do it that way around here," or "That's never worked in the past," or "Why don't you calm down," or "You'll lose that enthusiasm once you find out how it is in the real world." What a tragedy! You can see where putting our enthusiastic people—whether new to the business or veterans—into the wrong hands for mentoring can become a negative to their sales mindset and to your sales culture.

During interactions with the buyer, enthusiasm is critical. Now, I'm not talking about jumping up and down or overexaggerating your tone of voice. Those things aren't believable to the buyer. What I am talking about is being excited when you talk about your product, your company, or your Brand. Showing confidence here can be as simple as looking the buyer in the eye and assuring her that you will take care of any problems that arise with the product. As salespeople, you should act as if it should be important for the buyer to be associated with your company or to proudly own your Brand. Look at it this way: if you can't get excited and enthusiastic about your own Brand, then how can you expect the buyer to do so? There are far too many salespeople walking our planet looking and acting as if they have just come from a funeral, rather than as if they are headed to a party.

Be enthusiastic. It's contagious.

The second E in E^2 stands for *experience*. Experience is street smarts, the "been there, done that" mentality. It is your ability to convey to the buyer that you understand his issues because you have been there; you have experienced similar situations, thoughts, feelings, and buying transactions. It is invaluable in sales, yet it is often underutilized. Let me illustrate.

Have you ever been around veteran salespeople who are very experienced, yet who seem to be complacent or in a rut? Why do you think that happens? You might give one of the following answers:

- They have been doing their job for so long that they are bored.
- They have been calling on the same people or selling in the same industry for years, so it seems as if nothing new ever happens.
- They give the impression that there is nothing that they haven't experienced, so they have been lulled into complacency.

Now, I believe those are fairly accurate answers or even soundtracks within these salespeople's heads.

My best advice to salespeople who find themselves in this situation is twofold:

- Life is about learning curves. Why has yours stopped? The truth is that you didn't get where you are by chance, but rather by building some good skills, habits, and experiences in the street. Your experience may be working against you as you try to learn something new—something like my concept of Brand selling. If you are in that boat, my advice to you is to *relax* and try to remember why you enjoy your job or what it was like when you first started.
- Challenge yourself to adopt this line of thinking:

  Success is a journey, not a destination.—Anonymous.

- You never quite arrive, and that always gives you another goal to conquer, another experience to have, another piece of knowledge to give back to the buyer.

Also, I have found that many salespeople believe that only experience within the specific industry you are calling on can work for you. Having sold in many industries with many different products and services, I can safely say that this assumption is largely false. Selling experience is generally a transferable skill; it goes with you from sales role to sales role. So if you have prior sales experience, use it to your advantage.

Finally, when you combine experience with enthusiasm, you have an incredible sales weapon. Have you ever been around a veteran salesperson who has both? Watch out, because this person has exactly what any good sales leader would want to duplicate. She has the *multiplier effect of E^2*. It is quite simple: experience and enthusiasm are an unbeatable combination in a veteran salesperson.

The *K* in E^2KG stands for *knowledge*. It is rooted in the specific industry, product, or customers that you are calling on. Knowledge generally has to be earned and gathered over time—the time needed to understand and be exposed to the products and the customer base. (Knowledge generally is not a transferable skill unless the new industry or product being sold is very similar to that sold in the sales rep's last job.)

Knowledge is also one of the biggest roadblocks to selling from the heart. Part of the reason for the lack of transfer to the heart is that most salespeople approach job knowledge, and product knowledge in particular, from a logical standpoint. That is, that they are more concerned about their product or service and pushing its features and benefits to the buyer than about anything else. Why not? They are taught to be product experts. They are taught to watch others who are good product presenters. They are taught to read marketing and sales flyers, memorize key facts, and regurgitate those facts to the buyer. They are taught to beat the competition by understanding and selling against its product weaknesses. The bottom line is, they do what they are taught because they know no better. They use their heads more than their hearts when it comes to knowledge.

Now, please don't get me wrong. As you know by now, I am a big advocate of strong product knowledge skills and selling benefits to the buyer. However, those good things can quickly be overdone; the strength can become a weakness. I have personally seen buyers' eyes glaze over when they are being inundated with the latest feature and benefit knowledge pitch or quality story from a salesperson. The worst part of that common situation is that the salesperson does not think she is doing anything wrong.

Knowledge adds credibility to your experience and will increase your confidence in the product, the Brand, and your company, but it needs to be utilized as an overall part of the strong E^2KG.

The *G* in E^2KG stands for *growth*. Growth can be as simple as an attitude about the sale or business, a strategy to help a business through "growing pains," or a way to help the buyer to grow personally. For instance, the buyer may grow through education provided by the seller, or by gaining a new approach to applying the product knowledge to a problem in his business. Also, a consumer may find it easier to fix a home-improvement problem—a leaky pipe, an infestation of wasps, a painting or drywall project. Simply put, a positive attitude on the part of the seller regarding the buyer's ability to use the product, grow personally or professionally, or simply just see himself in a better light all work toward the growth mentality.

Growth mentality is the wild card in the E^2KG heart formula. It is what separates the average from the good and the good from the great salespeople. It is an intangible asset that means that the salesperson is always looking for ways to help the buyers, grow their businesses, and find solutions to their problems. It is largely founded in the salesperson's heart, in her attitude toward her job, her buyers, and her life in general. It is rooted in an abundance mentality.

Black & Decker instills the growth mentality into its salespeople. The Accessory Division had a saying that encapsulated it perfectly: "Own the Wall." That meant that we wanted to grow their business profitably and at the same time lock up as much retail space as possible for our company and "mind space" for our Brand.

Balancing the Teeter-Totter

The previous discussion of the E^2KG formula points out that the more enthusiasm, experience, knowledge, and growth you show as a salesperson, the more trust you will build with your buyers, and once that is established, the buyers will see that you care about them and that you know their needs. Ultimately, the higher your E^2KG is, the more confidence you will convey during the sales transaction. Now the teeter-totter looks a little different, doesn't it?

What most salespeople and leaders don't realize is that a strong E^2KG offsets Buyer Mindset 2 and effectively balances the power on this sales teeter-totter (see Figure 6.2).

The astute salesperson quickly sees this offsetting nature of a strong E^2KG when it comes to balancing the power of the buyer. When your E^2KG is stronger, in effect, you are gaining in confidence, and the buyer perceives this when you communicate during the sales interaction. This increased confidence knocks out the three main reasons that buyers don't buy—they don't trust, care, or know—and ultimately builds buyer trust in you the salesperson and in your company.

Not only is E^2KG important during any sales interaction, but I have found it to be increasingly important when selling the Brand. Why? Mainly because most salespeople are not used to selling the Brand intentionally, so the experience and knowledge components of E^2KG are underdeveloped or still need to be strengthened. This development will happen in a number of ways:

THE BALANCED "TEETER-TOTTER"

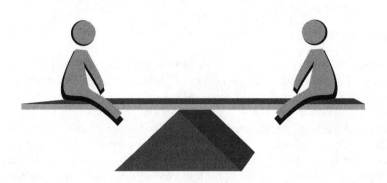

Buyer	Balancing the Power	Seller
Don't care	*with*	Enthusiasm and experience
Don't know	*with*	Experience and knowledge
Don't trust	*with*	Growth

FIGURE 6.2

- By listening more intently to customers and how they perceive the Brand. This builds experience with the Brand.
- By understanding how your company views the Brand and the message that it wishes to convey in the marketplace. This builds knowledge of the Brand.
- By focusing on enthusiasm and growth—which are both huge heart issues—and allowing your Brand experience and knowledge to be built over time.
- By following the Brand Staircase model outlined in this book.

Companies that start to believe this understand the heart issue deeply and how it ultimately affects the Brand sale. Their leaders understand that this needs to get into the salesperson's bloodstream. The best companies I have worked with make this part of the culture by constantly asking their salespeople, "How's your E^2KG?" Since I have been teaching this concept in workshops, I have had numerous people, including vice presidents and CEOs, ask me to spend more time on the subject because it gets at the essence of a strong sales mindset.

Key Points

Before they can effectively engage in Brand selling, salespeople should be well acquainted with the notion of buyer's mindset and their own mindsets regarding Brand selling. Mindset is defined as a mental attitude, a fixed state of mind, or an inclination. Buyers, like all of us, are complex human beings who enter sales transactions with their past experiences, opinions, history, preconceived notions, and belief systems. It is our job as salespeople to unravel the mystery behind the buyer's mindset and motives. In doing so, we will understand, respect, and interpret correctly where the buyer is, in order to find a way to best connect him to our Brand.

The three universal Buyer's Mindsets are

1. Buyers reserve the right to decide with whom they will open their wallet.
2. There are three reasons that buyers don't buy: they don't trust, don't care about, and don't know the seller and the product.

The mindset linked to Brand selling:

3. Buyers primarily enter on one step of the staircase: Price, Style, Quality, or Brand.

To understand effective Brand selling, you need to understand not only buyers' mindsets, but also your own mindsets—the sellers' mindsets and how they interact with the buyers' mindsets. Selling starts with the salesperson's mindset—how he envisions the sale, the buyer, the flow of the conversation, and the connection being made to the Brand.

Professional salespeople are wired to have strong and positive sales mindsets concerning the brands they represent.

Sales Mindset 1: Selling starts long before you first engage the customer.
Sales Mindset 2: Salespeople don't need a lobotomy, they need a heart transplant.
Sales Mindset 3: E^2KG—experience and enthusiasm, knowledge, growth.

There is a balance of power that mentally takes place for salespeople when they are able to keep their E^2KG pumping strongly during interactions with buyers. This balance earns them the right to do business with the buyer. Essentially, experience and enthusiasm balance out the buyer mindset of "don't care." Knowledge balances out "don't know." Growth balances out "don't trust."

The higher the E^2KG, the higher the salesperson's confidence will be, and the higher the buyer's trust will be. We need to instill in our people today this idea: *professional* salespeople need to become the biggest Brand ambassadors in the company.

CHAPTER 7

MOTIVES

W hen do you usually hear the word *motive*? When it's associated with something negative or bad:

- Her motive was revenge (Webster's descriptive phrase using "motive").
- His motive was to rob the bank.
- The teenagers' motive was to stay out later at night.

The list could go on and on. It seems you never hear about positive motives like

- Their motive was to help disaster victims.
- His motive was to slow down to avoid a speeding ticket.
- The leaders' motive was to strive for peace in the Middle East.

Somehow our culture has put a negative spin on motives. What I am driving at here is that *motive* sounds negative and in some cases manipulative, yet it is not. We all have our motives for doing things. A motive (in and of itself) is not by nature a bad thing. It simply is a factor in determining how people make choices and decisions in life. Most importantly, this includes the decisions of the buyers we sell to, and it is up to us to acquaint ourselves with the mental processes that translate into motive on the part of the buyer.

The Buyer's Bull's-Eye

Before we get into the specific motives of buyers that I and others have observed over the years, allow me to introduce you to a model that I use in my classes that gives you a concrete picture of the mental landscape that the buyer inhabits. I call it the *buyer's bull's-eye*, and it contains two important elements: mindset and motive (see Figure 7.1).

BUYER'S BULL'S-EYE: MINDSET TO MOTIVE

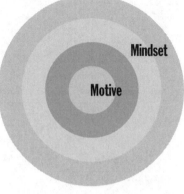

FIGURE 7.1

This bull's-eye can serve as a guide so that I can build a mental picture for you of how the buyer thinks, feels, and acts. The following definitions and Figure 7.1 help us understand the sales interaction from the perspective of the buyer.

- *Mindset.* A mental attitude, fixed state of mind, or inclination
- *Motive.* Something that influences a choice, prompting an action or *intention*

These elements work together. Notice that the mindset is on the outer edge of the target. This is where buyers figuratively enter the sales interaction, and also where they will start to come into focus in our scope. As you move toward the center and take aim at the motives, the buyer's original mindset will fade away and the well-trained salesperson will focus on the center of the target—the motive. To do so, you will now need to understand how the buyer thinks, feels, and acts based on what she does or says *during the interaction*. As salespeople, our job is to uncover and/or confirm buyers' motives. In this chapter, we define the most common motives.

Now, it is no coincidence that I have illustrated the concept of the relationship of mindset and motive by using a bull's-eye with "motive" in the middle as the primary target. I grew up in Montana. One of my avocations is the outdoors. I like to camp, fish, backpack, hike, ski, and hunt. Hunting requires a target and a considerable amount of preparation, good fortune, and skill to be successful. One generally unnoticed part of successful preparation is making sure that your gun is "sighted in," meaning that your gun is on target. Your goal in sighting in your gun is that when you look down the sights or through the scope and focus on the target, your bullet travels in a true path and hits the center of the target. The goal is the same whether you shoot for fun, for competition, for target practice, or for hunting big game. It is fundamental—a gun needs to be sighted in before a shooter can be successful.

Interestingly enough, when guns first come from the factory, they are seldom accurate and on target. The shooter needs to have target practice to sight in the gun in order to expect any level of success whatsoever. Guided by the gun manual and scope adjustments, the sportsman shoots at the target and adjusts, shoots again and adjusts, until he is on target. It usually requires multiple attempts before the shooter can hit the bull's-eye.

This example is analogous to our selling situation in a number of ways:

1. The target represents our goal: to secure a sale.
2. The salesperson needs to practice and focus on the bull's-eye by taking shots at it in real selling situations.
3. The focus needs to be on the motives of the buyer—at the center of the bull's-eye.
4. As we sight in on the bull's-eye and get more proficient at focusing in, our shots will move from the outer circle of mindset to the inner circle of motive. We will thus be getting at the real reasons that buyers purchase.

I know this all sounds good in theory, yet in reality, most of us as salespeople haven't taken close aim at the target yet. We haven't focused through our "scope of experience" to land on the target, much less hit the bull's-eye where the buyer is choosing to act. Instead, many salespeople choose to focus on the features and benefits of their products, never giving a thought to the buyer's mindset or inclination toward Price, Style, Quality, or Brand when entering a transaction.

This has to change, especially if salespeople want to be successful at selling the Brand. Why? Because Brands are mostly emotional, as are motives. If we don't find a way to connect with the buyer through her motives, then it is unlikely that we will get to the real reason she is buying and thus secure the Brand sale. Remember, the motive is where the buyer acts or is prompted to action; it is truly the reason(s) she buys.

Motives influence actions toward mindset in several ways. In this chapter, we gain an understanding of the buyer's motives and apply the correct approach to them during the sales interaction. Let's start by reviewing the most common types of motives we observe as salespeople.

Emotion and Logic: Two Kinds of Motive

In participating in and studying the profession of selling for 25 years, I have found that motives break down into some basic categories that revolve around logic and emotions. The main logic motives fall into the categories of savings and production, and the main emotion motives fall into the categories of personal and power (see Figure 7.2).

Motives That Appeal to Logic

- *Savings: time.* Customers buy a product because it makes household chores go more quickly, saving them time. These are products like a bigger mower, a better vacuum, a stronger power washer, or an easier-to-assemble Christmas toy.
- *Savings: money.* Customers always shop the sales to get the best price possible. This saves money, which makes them feel good, stretches their budget, and gives them more money to spend on an upcoming vacation.
- *Savings: hassles.* Customers buy a compatible or upgradeable component for easier installation. They buy an extended warranty to take the hassle out of the product if it breaks down, thus also limiting their risk. They buy insurance coverage for a cell phone to minimize headaches if it is lost or stolen.

COMMON MOTIVES

Focus on Motives—the real reasons people buy

APPEAL TO LOGIC
Savings – time, $$$, hassle
Production – more efficient, better results, more output

APPEAL TO EMOTION
Personal – job easier, look good, save face, more leisure time
Power – control, recognition, approval

FIGURE 7.2

- *Production: more efficient.* Customers buy an economy car to get a more efficient motor or better gas mileage, which also saves them money. They buy a universal remote that makes their channel surfing on their home theater system more efficient while entertaining guests. They adopt a business process that makes their supply chain more efficient.
- *Production: better results.* Customers purchase luggage that lasts longer and holds up better under the rigors of travel. They buy a higher-end camera, stereo, or TV because it has high-resolution pixels, sound, or pictures. These better results are pleasing to the eye.
- *Production: more output.* Customers buy an electric power tool because it has more torque, output, or power than a hand tool, making their job easier and quicker. They buy a high-end mixer for the kitchen because it can make larger batches of cookies or blend drinks more quickly or puree more smoothly, thus feeding the troops better.

Motives That Appeal to Emotion

- *Personal: job easier.* Customers buy a home-improvement guide that makes their house remodeling job or do-it-yourself project much easier. They contract out that same job because they are no good at such projects and they want to make their life easier. They buy a gas grill to replace their coal hibachi to make their job of flipping burgers simpler and possibly give better results.
- *Personal: look good.* Customers buy clothes that appeal to their taste for fashion and that they get compliments on. They purchase a gift to be seen favorably by a significant other—to look good in that person's eyes.
- *Personal: save face.* Customers buy flowers to make up after a fight. They buy a "guilt gift" to show that they care. They try to keep up with the Joneses by buying a similar item to keep pace with the neighbors.
- *Personal: more leisure time.* This is a common aftereffect of another motive. For instance, by paying a housekeeper, people free up their schedule, allowing more leisure time. They may buy into a time-share condominium in order to use their leisure time strategically.
- *Power: control.* People may buy an electronic organizer to have more control over their time. They may purchase the services of a financial advisor to better control their finances or plan for their future retirement. They may purchase a home security system to have better controls and safety around their house.
- *Power: recognition.* Customers may buy an expensive outfit or suit to be recognized at a special event—a homecoming dance, wedding, or

bar mitzvah. They may donate to a charity or fund-raiser for personal recognition.

- *Power: approval.* Customers may purchase a gift to win the approval of a girlfriend, a parent, a relative, or even a child. They may buy almost anything to win the approval of others.

Whew! After reading through those, I'm sure you can see how they can work together. I also bet you are asking yourself a few questions, such as

- Could this list go on and on? Absolutely!
- Do I believe there could be more motives out there? Probably.
- Can buyers have multiple motives? Yes, and they often do.
- Would you like to become behavioral psychologists in order to do your job? I seriously doubt it.

So, why in the world did I take the time to run you through that short list of motives?

There are a couple of very good reasons:

- Most experienced salespeople quickly understand these motives because they have seen or heard buyers talk this way or act this way. However, the tragedy is that very few salespeople really work these words into their sales language when talking about their products and then actually sell to the motives of the buyer.
- I have found over the years that we intuitively understand these motives, but we do not intentionally use them in our sales process.
- I have also found that most salespeople need a frame of reference to help them categorize these motives, thus making it easier for them to put these motives into their sales process.

We discussed mindset at length in Chapter 6, and you now have a sense of the main aspects of motive. Let's look at some examples of how they interact.

Interaction of Mindset and Motive

When I was first married, my wife and I had different mindsets (inclinations) about purchases for the house. I was usually concerned about price. I was thinking, "Can we afford it; is it within the budget?" She was usually concerned with quality and thus was thinking, "Will it hold up; what is the warranty; where do I take it for service if it breaks?" When we went on shopping excursions for furniture, we were coming from two different places mentally.

What I found was, the bad salespeople would get caught between selling me on price and making sure she was happy with quality. Very seldom could they please us both, and we usually left without purchasing. Now, the good salespeople worked hard to find out whose mindset was more important: mine on price or hers on quality. Then they would approach us based on that mindset. In addition, the better salespeople worked hard to get us to the same mindset of quality by appealing logically to my intelligence, usually by speaking of the benefits of a longer warranty, better durability, and so forth. However, the very best salespeople did both of those things and also went one step further: They focused on our motives. They asked questions like, "Why is quality important to you, Mrs. Stiff?" When she replied, "I want this furniture to last through the years as our kids grow up," or "I don't want to have to replace it every other year," or "We like to entertain guests at our home, and I want them to be comfortable," the salesperson was getting at her motives: pride of ownership, making the house into a home, making her job of mothering and raising a family easier, making it easier to entertain friends, and taking the hassle out of having to replace furniture. Once they got to these motives, we were done; the sale was made, and the price didn't matter.

The greatest furniture salesperson who sold the Brand most effectively was Kristen at Ethan Allen. We had experienced a house fire, and she was there to help us with the furniture replacement. She understood the emotions of the event and could have sold us in the showroom, yet she took the time to come to the burned house, look at the charred rooms to make recommendations, and help us dream again about the possibilities of a rebuilt home.

- She understood our *mindset* (inclination) as she got to know us. My focus was on price and budget; my wife's focus was on quality. Yet, she wasn't pushy; she didn't wave the Brand in front of us or disrespect our budget (our wallet).
- She tied into our *motives* based on logic: the ability to find a showroom almost anywhere we moved within the country—a place where we could add to our current line of furniture and repair or replace it as necessary.
- She tied into our *motives* based on emotion: of family, recovery, rebuilding, and hassle-free shopping. She understood the wisdom of emotions and made our rebuilding job easier by providing a high-end, "one-stop shopping" experience.

Put Yourself in the Buyer's Shoes

The point is simple: think about your own buying experiences, and put yourself in the buyer's shoes for a minute. Think about the last time you traveled for business or pleasure. There are three or four basics that a traveler needs while on the road: a hassle-free flight to his destination, a decent night's rest, a good cup of coffee (or tea) in the morning to get him going, and a decent meal to keep him going during the day. Let's examine a few of them while reflecting on the choices we can make with the buyer's bull's-eye in mind.

- *Air travel.* As a buyer, you have many flight options to look over. The decisions among them have to do with your past experiences as a flyer (mindset), whether your company is paying for it (first class may be an option) or you are footing the bill (a low-cost airline with less amenities) (motive of logic), and lastly how it all ties into your motives. Your motive may be to save money, so you book online because it is coming out of your own wallet, or it may be to have a hassle-free flight or get frequent traveler points for a future personal vacation, so you spend more money on business travel now to enjoy a better vacation later. Either way, there are multiple options for the buyer with multiple motives being exercised.

- *Hotels.* Again, there are many options available to you. Your *mindset* may be to "stay at the same place I always do when I fly to Chicago" because it is easy to access from your client's office, it has the right business services for you, and, most of all, it feels like "home away from home," or because it is impressive to your clients and therefore makes you look good, or because you just really like the people who work there and have never had a bad experience (all *motives*).

- *Coffee.* You can get a cup of coffee around any corner in a major city. However, your mindset may be that you have always trusted the way they brew coffee at Joe's Diner or that you want to visit a Starbucks. Now, those two coffee "experiences" come from different viewpoints—not good or bad, just different. Some people view a cup of coffee as just that: low cost, straight up, and regular with no gimmicks; while others view it as a "flavor experience" that they are willing to pay a premium price to receive. Some people even view drinking coffee as a social experience where they meet friends. All are strong motives for their lives and habits as buyers.

You see the constant interplay between mindset and motive for the buyer. It is part of our daily lives; it threads through our "buying fabric." Now, these daily transactions don't all require a direct salesperson's intervention, yet they are still instructive for looking at this concept as you encounter buyers who do interact with salespeople to purchase goods and services. In those cases, most of us have had similar experiences where the more the salesperson understands the buyer's mindset and motive, the easier it is for the salesperson to relate to the buyer—hit the target and start to sell her on the Brand.

In the next chapter, we'll talk about what you need to be thinking about next in order to move—or migrate—the buyer from where he is now mentally to where you want him to be—at the beginning of the Brand Staircase.

Key Points

- A useful way to think of where the buyer is coming from is for the salesperson to think of the image of a target, or bull's-eye, that contains mindset and motive.
- To be successful in using the buyer's bull's-eye, you need to connect to what the buyer is thinking and feeling as she enters the sales transaction (mindset). Then you need to focus your sales efforts on understanding and uncovering her motives.
- As we sight in on the bull's-eye and get more proficient at focusing in, our shots will move from the outer circle of mindset to the inner circle of motive. We will thus be getting at the real reasons that buyers purchase.
- We defined motives and categorized them based on logic and emotion:

Appeal to Logic:	Savings—time, money hassle
	Production—more efficient, better results, more output
Appeal to Emotion:	Personal—job easier, look good, save face, leisure time
	Power—control, recognition, approval

CHAPTER 8

MIGRATION

Ultimately, our job as salespeople is to identify the step of the staircase on which the buyer entered, and then help him move toward the Brand. If we don't help him move from that step, he is likely to buy the product based on his entry-point mindset, which we discussed in Chapter 6. Also, if you are trying to sell your Brand, then the other three choices aren't likely to benefit you as the salesperson. That is, buyers will continue to buy on the basis of Price, Style, or Quality. Thus, our job is to help them move or *migrate* toward the Brand.

We also talked about the salesperson's mindsets in Chapter 6, and we suggested some changes to your mindset before you enter the transaction. Then, in Chapter 7, we talked about the extremely important notion of motive. Motives are the biggest reasons that buyers purchase; thus, they are the key to migrating the buyer. So, how do we work motives into the sales process? We need to look for firm evidence from the buyer, and we need to ask good questions. That is where we are headed next as we meet the buyer face to face in Chapter 9.

You see, all of this preliminary groundwork on mindset and motives was done to help you realize the importance of prethinking your selling interactions. Keeping these buyer and seller mindsets in your working memory when the buyer actually enters the sales interaction is invaluable. Once the buyer enters the face-to-face interaction, the game changes, and you have to think and feel like a Brand salesperson. The ultimate action you will take as a Brand salesperson is the migration of the buyer, whether it is an individual consumer buyer or a trade buyer.

Accordingly, this chapter brings together three main ideas:

1. The concept of migration and the importance of *helping the buyer migrate* from his entry point (mindset) toward the Brand step of

the Staircase, where you can more easily start the Brand conversation (uncover his motives) and sell downhill.

2. The question of *customer loyalty and its impact on migration* and how we view the Brand Staircase.

3. The idea that loyal customers don't just buy the Brand; they experience it. We will delve into the power of a buyer experiencing the Brand.

What Is the Importance of Helping the Buyer Migrate?

When I was growing up in Montana, I used to witness a mass migration of Canadian geese out of the cold North Country toward the warm climate of the Deep South in the late fall. Mystified as to where they were going, I asked my dad one day.

"Where are the birds going, Dad?"

"Son, those are geese. They are migrating south for the winter."

"Why?"

"Because it is too cold for them to survive up north. In other words, if they want to live, they have to move."

"What causes them to move?"

"The weather changes, and their bodies just know that it's time to go. Plus the older geese teach the younger geese to migrate, just like I'm teaching you now."

I don't remember much beyond that, but I do remember thinking, "They move from the cold to survive."

I think that buyers are much like geese in this sense:

- Many of them are "out in the cold" when it comes to your Brand.
- They need to move or migrate from the step of the staircase that they entered on toward the Brand step if we are to be successful in selling the Brand.
- As salespeople, we need to be their "weather catalyst," giving them a reason to move into the warmth of the Brand and its experiences and promises.

What this means to us as salespeople is that we can act as the primary catalyst for the buyer when it comes to our Brand. If we want to be successful, then we need to help change the buyer's thinking (just as the weather changes the goose's thinking) to help the buyer migrate toward our Brand (see Figure 8.1).

The word *migration* has many meanings. *Webster's American Family Dictionary* defines *migration* as "to pass periodically from one region or climate to another, as certain birds, fishes, or animals . . . to change

MIGRATING ON THE BRAND STAIRCASE

FIGURE 8.1

position . . . to change location periodically, to move from one location to another." Buyers need to change location periodically, and as sellers we need to help them.

When I'm with salespeople and sales leaders in a Brand selling workshop, and we start discussing this migration topic, there can be some "push back" from the group. It comes in the form of statements like these:

- "Wait a minute. I have seen some buyers who were convinced that they knew enough about our product to make the decision on their own. I've even seen buyers who showed little interest in talking with me, to the point that they almost shunned me (the salesperson)."
- "I have attempted to sell buyers who were so set on their Brand that there was no way they were going to change."
- "Some of the people I have dealt with would not spend one penny over what their budget would allow, period."

I quickly respond to those objections by agreeing with them, but with a few exceptions. Please recall that nowhere in our discussions have I said that Brand selling would automatically convert every customer to your Brand, or that it would be a magic bullet that would convert every

Price-minded buyer to a Brand-seeking shopper, or that there would not be any speed bumps or hurdles along the way.

Rather, being a realist here, I find it useful to add one more line of reasoning to answer these questions. The workshop participants then begin to consider different "migration scenarios" that help salespeople take more responsibility for making the Brand Staircase come alive. In dealing with many companies, I have found three truths about migration:

1. *Some buyers will migrate on their own. In that case, there is no need for a salesperson.* The reality is that in modern-day shopping, many buyers are well educated as a result of prior experience with a certain Brand. They probably have heard word of mouth about a product from other users or from a company's advertising and can make sound decisions on their own. As a matter of fact, many buyers choose to do that by shopping on the Internet or going to mass channels that provide many product choices and encourage unaided shopping and self-service. Thus, most of us who sell for a living will not usually encounter these buyers.

   Exception: There are times when "migrate-on-their-own" buyers do cross your path, especially when they are shopping you versus the competition but would like to decide on their own. Periodically, these buyers find out that they need more education than they originally expected. They then become buyers that we can intercede with and possibly influence toward our Brand.

2. *Some buyers will not migrate at all. In this case, again, there is no need for a salesperson.* You see, there are times when a certain Brand has become so entrenched as a big part of the buyer's lifestyle or choices that you cannot change the buyer's mind no matter what. For instance, your Uncle Harry is known as a "Ford guy," and under no circumstances (short of death, or serious illness) would he buy anything but a Ford vehicle.

   I have also found that certain people will stick very closely to their budget or Price mindset no matter what. Again, these people are very hard to convince that there is a need to migrate from their entry-point mindset.

   Exception: I have seen times in my selling career where these "will-not-migrate-at-all" buyers will look at another possible product or Brand. Usually, this happens when they have had a recent bad experience concerning the quality of the product with a favorite Brand that they blindly trusted in the past. Normally they will stay with that Brand unless we give them a reason to look further. In other words, we need to provide new evidence for another Brand that would make it worth switching to. In this case, there is an obvious need for a salesperson.

3. *Many will need help migrating. In this case, there is a big need for a "Branded" salesperson.* The good news for salespeople is that the vast majority of the buying population falls into this category. They are people who are part of our Branded society who realize the depth and breadth of choices available to them and are going to buy accordingly. They are generally open to manufacturers that have built the latest and greatest products—a "new and improved mousetrap"—and they check consumer reports or trade magazines for the best-quality products. They shop the sales and compare prices, but they are not willing to sacrifice the value in the products and Brands that they buy without good reason.

In summary, there are key questions to be asked by you the salesperson:

BUYER MIGRATION—KEY QUESTIONS
1. Where do buyers enter on the staircase?
2. Will they migrate toward the Brand?
3. Will you or the competition help them migrate?

Now, when we finish this discussion during the workshop, the interesting observation I have made is that the buy-in within the room skyrockets. Why? The salespeople start to realize that it's their job to help buyers in the migration process, and furthermore, that if they don't, someone else will—the competition. Let's illustrate this by taking it one step further.

The 80/20 Rule Applied to Migration

There is a universal rule within sales and leadership circles that has been simply named *the 80/20 rule.* It states that normally, in any given territory, on average about 20 percent of your customers will give you 80 percent of your territory's volume. This means that a small percentage of the customers dominate or contribute a large percentage of the sales dollars.

During conversations about growing the territory's or category's business, sales leaders will typically challenge their salespeople with this type of question: "If you are going to grow your territory or market share, then what is happening with the other 80 percent of the buyers who are not currently contributing to your sales numbers? If you could get just another 10 percent of the noncustomers to start buying from you, then your quota or sales goals would be much easier to reach, wouldn't they?"

This same line of reasoning applies to the Brand Staircase: buyers enter with a primary mindset of Brand, Quality, Style, or Price. Some are willing to change their mindset; some are not. My experience in multiple industries has shown that buyers who will migrate on their own and buyers who will not migrate at all are in the minority. These buyers represent the two extreme mindsets, Price and Brand, and include about 20 percent of the population. The remaining 80 percent of the population, or the vast majority of buyers, will enter on the Style or Quality mindset. Thus the pattern follows the classic 80/20 rule. See Figure 8.2.

So, let's say that you get serious about migrating buyers who entered on steps other than Brand. Ask yourself a couple of questions:

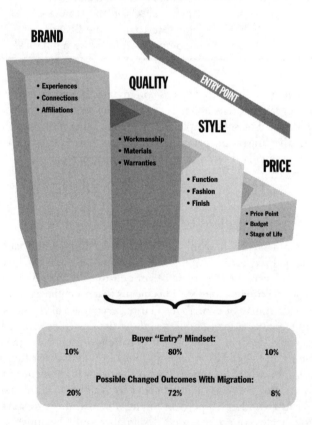

FIGURE 8.2

- What if I could help just 2 percent of the buyers migrate from Price toward Brand?
- What if I could help another 8 percent migrate from Style or Quality toward Brand?
- What could it mean to my sales numbers if another 10 percent of my potential buyers got serious about the Brand and migrated there?

I then speak directly to the sales managers and leaders who supervise salespeople and ask these questions:

1. Imagine if you had a shot at 10 percent more of the market.
2. Imagine if you had the breadth of line to cover all of the price points in a category of product. That is, you were able to bring to the market products that cover the opening, mid, and high price points, and, not coincidentally, also cover the other main mindsets on the Brand staircase—Style, Quality, and Brand. Would that give you some sweet options or what?
3. Imagine if your salespeople were committed to Brand migration and your store personnel and the salespeople of your distributors, dealers, and agents were Brand ambassadors.

Many heads are nodding in agreement. They see the logic. Some feel the pain. Others start thinking about those customers that they could start helping to migrate.

How Loyal Are Your Customers? Do They Really Need Help Migrating?

Questions of customer loyalty and ways to improve it are constant topics of discussion within the sales community. Good salespeople are always examining their customer base with an eye on improving its loyalty. As a matter of fact, most great salespeople have made customer loyalty an art form. But what does customer loyalty have to do with the Brand Staircase and migration? Well, let's explore that for a moment.

In my company's Brand selling workshops, our first exercise on buyer mindset and the need to migrate asks salespeople to think about their top 15 buyers. This is an exercise that you may benefit from as well. First, identify your buyers by the various levels or amounts of business they give you as a salesperson and then write down the customer names on 3 × 5 cards of different colors based on their level of business. We break it out like this:

- *Loyal customers* (light blue cards) give you their business almost all the time. These buyers tend to shop you regularly, they will call you to put aside product for them, they don't miss a sale or promotion, they may tell you openly that they buy most of their goods from you, they know you well, and they have probably established a personal friendship with you.

- *Developing customers* (purple cards) give you their business about half the time. These buyers are less regular than loyal buyers, yet you see them during major sales, and you know that they are buying from you and also buying from one or several major competitors. They may not be bashful about "shopping the field," and you know that they have potential to buy more from you and your company.
- *Occasional customers* (pink cards) give you their business only some of the time. They are seen infrequently, and thus you imagine that they must spend their money in other places rather than with you. They may be a mystery for you to figure out or be elusive in their buying habits, but they have great potential to do business with you.

Normally, salespeople can easily identify and categorize these 15 customers/buyers. This personalizes the learning for them, catapults them into their own sales world, and puts the emphasis right where it should be—on their customers.

Next, duplicate this information on a chart similar to the one in Table 8.1 in order to track how the Brand Staircase applies to your customers.

TABLE 8.1 List 15 Customers at Various Levels of Business

5 occasional customers—some of the time
5 developing customers—more of the time
5 loyal customers—almost all the time

Loyal (blue cards)	Developing (purple cards)	Occasional (pink cards)

Now, set these customers aside for the moment and review the first three steps—Price, Style, and Quality—on the Buyer Stair-Step (Chapter 3).

Pull out your 15 customers again. This time, however, go back to mindset and identify the *primary step* on which each buyer enters the staircase. Determine how these buyers normally buy, and identify the step that has the most influence on their choice: Price, Style, or Quality. Then, place a colored dot that matches the color of the step you chose for each customer: Price (red), Style (yellow), or Quality (Blue).

Go back to the customer chart one last time—this is your opportunity to change any customer by placing a new dot over the top of your first choice, with one exception: you can now add an orange dot that represents the Brand mindset. You may be surprised to find that very few dots change color. I've found in workshops that in most cases, one or two buyers may be buying based on the Brand, but the majority are buying based on the other three steps.

Now, imagine a salesperson looking at 15 of his customers on Table 8.1 in a kaleidoscope of color. He now has a visual picture of how much business he does with customers and the mindset that most of his customers buy from on a daily basis. While observing their charts, we ask the salespeople at our workshop the following questions:

- What trends do you find in your results?
- Where do your loyal customers fall on the Brand Staircase?
- What would it take to move a customer from occasional to developing, or from developing to loyal?
- What customers are at risk, and why?

You can imagine that the answers are very interesting and widely dispersed. But if nothing else, they are eye-opening and start the discovery process for salespeople to individually rethink their customers, buyers, and marketplace. Figure 8.3 pulls customer loyalty and buyer mindset together.

We also are able to make some consistent observations and connections when we debrief this exercise:

1. Salespeople generally know their regular customers quite well and can intuitively determine their level of business (loyal, developing, or occasional) and then place them on the staircase.
2. Salespeople are able to mentally meet each customer on the staircase by physically placing a colored dot representing that customer's entering mindset (Price, Style, Quality, or Brand) next to the customer's name.
3. Now, at a glance, salespeople can look at their customer base and recognize patterns of buying behavior based on the components of

CUSTOMER LOYALTY AND BUYER MINDSET

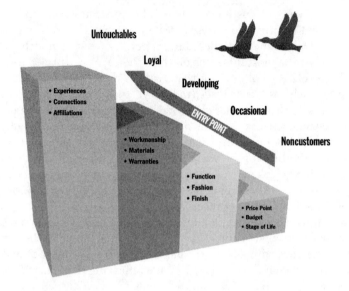

FIGURE 8.3

the Brand Staircase. They also recognize a stronger need to sell the Brand and strategize how they might be able to move customers toward the Brand. As a matter of fact, most salespeople are surprised by how little their buyers are buying based on the Brand or how little they are selling the Brand.

4. The further you move a buyer up the staircase toward Quality and Brand, the more loyal that buyer tends to become. Eventually buyers may become almost untouchable in their allegiance to your Brand, much like the "Ford guy" we mentioned earlier. At the other end of the staircase, we may have room to attract noncustomers to the staircase as a way of broadening our market share.

5. The Brand Staircase is merely a concept until we do this customer exercise. The mere act of placing their customers on the chart brings the staircase alive for the average salesperson. Now, with their top customers present on the Brand Staircase, salespeople realize where their buyers are currently, how far they need to go, and the power of starting to intentionally migrate them to the Brand. *The Brand Staircase has now become a selling tool for growing their customer base.*

How Does a Customer Become Loyal?

It seems that a big ingredient of customer loyalty is experiencing the Brand. Put another way, from the perspective of the salesperson, Brand names should be the salesperson's easiest marketing and sales tool to help buyers experience and associate with certain activities that relate to a particular product. As I have said more than once in this book, salespeople tend to sell everything but the Brand. Often the reason a sales interaction fails is because the salesperson sells on the Price, Style, or Quality of the product. We are too product-focused, because as salespeople that's how we grew up—just give me the product and let me sell!

Instead, if we really want to find the key to increasing customer loyalty, then we should connect our customers to the experience of our Brand, not just the product. We would be well advised to take a lesson from some Brands that we see in the marketplace that do this well.

Allow me to illustrate.

Douglas Atkin, author of *The Culting of Brands: When Customers Become True Believers*, aligns directly with that thinking. "And it's the brands that are recognizing the power of human interaction that are becoming the heroes of business." He goes on to highlight a direct quote from Dave Barger, the president and chief operating officer of JetBlue. According to Barger: "It's the People, not the Planes. You can be a part of a well-funded start up, have all new planes, a cool product, leather seats, live TV, cool snacks. But none of it matters. The people are the Brand . . . you are the Brand as a person." Atkin goes on to note, "Fortunately, the people running the company realize that as important as the substance of the customer experience is (the TV, comfortable planes, the low prices), it's the *core members* of this rapidly growing cult brand, and their interactions with customers, that are making the difference. It's not the stuff. It's the staff that is driving these results" (p. 37).

At DeWALT, we launched an end-user marketing approach that coincided with the launch of the product line. We used to say that we wanted to be where the user *works, lives, and plays*. So, we did just that:

- We went where they worked—we went right to the job site where they were building homes and demonstrated power tools and accessories.
- We went where they lived—we went to the NASCAR races, to the professional rodeos, to the speedboat races where they were enjoying their leisure time.
- And we went where they played—we went to their local lumberyard on a weekday with three things in mind: food, fun, and free stuff. We fed them lunch, we had some fun, and we gave them a free hat.

It got to be so much fun that users clamored to be there and be part of the action. One example of the fun part was the DeWALT Challenge. It was a contest using a cordless drill. We set up a competition among the customers. The challenge was to see who could drive the most 1¼-inch drywall screws into a piece of drywall in 10 seconds. We literally used a stopwatch, and the winner received what was to become a coveted goldenrod DeWALT T-shirt that said in bold black letters "Guaranteed Tough" with the inscription "DeWALT Industrial Power Tools." Now, I ask you, what construction worker wouldn't want to win that T-shirt, parade around in it at work, and have bragging rights for weeks to come? As a matter of fact, the users actually became walking billboards for our Brand. Everyone wanted to be a part of it. The enthusiasm was incredibly high, the excitement was contagious, and the best part was . . . the users of our product helped us create it, and the competition could not duplicate it. Why? Because it had become associated with our Brand alone. We had claimed the "first mover advantage," similar to Apple's innovation with iPod. Thus, we had seized the opportunity, as the first manufacturer in the marketplace, to claim that advantage. It would be very difficult for anyone else to duplicate it.

- We extended the Brand beyond the workplace—beyond the 8-to-5 job—and the users welcomed us with open arms.
- We sponsored events that were exciting to attend and that were part of how our buyers were already living their lives or part of how they wanted to live their lives.

At DeWALT we sold beyond the product; we purposely connected with people's lifestyles and experiences. We made an emotional connection with customers that extended beyond their workday into their leisure time, beyond their trade to affiliate with their lives. The Brand led them to perceive a power tool company as a partner at work and a friend after hours. If I hadn't lived the experience, I might not have believed that it could happen. It was powerful, and it can be powerful for your Brand, too.

The end result of Black & Decker's market launch of DeWALT was one of the biggest turnarounds recorded in marketplace history. It is now a Harvard Business School case field study on how to use a strong Brand and end-user strategy to take back a market.

Over the last decade, this type of Brand experience has become more common. People don't want to just buy products or services—they want to experience them, they want to connect with them, they want to associate or affiliate with them. Why do you think the credit card companies all want co-sponsors now? What I mean is that the credit card industry has gone to something called affinity marketing, which basically means that you can get a card with the logo from your alma mater, be it Wake Forest or Harvard; your favorite store, whether it is Bass Pro Shops or Victoria's Secret; or your favorite sports team, which could be the Baltimore Ravens or the Boston Red Sox. People have carried over their lifestyles into an ongoing experience with the Brand.

Let me give you some more examples.

Waterford Crystal is a high-end manufacturer of exquisite crystal products based in Ireland. In every box of its expensive crystal pieces, it places a beautiful silver embossed card with a seahorse on the outside. The inside inscription reads:

Our Mark of Excellence . . . Waterford's pursuit of design excellence is forever steadfast in a world of wavering standards. Always beautiful, ever functional, we strive to fulfill your aspirations. Every piece is manually checked an average of 4 times to ensure it arrives to you in perfect condition. Seek the Seahorse stamp of excellence, which can be found on every piece of Waterford, our guarantee to you. For you, for now, forever. Enjoy.

Wow! I feel like I just got married, not like I simply bought a piece of crystal for my dining room table or living room. Do you think these folks believe in their products? Yes, emphatically. But, even more important than that, they believe in the experiences and aspirations that go along with their products.

Beretta is a five-hundred-year-old Italian-based company with a passion for making high-end, well-built firearms—mostly shotguns and pistols. I had the good fortune recently to visit Beretta USA. I was given the local tour by my contact, the vice president of sales and marketing, and after lunch we were to meet the president of the U.S. operation. At lunch, we started talking about hunting. I was the more seasoned hunter, so I was telling him of my hunting adventures in Montana and how I viewed the experience overall.

I said, "For me, the hunt is about the experience—not the kill. It's about the cold mountain air, the anticipation of waiting, watching the dogs work the fields and point upon finding their prey, the adrenalin rush of seeing animals roaming wild in the wilderness, the preparation and gathering of your gear, the camaraderie of the hunting camp, and the story telling at night."

So, having relived the mountains over lunch, I expected to meet the president after lunch and talk about guns, my services, and leadership on his team. Boy, was I wrong! After Pat introduced me and we shared pleasantries, I noticed an antique Beretta handgun sitting on the president's desk. I motioned to him as if to ask, "Can I pick up this priceless artifact?" I mentioned that I loved hunting, and he nodded his head in approval.

Before I could say anything else, he announced to Pat and myself, "You know, Dan, we don't sell shotguns; we sell experiences!" I glanced at Pat, and we both smiled. He continued, "It's not about the guns; it's about the experience you have when you're out using the gun." He went on to explain Beretta's brand to me by handing me a brochure. It called out to me the "Brand DNA" and focused in on eight words, none of which included the word *gun:* Reliable, Passionate, Craftsmanship, Italian, Innovation, Integrity, Responsible, and Authentic.

It went on to say:

At the core of Beretta is a passion.

An understanding of the wild places.

The cold fields of autumn. The high grass and the low marsh.

Rain and sun. Man and dog.

It's an understanding that is pure and real. It lives in the deepest reaches of the hunter's heart. The innermost corners of the shooter's soul.

And it is everywhere. A field in Tuscany. A lake in Wyoming.

The flash of a tail. The thunder of wings . . .

Need I say more? Did you not go to that place, even if only for a moment?

My only questions for the president were these:

"Do your salespeople know how to speak this language, use these words?" The answer was no.

"How long would it take them to learn how to speak this language?" The answer was two years.

The bottom line here is simple: the Brand has a language all its own, an experience that transcends the product, its showroom, its packaging, or its warranty. We talked about this extensively in Chapter 2, and one of the goals of this book is to get you to speak it. As salespeople and sales leaders, if we are to be successful at selling the Brand, it is our job—or even our duty—to make those experiences come alive for buyers by helping them migrate toward our Brand.

Think about the examples from JetBlue, DeWALT, Waterford, and Beretta. The end users or buyers of those products are certainly buying more than a flight, a tool or accessory, a piece of crystal, or a shotgun. At the core of their purchase decision is an alignment with the

Brand—the experiences that the Brand declares, the affiliation with other users of the Brand, and the direct and often emotional connection with the Brand.

In the next part of this book, we will offer you many ways to practice migrating the buyer to the Brand using the principles we have laid out up to now. Stay tuned!

Key Points

As professional salespeople, it is our job to meet the buyer on the Brand Staircase and determine three major things through the face-to-face interaction:

1. **How to migrate the buyer.** Migration is the act of helping the buyer move toward the Brand. There are three main migration scenarios for buyers:
   - *Some buyers will migrate on their own.* In that case, there is no need for a salesperson, unless the buyer is competitively "shopping us."
   - *Some buyers will not migrate at all.* In this case again, there is no need for a salesperson, unless the buyer has had a recent bad experience with a favorite Brand, and we can provide new evidence on our Brand.
   - *Many will need help migrating.* In this case, there is a big need for a "Branded" salesperson. Fortunately, the vast majority of buyers fall into this category. The main question in migration becomes, who will help buyers migrate, you or the competition?
2. **How to improve customer loyalty.** We debated the level of customer loyalty based on which step of the staircase the buyer entered and the amount of business that the buyer is doing with the salesperson. We then made some connections with the need for migration. Now, with their top customers located on the Brand Staircase, salespeople realize where their buyers are currently and the power of starting to connect them to the Brand intentionally. The Brand Staircase is now a selling tool, not just a model.
3. **How to tie into buyer experiences with the Brand which go beyond the product itself.** We told some brand stories and discussed the experiences that people had with those brands that separate them from the competition. The power behind experi-

encing the Brand is that it drives customer loyalty. The buyer affiliates not only with the product that you sell, but also with the enjoyment that she receives from the experience, which goes far beyond the product and its specifications. Lastly, it is those unique experiences that make it difficult for the competition to duplicate your Brand.

PART 4

SELLING BRANDS IN THE BUSINESS-TO-CONSUMER SETTING

THE LIFESTYLE CONNECTION

I n the first eight chapters, we have built a universal understanding of selling the Brand. In general, we have focused on the most common denominator for all of us, selling to the consumer, because we all can understand it as consumers who purchase Brands, products, and services daily. This also has created a foundation of knowledge and skills for us to build upon that applies equally to selling Brands in any of the other channels.

However, it is important to note that the Brand is sold differently depending on the channel in which you mostly sell: consumer, trade, service, or crossover. In this chapter, we begin to make these distinctions by discussing an issue for the consumer—lifestyles. Later chapters are more specifically focused on business-to-business concerns. In order to ensure that you make the right turn in your Brand selling journey, I want to spend a few minutes being your tour guide before you proceed. Let's begin by comparing the big consumer Brands to trade Brands.

The Big Differences between Consumer and Trade Brands

Consumer Brands have a direct impact on our lifestyle, including how we spend our leisure time and our discretionary income. *Trade Brands*, on the other hand, *seldom* have a direct impact on our personal lifestyle. They are usually purchased by professional buyers who have responsibility for the profitability of a product line or service category, and, importantly, who are buying for their company, not for their personal use. A more specific breakdown follows:

Consumer Brands	Trade Brands
Buyer emphasis	
Buying for self, using the product	Buying for a company, not using the product
Casual, arm's-length relationship	Ongoing, businesslike relationship
One-time or periodic sale	Repeat sales and/or regular call pattern
Many product/service choices	Fewer product/service choices
Sales direct to consumer	Sales to distribution/resellers/trade users
Brand emphasis	
Brand is visible to the public	Brand is invisible to the public
Brand usually is advertised in mass media	Brand usually won't be advertised in mass media
Brand image is built by media and company and supported by salesperson	Brand image is built by company and driven by salesperson
May represent multiple Brands	May represent fewer Brands

Thus, if you sell consumer Brands, the best path to take is to read Chapters 9 and 10 on lifestyle questions and business-to-consumer selling. If you sell trade Brands, then the best path is to read Chapters 11 and 12 on the business-to-business selling environment.

It is important to note here that salespeople who represent *crossover Brands* can sell in both of these settings. This can make their selling roles more complex because they might be selling the Brand as a trade Brand to distribution one day, then as a consumer Brand to the end consumer during a weekend show. If you sell crossover Brands, it would be wise for you to cover all four chapters.

Service Brands, on the other hand, can be sold in either channel, depending on the end user of your service. For instance, if you are selling services to the consumer, such as lawn care, haircutting, personal grooming, health and fitness, or travel and leisure, you would line up mostly with Chapters 9 and 10. However, if you sell professional services to business owners, such as accounting, legal, or engineering services, then you should refer to Chapters 11 and 12.

No matter which path you take here, I will meet you at Chapter 13 to talk about the Brand's impact on the culture and vice versa.

The Lifestyle Connection for Consumers

In the business-to-consumer setting, the key to connecting with the Brand is to understand the buyer's lifestyle choices first. This should be a primary focus for the Consumer salesperson to help him connect with the Brand through a full understanding of the importance and meaning of lifestyle choices. You may recall that we introduced an important sales mindset in Chapter 4 that is worth repeating here:

> People are not just purchasing a product,
> but rather supporting a chosen lifestyle.

All of us have lifestyles that we pursue, aspire to, or want to affiliate with—*whether we do so intentionally or not* is the question. Most of these lifestyles are uniquely our own. We also affiliate with others who share similar lifestyle needs—for instance, the Harley-Davidson Hog owners, the chat rooms for PC users, and the priority clubs for frequent travelers, to name a few. On the other hand, a product can do something for the customer but may not fulfill that lifestyle need unless we intentionally help customers connect to the Brand we are selling through the product.

The key to this new perspective is not to forget about product knowledge, but rather to learn firsthand each day what customers are looking for in a great Brand. Learn how they use Brands every day, how they apply Brands to their lives, and which Brands they would love to try if they could. Learn which Brands they affiliate with, where they connect with those Brands, and, most importantly, why.

One of the most valuable things I learned from my mother was the concept of *learning curves.* She taught us that you can learn from everyone you interact with in life—friends, neighbors, siblings, elders, teachers, strangers, and even enemies. Over the years, I've expanded those learning curves to include vendors, peers, other salespeople, users, buyers, and even customers. Life is about learning curves—how fast you ascend them, how much you pay attention to them, and how much you learn from them along the way. The question is, are you willing and able to learn from your customers about their lifestyle choices and connections with your Brand? Are you willing to apply those learning curves to your daily sales life right now? The main vehicle to help our learning curves is to ask great questions. That's where we are headed next.

Getting at Lifestyle through Good Questions

If there were only one skill I could teach to salespeople, it would be questioning and listening. Why? Because questions stimulate thought, get information, and encourage people to talk. They also reveal your curiosity, reflect that the person's opinion is important to you, and show people that you care. Many of the greatest leaders of all time in their professions were great questioners and not shy about it. These famous people once said about questioning:

"If only I had the right question, if only I had the right question."
—Albert Einstein

"Sometimes the question is more important than the answer."—Plato

"Do you have any questions for my answers?"   *—Henry Kissinger*

"Find the right questions. You don't invent the answers—you reveal the answers."   *—Jonas Salk*

"Much is lost for the want of asking."   *—Madame Curie*

"I cannot teach anybody anything, I can only make them think."
—Socrates

Now examine that list of people. You could easily argue that every one of those key leaders already had many of the answers for his or her profession, yet all of them still valued the questioning process above their answering expertise. They understood that statements and answers get at the *head*, and that questions get at the *heart*. Imagine if every profession were as grounded in learning more, asking better questions, listening well, and giving targeted answers when the need arose! The world would be a better place.

I believe that as salespeople and sales leaders, we can learn great things from these leaders about how to approach our buyers. I believe most of those leaders thought that life is a mystery, that it is a curious thing. Every person who walks the planet has a bundle of experiences, by choice and by chance, that together make up her story. Let's connect the dots to lifestyle questioning and how it gets at the Brand.

There Is A LOT to Lifestyle Questioning

Armed with the importance of asking good questions, how do we help consumer buyers accommodate a lifestyle? I have found that the foundation for asking good lifestyle questions is rooted in four things. We have named them:

THE BRAND RULES OF ENGAGEMENT
Asking, Listening and Observing, and Talking

The *Brand Rules of Engagement* involve four simple forms of communication that signify the need to engage with each customer. Every seasoned salesperson has dabbled in these verbs—Asking, Listening, Observing, and Talking (A LOT)—at various classes he's taken or workshops he's attended. However, understanding these verbs doesn't mean that we apply them as part of our language. They might seem like common sense, however, they are not common practice. The reality is that few salespeople apply these verbs to selling their Brands because they haven't been taught how to do so. That is, they haven't been taught how to interact with or engage the buyer.

Before you check out on me, thinking that you've already been through a class on asking questions or listening, read on! The big difference here is the big differentiator—the Brand! Of the four skills, we will now laser focus on two main things (see Figure 9.1):

CONNECTING LIFESTYLE TO BRAND

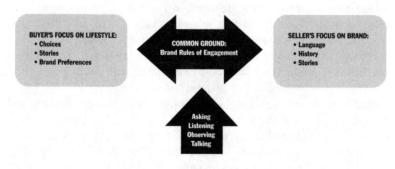

FIGURE 9.1

1. The lifestyle that the buyer is leading or aspiring to lead
2. The Brand you represent and how to bring it alive to meet that lifestyle need

You may be saying, "This is an interesting and unique approach, but why does it work?" Well, it is probably more instructive to look at why the old way wasn't working. The source of my findings comes from two areas: field sales calls and conducting Brand Selling workshops.

When I first started mentally working through the foundation of this Brand Selling program, I went on multiple sales calls with customers to determine what was going wrong with the way people were currently attempting to sell their Brand. I found a pattern. I then found a very similar pattern in the workshops I teach as salespeople begin to uncover new Brand selling habits to replace the old. The findings were very interesting. Let me explain the findings, then contrast them to the A LOT lifestyle questioning approach.

When salespeople asked questions, they did so only to start the conversation, and they dug only deep enough to uncover the basic needs of the buyer, which was similar to what their competitors were doing. Many of the questions weren't even open-ended in nature; thus, they didn't stimulate the buyer to deeper levels of conversation. Instead of getting into an engaging conversation with the buyers, the salespeople found themselves in an artificial, surface-level discussion that always went back to product.

Salespeople tended to listen only for what they wanted to hear, which left them with only half of the picture. Unfortunately, they also talked twice as much as they listened. Put another way, we have two ears and one mouth for a reason—to listen more than we speak. Unfortunately, some salespeople have missed that lesson. Thus, in interactions, it was hard for many buyers to get their own stuff in—that is, their lifestyles, stories, or Brand preferences.

As to observing, the salespeople overall seemed blind to nonverbal communications—the signs that the buyers were making beyond the words that they were saying. It was as if the nonverbal messages were hiding in plain sight. Even a simple observation skill, like observing what the buyers were wearing, was in large part absent. The skill of observing and assessing what the buyer was doing during the interaction, how she was acting, and the messages she was sending along the way was largely overlooked or undetected.

Finally, in terms of talking, salespeople tended to default early and often to taking over the conversation. Their verbal skills were good, but overdone. When they did start telling the story, they usually went to regurgitation of product features instead of Brand buildup. The talking became very feature and benefit driven. The need to teach salespeople how to talk to their buyers was overshadowed by the need to teach them what their focus should start with—the Brand.

So, as we transferred this learning to the development of the Brand selling concept, we needed to make some adjustments so that we could start selling differently and get off on the right foot. First, we needed some new language to help us become intentional about selling with the Brand first and using the Brand Staircase. So I coined the phrase *lifestyle questions.*

Next, we went back to the Brand step of the staircase and developed some visuals in the form of orange Brand cue cards that contain the Brand Rules of Engagement. You will see these unfold shortly.

The third step was to make the process operational for sales teams that were now focused on Brand selling to their buyers. Their salespeople needed to be a team that spoke the same Brand language around lifestyles on a daily basis *without* making them into a band of puppets or having them become too "scripted" in their approach. Let's begin now to understand the fundamentals that bring lifestyle questions alive. In Chapter 10, we will focus on dealing with buyers at each step of the Brand Staircase and applying these skills.

Asking

Asking questions is a key skill set for a good salesperson. The goal of asking great questions is to get the customer to talk openly about his life.

> - People love talking about themselves, if you just give them a chance.
> - There is no life story or experience more important to people than their own.

The bottom line is simple: people love to talk about themselves and their lives if we will just allow them to do it. I know that sounds basic, but I am always dumbfounded by how many salespeople know this little insight but don't practice it. So, our first goal is to get buyers talking about themselves. That is the first Brand Rule of Engagement (see Figure 9.2).

In Brand selling, the focus of the questions is initially centered on Brands in general. Then it moves specifically toward the particular Brand as it relates to experiences, connections, and affiliations.

> Lifestyle questions center on the Brand and the buyer's
> Experiences from the past
> Connections to the present
> Affiliations for the future

FIRST RULE OF ENGAGEMENT

When ASKING...

- Engage them from the beginning
- Get them talking about their life

Ask open-ended Questions around Brands including:
- Experiences from their "Past"
- Connections to the "Present"
- Affiliations for their "Future"

Build Trust early

FIGURE 9.2

All three of those are powerful motivators for buyers because the buyers have already lived those experiences, are currently looking for a brand connection, or wish to affiliate with a brand in the near future. Yet as salespeople, we overlook or undersell the value of this connection every day, simply because we don't help buyers find ways to associate with our Brand.

The need to connect buyers to time is also important here—the past, the present, and the future. This concept is one of the most powerful, yet simple, parts of our association with Brands. You see, every one of us is a walking, living, and breathing combination of past experiences, personal history, and aspirational dreams. We all have a past, live in the present, and have some unfulfilled dreams for our future. So, the minute someone walks through the front door of your establishment, walks up to your booth at a show, visits your showroom, or escorts you into her office, we have one simple goal in mind, and that is to unpackage those experiences, connections, and affiliations by asking good lifestyle questions to help us understand the Brands that are most aligned with the buyer's expectations.

So how do we do that? Let me give you the top tips to get you started by examining a retail store setting, one that we can all relate to as a buyer and most of us as a seller.

WHEN ASKING:

Point 1: Engage the Buyer from the Beginning. Make the customer feel at home, important, and comfortable. Remember, first impressions are lasting for most people, so give a positive first impression by showing sincere interest in the buyer. Your goal here should be to prepare him for a conversation about Brands. So get him talking about his life by asking questions about his opinions. For instance, three strong conversation starters in a retail store environment are

- "What brings you to our store today?"
- "I see you're looking at XXX Brand; have you experienced it before?"
- "I see you're looking at XXX Brand; what do you like about it?"

All of these questions immediately engage the buyer and start a conversation about his experience or interest level with Brands. They make an instant association with Brands, and probably with your product. They also ask the buyer to think about his purpose, his past, and his convictions.

Exercise: Write an opening question that would engage the buyer from the beginning in your particular selling environment.

Point 2: Get Buyers Talking about Their Life. As the conversation develops, get buyers talking about their experiences with other Brands in the past. Your goals here are to

- *Talk about their lives, not your product.* Remember, it's their experiences with the Brand and perceptions of the Brand that really matter.
- *Ask two or three great lifestyle questions to encourage buyer engagement.* These questions should lead to follow-up questions and an engaging conversation with the buyer.
- A LOT does not refer to a lot of questions asked of the buyer; *rather, it refers to a lot of engagement with the buyer.*

I have found questions like the following to be very effective in the store environment:

- "Tell me about your favorite products or Brands within your home."
- "Describe for me a purchase you made of a good Brand lately. Why did that end up being a good decision for you?"
- "What do you think of when you think of Baldwin/Kohler/JennAir/ Corian . . . ?"
- "If there is one Brand that you have always wanted to purchase for your house, but have had a hard time affording or justifying paying so much for in the past, what Brand is that, and why?"
- "I see you pulled up in a BMW/Mercedes. . . . If you don't mind, tell me what you like about your luxury vehicle. Are you looking for a similar Brand experience in your home furnishings?"

These are great follow-up questions that keep the conversation going or ask the buyer to associate with other Brands. This gives you a feel for how the buyer's lifestyle is influenced by Brands.

Point 3: Ask Open-Ended Questions around Brands That Include Information about Experiences, Connections, and Affiliations. The deeper the conversation goes, the more you have earned the right to be specific about lifestyle. As you progress further, many of these questions get at the buyer's stage of life and living circumstances. Your goal here is to keep the dialogue rolling and the conversation flowing comfortably. Common questions to be asking at this stage include

- "Describe for me your neighborhood/home/housing development/ remodeling project. Is it new? Are there many young families? Is it transitory or well established?"
- "What type of home do you live in? What is the size? How many rooms are there? Describe the layout. Are you happy with the style? If yes, what do you like about it? If not, what would you change about it?"
- "I can help you understand the security issues relevant to your neighborhood if you will tell me about how you want to protect your family. How many children do you have? What are their ages?"
- "What stage of construction are you in? What size is the remodeling project—how many rooms, how many square feet?"
- "How do you like to spend your leisure time?"

Obviously, some of these questions would be more appropriate and comfortable for both parties in an established buyer/seller relationship. Also notice that the questions have gotten progressively more detailed and tie into the conversation and flow nicely. All of these questions are open-ended in nature, which allows the customer to talk freely about her experiences, connections, or affiliations with a certain Brand. They provide evidence about the buyer's story and build a tapestry around her life.

Exercise: Write two questions that are open-ended and get people talking about their life and their association with Brands. Make the questions specific to your selling environment.

_____

_____

_____

_____

Point 4: Build Trust Early. Now, some of you might be saying, "I don't understand how you can uncover or talk about someone's lifestyle without being intrusive. In other words, isn't it kind of delicate to be asking about someone's lifestyle, especially when she was a stranger when she entered your world?"

That's a good and relevant question. The answer is: it depends, meaning that yes, it can be delicate, but no, it should never be intrusive. This is where we need to use our listening and observing skills, which will be covered next. However, I believe it's all about trust between buyer and seller, which goes back to our conversation about Buyer Mindset 2 (don't trust, care, or know). Here are some action items you can use to help you build TRUST.

- *Test.* Allow the buyer to test the waters with you. Be OK with the moments of silence when you know you are being tested. At the same time, you have the right to test the waters with him within reason. Follow the Golden Rule: ask questions that you would be willing to have others ask of you in a similar situation.
- *Rapport.* Find easy ways to get to know the buyer. Get good at names, and use them often. Notice simple things about the buyer's demeanor and respect her by honoring her pace, space, and countenance: Is she hurried, casual, businesslike, impulsive, funny, serious, or quiet? Above all else, be sincere. Ask yourself: how would I want someone to deal with me if the tables were turned?
- *Understanding.* Gaining a keen insight into the buyer and how he lives his life is important to understanding how your Brand can help fit his lifestyle and meet his needs. Remember that you are an educator. It is quite natural for you to expand your understanding of the buyer, and if this is done respectfully, it will feel natural for the buyer, too. Ask yourself: "What do I know about the buyer already? What do I need to know? Based on that, what do I need to ask?"

- *Simple*. Keep things simple and focused on the buyer, not on you or your product. Remember that most of the salespeople that buyers encounter will quickly focus the conversation on their company, their product, or themselves. Be different from those salespeople. Be careful not to dive into your product with complicated specs, features, benefits, and explanations.
- *Time/timing*. Give buyers time to answer your questions. Don't rush this stage by answering your questions for them, reading their mind, or anticipating the next thing they will say. Don't waste their time, respect it—give it back to them if you can. When it is time for you to talk, have a short version of your Brand story that communicates the two or three key reasons your Brand can fulfill the buyer's lifestyle needs. Be aware of your timing with questions and appropriate comments.

The bottom line here is that building trust takes time. It's only human nature to test the water with others, especially in a new relationship. It's also very natural, if it's done sincerely.

I witnessed this firsthand when a rep who had gone through the Brand Selling workshop called me to report, "The interesting thing for me has been the actual openness with which I have seen people share about their lives with this Brand selling process. I was floored by how open people were and how much I learned about them in a short period of time. As a matter of fact, by the time most of the people left the store, I would say I had built a trusted relationship with them."

Exercise: How have you built trust in the past with a new buyer? Write yourself a short story about what you remember about a particular sales event. Try to identify what you did and didn't do with respect to testing, rapport, understanding, simplicity, and timing.

_____

_____

_____

_____

Listening and Observing

One of my favorite quotes is attributed to Abe Lincoln: "Better to be silent and thought a fool, than to speak up and remove all doubt." Isn't that so true of us as salespeople?

One of the bigger challenges in selling a high-end or Brand-driven product is listening for the buyer's perspective as she "enters the aisle," to gain a clear understanding of the customer's/buyer's mindset when we first engage her. Will she be price-sensitive, looking for a particular style, dropping Brand names left and right, know exactly what she wants, or simply ask for a certain product or brand when you first encounter her? To deal with that, you need to listen for clues and observe buyer behavior involving the buyer's mindsets, which is the Second Brand Rule of Engagement (see Figure 9.3).

Listening and observing comes down to reading people and the messages they send you and then connecting those messages to their lifestyle and the Brands that you sell. Let's break this down a bit here.

WHEN LISTENING AND OBSERVING

Point 1: Listen for Clues. The salesperson will hear clues to which buyer mindset is dominant by listening to the buyer and mentally noting what we hear him say. The clues we hear will guide us during the conversation. Remember, you are listening for both words and tone. Words are "what he says," whereas tone is "how he says it." Both matter here if you are to get the proper picture.

Remember our discussion about mindsets in Chapter 7? Here is where we can put that discussion together with some practical examples. The following are some common buyer mindsets:

SECOND RULE OF ENGAGEMENT

When LISTENING and OBSERVING...

- **Listen for clues to Buyer Mindset ("What we hear them say")**

- **Look for Visible Sales Signposts ("What we see them do")**

- **Wait for Probable Outcomes ("What they may do")**

FIGURE 9.3

Price buyer mindset:

- "I'm building a new home; I have $500 to spend on _____."

Style buyer mindset:

- "I want a good-looking _____."

Quality buyer mindset:

- "What kind of warranty does it have?"

Brand buyer mindset:

- "I'm used to buying the top end, and I'm not bashful about saying so."

Exercise: What have you heard buyers say in the past that would indicate a certain mindset?

_____

_____

Point 2: Observe Visible Signs. Are you a people watcher? I tend to be. Why? Because I am fascinated by what people do and how they act. It is especially interesting to watch people on a busy travel day at the airport or shopping at the mall. Sometimes I think it would be instructive to teach a "people-watching class" out at the airport just to demonstrate the significance of paying attention to people's nonverbal behaviors.

Often, salespeople don't look for visible signs (strong nonverbals, including buyer actions). I call them *sales signposts* that come from what the buyer does concerning the product. They can also guide us during the conversation. For example, here are some visible signs at each stairstep based on what we see the buyer do:

Price visible signs:

- The customer looks at products at a particular price point first.

Style visible signs:

- The customer is found comparing products and their function, fashion, or finish.

Quality visible signs:

- The customer is reading the warranty, packaging, or detail information about the product or the manufacturer.

Brand visible Signs:

• The customer drops other Brand names during the conversation (Kohler, Corian, JennAir . . .).

Exercise: What *visible signs* have you observed in your sales interactions that would indicate a certain buyer's mindset?

Price mindset_____

Style mindset_____

Quality mindset_____

Brand mindset _____

Point 3: Probable Outcomes. The outcome of most sales efforts is driven by whether the buyer stays on the step where she entered or moves to a different step on the Brand Staircase. For example, if the buyer enters with a buyer's mindset based on Price and the salesperson allows the buyer to stay there, then what will the logical outcome be? She will probably buy a lower-priced item and maybe not even consider anything else. But what if the salesperson were to help her migrate up the staircase or, better yet, start at the Brand step and sell downhill? A much better outcome! Essentially, the salesperson would have educated the buyer and helped her associate with the Brand.

Thus, by asking creative lifestyle questions, you can understand the buyer's mindset and identify the visible signs that indicate her location on the Brand Staircase. Then the salesperson's role is to work the Brand story into his conversation in order to effectively migrate the buyer to the Brand step of the staircase, thus creating better outcomes in the aisle.

The primary way you engage the buyer is through asking good questions and through your listening and observing skills. By the time you begin to understand the buyer's lifestyle, you also have a clearer picture of what your Brand might do for her. Your job then is to connect her to your Brand, to make it clear why she should affiliate with your Brand, and to help her experience your Brand. This is when we need to start talking, when we need to bring our Brand story alive.

Talking

The Third Brand Rule of Engagement focuses on talking respectfully with the customer (see Figure 9.4).

THIRD RULE OF ENGAGEMENT

When TALKING...

- No "Throw Away Comments"
- Use Energy, Enthusiasm, and Emotion
- Be Intentional about Brands
- Use Brand words that convey emotions not logic – Such as:

  - Peace of mind
  - Security
  - Craftsmanship
  - Heritage

  - Aspiring
  - Discriminating
  - Exclusive
  - Prestige

FIGURE 9.4

There are times when salespeople can talk most effectively, and generally those times come later in the sales interaction. However, this doesn't mean that you don't verbally engage until the exact right time late in the interaction.

On the contrary, here are some good reasons to talk early in the conversation:

- To build rapport and trust
- To start or continue the flow of conversation by asking lifestyle questions
- To create a comfortable environment in which to engage the buyer

WHEN TALKING:
Point 1. No Throwaway Comments. What I mean by this is, don't use any comments that add no value to the conversation. A common one is the "Can I help you?" opening. The throwaway opener has always bothered me. The phrase "Can I help you?" is at best a throwaway comment. It is not creative or engaging, and it is easily dismissed by the average buyer.

It begs the person to respond with the standard response of "No, I'm just looking," which really translates into "No, leave me alone."

Buyers are building a first impression of you from the minute you start talking. The fact of the matter is that most buyers have come to your place of business for a reason—to find a product or a Brand, and hopefully to have a good lifestyle experience. It is much better to engage them in conversation than to throw words at them.

In contrast to the throwaway opener, the good Brand salesperson uses creative openers to start the conversation. I have already mentioned a few good opening questions under Rule 1—Asking: "What brings you to our store today?" or, "I see you're looking at XXX Brand; have you experienced it before?" Some others I have found to be effective include: "Good morning. What Brands can I help you find today?" or, "Have you shopped our store for your favorite Brands before?" or, "As you casually shop our store today, I can share with you the stories and history behind our best Brands. Would that be helpful?" or, "Hi. You look like you're in a hurry. Can I help you by quickly educating you on the Brands we carry?"

These questions tend to help buyers get caught up in a conversation with you about Brands and also show them that you are willing to make a different and better effort than the average salesperson. I can also tell you from experience that any of these questions will set you apart from other salespeople.

At LPD Inc., customers have told us in buyer surveys that their time is very valuable and that salespeople's comments need to be value-added and focused on their lifestyle and buying needs, instead of salespersons' clichés—like the generic comment, "That looks good on you." Let's get creative here and start differentiating your Brand from the first words you speak to the buyer!

> You can help change a buyer's mindset by connecting
> with him on simple things—even the greeting.

Exercise: What are some creative *opening questions or statements* that you have used in your sales efforts?

_____

_____

Point 2. Energy, Enthusiasm, and Emotion. I encourage salespeople to exhibit the three Es when talking: energy, enthusiasm, and emotion. Of course, this relates back to the salesperson's E^2KG. It includes how we use our voice, tone, and facial expressions. It also includes our overall excitement about our products and services.

One quick point on enthusiasm and emotion: both come from within, from the heart. As a matter of fact, they correlate very closely when properly defined:

- *Enthusiasm* is lively, absorbing, eager involvement
- *Emotion* is a strong agitation of the feelings

When you combine those two, you will surely engage the buyer. One good lesson I have learned over years of selling is a simple little phrase: "Act as if!" The mental track goes something like this: When you are

- Seeing the tenth buyer that day and are getting bored, "act as if" she is your first buyer.
- Reciting the same answer to the same question for the fifth time in a row, "act as if" it is a fresh idea.
- Listening and observing for longer than your sales personality normally permits, "act as if" this particular customer is the most important person on the planet at that particular moment.

In other words, there are times when you need to talk yourself into having the right E^2KG. You have to bring energy, enthusiasm, and emotion to the party. It is your contribution to a successful sales interaction with the buyer.

Exercise: How do you coach yourself to have a good E^2KG? What are some practical ways that you can *add energy, enthusiasm, and emotion* to the conversation?

Point 3. Be Intentional about the Brand. In chapter 3 I made a comment worth repeating here: *We need to move from intuitive to intentional* when speaking Brand language. Every effort needs to be made to put Brand on the buyer's radar, by consciously putting it into our sales vocabulary. If you are willing to intentionally speak Brand language (as we talked about under points 1 and 2), then it will become a natural part of how you converse every day with the buyer. Please understand that this will not happen on its own. You need to be in charge of this change in your sales behavior. Believe me, you won't regret it!

Point 4. Use Brand Words That Convey Emotions, Not Logic. Remember our conversation about Brand not being part of our sales language? Our argument was that we aren't that comfortable with Brand words, so either we don't allow them to become part of our sales language, or we're not intentional enough in our use of them.

I was in the middle of teaching this point in a Brand Selling workshop. I had just described these Brand words and how they connect to good Brands: *peace of mind, security, craftsmanship, heritage, distinctive, aspiring, discriminating, exclusive,* and *prestige.* Suddenly a participant interjected, "Couldn't you take these words and associate them with just about any high-end Brand in the market? Wouldn't they tell a unique story for each different brand?"

"Yes, of course," I responded. "You mean like BMW, Corvette, Rolex, Maui Jim, Tiffany's, and Saks Fifth Avenue could all align with *prestige, heritage, distinctive,* or *aspiring.* Sure, that's a good point; these words are pretty good descriptors of most strong Brands."

Another participant interrupted, "But not all of those brands fit with all of those words."

I responded, "Exactly, nor would all of the people who associate with those Brands choose the same words to describe their emotions about their brand of choice. Now you can begin to see how flexible you as salespeople need to be at asking great questions and then personalizing the multiple Brands you sell to make the proper connections with the buyer. Obviously this list could change based on your unique Brand and how it is perceived by the average customer. You need to become a student of your Brand(s), and learn from your customers how they perceive the Brand and what words they would attach to it."

By the way, if I represented a manufacturer with a small number of key Brands, I would define the Brand using my own unique set of words. Collect specific words from all of your end users and buyers through any reliable method: market research, user surveys, customer/supplier panels, and so on. Your end users are closest to the product and have a keen sense of what the brand means to them. They can articulate it. Once you are clear on the words, get them to the lips of your salespeople. You'll be pleasantly surprised by the results.

Now, let me address three kinds of people that I usually encounter at this stage of the game concerning finding, developing, or implementing the Brand language.

1. *The Brand seeker.* This person has been searching for this concept of Brand selling for quite a while. She wants to get going with this selling approach, but she doesn't know the words that would best describe the Brand she represents. Her company has not invested

a lot of time, money, or resources in developing the Brand. So, she is in search of the right words.

Advice: Don't make the words up—if you do, they will be hollow. Don't rely only on your version of the Brand words from your experience as a salesperson. Instead, go ask the customers, buyers, and users of your products and services for confirmation. Take the time to ask and keep asking. After every sale, make it a habit to ask for the reasons the buyer bought the Brand. Keep track of the answers, and over a short period of time you will have confirmation of the Brand words.

2. *The Brand naysayer.* This person has sold logically for most of his life. He hasn't much believed what Marketing has had to say about the Brand or the ad campaigns it has produced. He is a "customer kind of guy." He listens to the customer's opinion and regularly feeds it back to headquarters.

   Advice: Keep listening to your customers. They are close to the Brand and can articulate it best. However take it one step further: get involved with end-user focus groups, customer advisory boards, or customer surveys. It is with those vehicles that you will hear it like it really is from groups of users. It will also be a good way to validate or negate the message being sent by Marketing on the Brand. Does it line up with the customers' perception? If so, great! Now start putting those words in your sales language. If not, take the voice of the customer back to Marketing and become a change agent around the Brand within your company.

3. *The Brand guru.* This is the person who has been in and around marketing for most of her life. She probably had a stint in sales and "carried the bag" and has since been involved with multiple ad campaigns and possibly even Brand and subbrand introductions. Her company has hired professional Brand builders to help build Brand touchpoints or strategies in the past.

   Advice: When was the last time you had your perception of the Brand verified by the customer? Have you had a chance to work in the field on sales calls, at trade shows, at buyer shows, or at end-user shows or events lately? Those ideas, plus the advice given to the naysayer, will help to verify what the consistent, emotional, and real language is for the buyers and users of your Brand.

I cannot emphasize enough here the need to be intentional with your Brand language and emotional word choices. Here's why: when you get intentional with a process like Brand selling, then you effectively make people "consciously competent" at their job. In other words, they are aware of the good skills that they have used (conscious), so that they can repeat those same skills in the future to be successful (competent). It does us little good if our people aren't consciously learning from their mistakes and victories. You need to be intentional about this language if you expect to leverage the Brand learning curve within your sales team or organization.

Exercise: Have you asked questions of your buyers that help *build your Brand language*—questions that can get at the customer's perception of your Brand? These questions can be utilized one-on-one or in a group setting, such as an end-user panel, customer forum, or customer-feedback surveys.

1. Why do you buy from us?

   Logical reasons

   _____

   _____

   Emotional reasons

   _____

   _____

2. What does our product or service do for you that no one else can duplicate?

   _____

   _____

3. What is your impression of our Brand? How does it improve your lifestyle?

   _____

   _____

4. How do we build trust and credibility with you as a customer?

   _____

   _____

5. If our company went away tomorrow, what would be missing in the marketplace?

_____

_____

6. If you have Brand loyalty to us, describe why.

_____

_____

7. If you have Brand loyalty to a competitor of ours, describe why.

_____

_____

8. What are we distinctively known for in the marketplace?

_____

_____

9. What blockbuster product or service was a breakthrough for us in the last five to ten years? Why?

_____

_____

10. If you could tell our CEO one thing about how to improve our personal connection with you the buyer, what would it be?

_____

_____

Tips for Effective Brand Selling

As you move from here into practice and utilization of the Brand selling process, here are some practical tips that you can use in your selling process. It probably goes without saying that no matter what the outcome, you need to finish well with the buyer. It is extremely important that you conduct yourself with sincerity, honesty, and professionalism, whether you get the sale or not. One of my customers said it best: "Anyone who enters here today may not be our customer yet, but could be tomorrow. Our Brands and our future depend on them."

Here are some tips on doing your homework as a Brand seller:

1. *Study and practice.* Many of you may feel like you're headed back to college right now (I prefer to think of it more as a Brand MBA from a streetwise practitioner). In a way, you are going back to school: you are building new habits that require time, energy, study, and patience to develop. There are no great shortcuts here. But there is good news: if you become a curious and dedicated student of your Brand, then your experience will kick in quickly and shorten your learning curve immensely. It has happened that way with Brand selling for other sales veterans, and if you've read this far in the book, then it will happen for you, too.

2. *Hit singles first, then move on to home runs.* Remember the analogy with curveballs that we used in Chapter 4? The optimistic salesperson may believe that he now can anticipate the price objection or should hit every curveball from the buyer, that every buyer should walk out having been sold, that every question should work, or that every buyer will have an open and honest conversation with him. That is very unrealistic—after all, we're all human. It's like expecting your kids to get an A in every subject, every time, every year.

   When you're beginning to sell Brand, it's much more important to improve along the way, to learn from your mistakes, and to sell your Brand with passion. We can't expect to hit a home run every time we're at bat. Hit singles first. The home runs will come as you improve your "Brand selling swing."

3. *Have fun with the process.* Sounds simple, doesn't it? Just have fun, and the rest will take care of itself. Well, simple isn't always easy, but we should strive for that in our day-to-day selling of the Brand.

   Let's put it another way: as a buyer, when was the last time you talked with a salesperson who was truly having fun in the selling process? If you are struggling to remember the last time, then you get my point. When you sell and have fun during the process, it is very attractive to a prospective buyer. It makes people feel comfortable, and it opens them up to have fun at the same time.

   I was talking with a store owner a couple of months after we had finished the Brand selling process. I was observing his salespeople in action, and I was intrigued by the fun people seemed to be having. People were smiling and gladly transacting business, even on some pretty expensive items. I asked him about any changes he had witnessed in his salespeople.

He responded, "My people are enjoying the selling now. They are making it more fun and with a purpose, to promote the Brands that are matches for the lifestyles of our buyers. By the way, shopping should be fun, not dreary. It's always amazing to me when people are surprised at having a good shopping experience."

So, as you move forward with Brand selling, look for progress with the process. Remember what your overall goals are with Brand selling, and look for improvement

- In *understanding* the Brand Staircase model
- In *understanding the buyer's mindset* upon entering the aisle, store, showroom, or office
- In then *communicating* to engage the consumer at the point of sale
- In then *asking good lifestyle questions* to qualify the buyer's need for your Brand and product
- In reversing the Brand Staircase and developing a "sell the Brand first" mentality

I am very sure that at this stage, you still have some questions, like: What happens when the buyer enters the transaction with a low–price point mentality and doesn't seem willing to change, to even get into the Brand conversation? She seems to have entered with her mind already made up.

What do you do when you, as the salesperson, get so tied up in features and benefits that you don't ask questions from the heart and you don't even make an attempt to be intentional about the Brand?

How do we articulate the Brand story? How do we get excited about it? What if the buyer doesn't want to answer any lifestyle questions?

That is where we are headed in the next chapter—how to deal with the tough questions and best practices.

Key Points

In this how-to chapter, we emphasize that the bridge to migrating a buyer from Price, Style, or Quality to Brand is through being aware of the buyer's lifestyle choices and asking good questions about them. The bottom line here is that the Brand has a language all its own that the salesperson needs to learn and speak.

Customers connect to Brands, not just products. Salespeople need to become Brand experts by connecting the Brands they represent to people's lifestyles. People are not just buying a product or service; instead, they are supporting a lifestyle.

The salesperson needs to establish good tools for getting at the connection between lifestyle and Brand. I call these the *Brand Rules of Engagement*. Through asking, listening and observing, and talking (A LOT), the salesperson can build the momentum to effectively engage the buyer and get at the buyer's real needs.

- A is asking lifestyle questions regarding the buyer's current lifestyle choices, current Brand favorites, and life stories or experiences.
- L and O are effective listening and observing. Listen for clues about the buyer's mindset, brand allegiance, and experience, and observe what the buyer might decide.
- T is talking to initiate an appropriate and effective conversation between buyer and seller. It should include starting the conversation by asking lifestyle questions and creating a comfortable environment in which to engage the buyer.

Finally, there are a few tips to help you with your brand selling process: study and practice, go slowly and build up gradually as your knowledge increases, and, most importantly, have fun.

CHAPTER 10

MIGRATING THE CONSUMER TO BRAND

When I'm with a group in a workshop, we define the difference between knowledge and skill as *application*. That is the point we are at right now—application.

At this point in the book, you may be asking

- How do we apply Brand selling in the trenches?
- How do I understand the evidence needed at each step in order to see the buyer's mindset?
- How do I work through the issues with buyers who won't migrate?
- How do I tell the Brand story?

In this chapter, we will answer those questions and give you some practical advice on how to migrate the customer to Brand. This includes the very important technique of how to tell the Brand story.

Brand selling is not a static model written from a script. As a matter of fact, it is an interactive model that is designed to promote dialogue and good conversation flow. Thus, in a way, the Brand selling process is like a job interview. In a job interview, the employer asks the job applicant a variety of questions to assess his background, his ability to handle a specific job, and characteristics that might make him successful. Eventually the interviewer has enough evidence to believe that there is an employment match, and then essentially starts selling her company and Brand to the interviewee.

In a similar way, the Brand seller is gathering evidence in a free-flowing conversation and then putting together the Brand story to tell the buyer. All the way through the interaction, the seller is gathering evidence from the buyer that could match well with the seller's Brand. However, just as in a good job interview, the main selling effort (talking/presenting) takes place at the end of the conversation, when the Brand story is told. Thus, the process is very flexible and, just like an interview, cannot be scripted; the Brand selling interaction could go anywhere within a buyer's background based on a variety of factors:

- The understanding that the salesperson uses in his assessment of the buyer's mindset at each step on the staircase
- The salesperson's anticipation of the buyer's willingness to migrate toward the Brand
- The extent to which the seller creates an environment in which the buyer can open up concerning her lifestyle and brand preferences
- How well the salesperson can communicate using the Brand Rules of Engagement covered in Chapter 9—that is, strong questioning and listening skills
- The extent to which the seller can tell the Brand story using intentional and accurate words that represent the Brand

We will cover each of these application points in turn and make you aware of the best practices that can be used in a jam.

Understanding Buyer Mindsets

You already have the basics on buyer mindsets, which we covered in Chapter 6. To sum up, we need to earn the right to open the buyer's wallet; we need to show her that we care, know, and can be trusted; and we also need to be able to determine the primary step on which she enters the Brand Staircase. Let's dig into the specifics for each step of the staircase: Price, Style, Quality, and Brand. Recall that we are looking for evidence that confirms the step that the buyer is on so that we can proceed with the migration process. That evidence comes in three forms that are gathered from our listening and observing skills:

- *Verbal clues:* Things we hear the buyer say
- *Visual signposts:* Things we see the buyer do
- *Probable outcomes:* Things the buyer might do based on your past experience as a salesperson or based on knowing the buyer because you have worked with him in the past

For the sake of this exercise, we will use a common example from the home-improvement category—accessorizing your home. Imagine a certain product in your home or living area that you would like to replace or upgrade. Keep that in mind while you walk through this example.

Price as the Buyer Mindset

When buyers enter with the Price mindset, we will recognize them by the following:

VERBAL CLUES
- "I'm building a new home; I have $500 to spend on _____."
- "I want a _____ that cost about as much as my last_____, which lasted three years."
- "Why is _____so expensive?"
- "Wow . . . why should I pay $100 for this product when the same thing from another manufacturer costs only $50?"

VISIBLE SIGNS
- Customers start at the lowest–price point products.
- Customers look at the higher-priced products, but very quickly move to lower-priced units.
- Customers talk the language of Price.
- Customers seem shocked that anyone would pay that much for a _____.

PROBABLE OUTCOMES (UNLESS WE HELP THEM MIGRATE)
- They will walk out with the cheapest product.
- They will be unwilling to listen to a Quality story.
- They never look beyond price, no matter what their ability to buy is.

Style as the Buyer Mindset

When buyers enter with the Style mindset, we will recognize them by the following:

VERBAL CLUES
- "I want a good-looking _____."
- "I'm changing my _____. I also need to change my _____."
- "I'm tired of the old design; what's a new and different look?"

VISIBLE SIGNS
- They compare looks and styles a lot.
- They ask many questions concerning finish or fashion.
- They seem to be looking for the right style, then deciding how much to spend.
- They may have brought their old _____ with them.

PROBABLE OUTCOMES (UNLESS WE HELP THEM MIGRATE)
- If their preferred fashion and finish can be found on a competitive unit for a lower price, they will probably go for it.
- They may never understand the Quality difference because the products "look the same."
- They may buy the "sizzle over the steak," i.e., choose finish, fashion, and function, the sizzle, and not care about the Quality, the steak.
- We "disqualify" buyers because they never hear the Quality story or understand the Quality difference.

Quality as the Buyer Mindset

When buyers enter with the Quality mindset, we will recognize them by the following:

VERBAL CLUES
- "What kind of warranty does it have?"
- "Is this as good as a _____ (another high-quality product)?"
- "I don't understand the difference in quality between these two products."
- "My last _____ tarnished, broke off, or didn't last—how can I avoid that this time?"

VISIBLE SIGNS
- Customers are reading the warranty, packaging, or detail information about the product or the manufacturer.
- Customers want to be educated and ask lots of detailed questions about the product, its warranty, and where or how it is built.
- Customers ask directly about the Quality or make reference to others who said that this Brand "lasts longer," "holds up well," or "is the one to buy."

PROBABLE OUTCOMES (UNLESS WE HELP THEM MIGRATE)
- They still make no connection between quality and value for the price, and still walk away with a competitor's product.
- They end up buying your product for part of the house (where Quality matters), yet buy a competitive brand for the rest of the house.
- They convert to your product based on Quality.

Brand as the Buyer Mindset

When buyers enter with the Brand mindset, we will recognize them by the following:

VERBAL CLUES
- "I'm used to buying 'the top end,' and I'm not bashful about saying so."
- "By the way, what is the price of this _____?" (asked very late in the conversation)
- "I live in Beverly Hills (i.e., a nice area)," or "I have a big house worth more than $500K."

VISIBLE SIGNS
- Customers drive up in a luxury or "pricey" car (Jaguar, Mercedes, BMW, or something similar).
- Customers have lots of "rocks on their hands," generally dress well, and so on.

- Customers drop other Brand names during the conversation (Kohler, Corian, JennAir, and so on).
- Customers deal with only one person at the store or require "private showings."

Probable Outcomes (They buy your Brand, or We Help Them Migrate from another Brand)

- You sell Brand first while qualifying the customer and assessing the competitive scene early in the sale.
- Buyers are already presold on a competitive Brand, and even if they are willing to listen to your story, they may be a really tough sale.
- The "why buy our Brand story" gets told early and sets the foundation for the sale and the standard for the buyers' quality decision.
- You win in many cases.

Putting the Mindsets into Practice

I was just finishing teaching this during a workshop when a participant walked up to me and said, "Not many of those outcomes are good for me at the Price, Style, and Quality steps!"

I replied, "Why not?" She gave me a puzzled look (indicating that I was teaching this stuff; surely I must be smarter than that). Then she responded, "Well, if a buyer comes in at the Price mindset, he may already have his mind made up and not spend more than his budget." I agreed.

"If a buyer comes in at the Style mindset, then he may buy based on the looks or fashion of the product alone and may not move off of that step." I agreed again.

The salesperson continued, "Or if he comes in on the Quality step, then he may just buy someone else's high-quality product instead of ours." I responded, "You're right, that could happen. I guess it all depends." Thinking she was getting somewhere finally, she asked in anticipation, "It depends on what?"

"It depends on you!" I responded. She looked at me in dismay. I went on, "You know your product, right? You know how to ask questions, right? You know how to build rapport, right? Now, you also know how to engage customers with the Brand Rules of Engagement, right? Then what is keeping you from being successful in moving (migrating) buyers from those lower steps of the staircase?" She was caught flat-footed. She needed help with migration. She, like many salespeople, had many of the answers inside, but we simply needed to draw them out. Remember, you are the *migration catalyst*. You need to give buyers a reason to migrate—to change posititon, to educate them as to why migrating would make sense and be a good decision.

In order to learn how to migrate your customers, try the following exercise. First, go back over each of the buyer mindsets. Do this by picturing a buyer that you have worked with in the past who was at each of these different mindsets. Now answer the following questions:

1. What verbal clues, visible signs, and probable outcomes have you seen with this buyer in the past?
2. Since you have worked with this buyer in the past, has there ever been a time when you were able to migrate her toward the Brand? If so, why did she migrate? What did you learn from that situation that you can apply in the future? If not, does anyone else on your team have a suggestion for how this person might consider migrating?
3. Brainstorm the best ways to move the customer from the step she arrived on to the Brand step. What would you say? How would you say it?
4. What have you included in your Brand story or language in the past? How would you get into that story?

Take a few minutes and work through this exercise with your key buyers in mind, using Figure 10.1 for reference.

MIGRATION EXERCISE

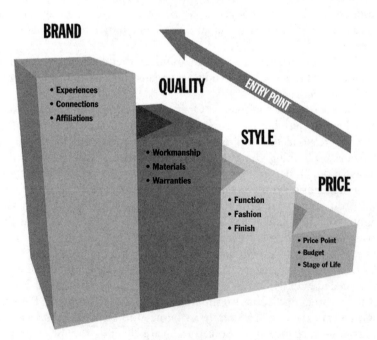

BRAND
- Experiences
- Connections
- Affiliations

QUALITY
- Workmanship
- Materials
- Warranties

ENTRY POINT

STYLE
- Function
- Fashion
- Finish

PRICE
- Price Point
- Budget
- Stage of Life

FIGURE 10.1

Price Mindset:

   1. Clues, signs, and outcomes:

_____

_____

   2. Learned from past migrations:

_____

_____

   3. Transition statements or questions:

_____

_____

   4. Brand story or language:

_____

_____

Style Mindset:

   1. Clues, signs, and outcomes:

_____

_____

   2. Learned from past migrations:

_____

_____

   3. Transition statements or questions:

_____

_____

   4. Brand story or language:

_____

_____

Quality Mindset:

1. Clues, signs, and outcomes:

_____

_____

2. Learned from past migrations:

_____

_____

3. Transition statements or questions:

_____

_____

4. Brand story or language:

_____

_____

Brand Mindset:

1. Clues, signs, and outcomes:

_____

_____

2. Learned from past migrations:

_____

_____

3. Transition statements or questions:

_____

_____

4. Brand story or language:

_____

_____

At this stage, an interesting thing happens when you start to challenge salespeople about what they know and how they use it in their selling process. I find that there are usually two primary camps here:

1. Most of the salespeople know more than they give themselves credit for during the heat of the battle. This exercise will bring it to the surface, and it will build their confidence.

2. Some of them draw a blank when it comes to this exercise for one of two reasons:
   • Because they don't have enough experience yet, so they are short of examples
   • Because they haven't learned from their experiences or are caught in a rut

My challenge to all of these salespeople is threefold:

• Take the TIME to migrate.
• Get good at Brand transitions.
• Practice using Brand language and Brand stories.

The power of this exercise is that it forces you to think about your role as it relates to your learning curve and migration. Let's take each of these best practices in turn, and then we will relate them back to the individual steps on the Brand Staircase.

Best Practices That Help Buyers Migrate

There are four key tips that I can give you that will help you with migration. Most of the time salespeople fail to migrate buyers because they don't *take the time* to migrate them. They rely on old selling techniques and product knowledge and miss the opportunity to talk about the Brand. So, when it comes time to migrate, keep this little acronym in mind:

T = testimonials

I = investigation

M = motives

E = educate

T = Testimonials

One of the more powerful selling techniques we can use to help people migrate is a satisfied user's testimonial about our Brand. Think about it. The buyer is usually looking for evidence that would support your Brand claims. Good testimonials from satisfied users are word-of-mouth endorsements. A satisfied user is the strongest and most unbiased piece of evidence you can provide. If you are selling today and you don't have a list of testimonials, then you have just buried one of your best sales weapons.

One of the best testimonials I heard as a buyer, and it was at a pretty stressful times of our lives, came from friends who had utilized a service that Nordstrom's provides called "the personal shopper." We had just been through a house fire, and we had no clothes. We needed to go on an unusual shopping trip because we weren't just buying a shirt or a pair of pants; instead, we were replacing an entire wardrobe. One of our friends told us that Nordstrom's provided a service that would allow us to work with one person on all our clothing needs. So, we dropped in to Nordstrom's and asked about the service. The store continued the testimonial by explaining the service, handing us a list of satisfied customers to call as references (testimonials), and asking for our approval to get our clothing sizes, which it would keep on file. We started shopping that night. You can't even imagine the amount of hassle factor that Nordstrom's removed from our shopping experience. It was migrating us toward its Brand through a "personal shopper" service that separated it from the other clothing stores we could have shopped at. To this day we still shop at Nordstrom's—mostly because of that one *experience*.

Exercise: What testimonials do you have that differentiate your Brand from the competition? Are you using these personal stories to help migrate buyers?

_____

_____

I = Investigation

Investigation is all about gathering good evidence from the buyer, using the Brand Rules of Engagement that we discussed in Chapter 9. Not to beat a dead horse here, but I am just amazed at the number of salespeople who have asked great lifestyle questions, but used very little of the information to help in the migration process.

Let me make a couple of important points here on questioning and the idea of *investigation*. Investigation by its very definition means that you are finding out important information from the buyer. It does not mean, however, that you are carrying on an *interrogation*. You are not overwhelming the buyer with so many questions that he feels that he is the accused on a cop show and you are Joe Friday, Dirty Harry, or a Crime Scene Investigator trying to break him down. When asking questions under the Brand Rules of Engagement, it is much better to ask two or three really great questions and have a focused and flowing conversation that is comfortable for both you and the buyer than to ask a multitude of questions and overwhelm the buyer. Investigate, don't interrogate.

Exercise: Think of an example of a buyer who did migrate to your Brand based on some strong information that you learned during your investigation:

_____

_____

M = Motives

We talked about the main reason people buy as their motive. We defined *motive* as something that influences a choice, prompting an action or *intention*. Once you understand that definition, it should be easy to start finding out exactly why it is that people buy from you in general and buy your Brand more specifically. However, I have found throughout my career that only the top salespeople take the time to understand motives. That, my colleagues, is the primary reason that they are the top salespeople (see Figure 10.2).

COMMON MOTIVES

Focus on Motives—the real reasons people buy

APPEAL TO LOGIC
Savings – time, $$$, hassle
Production – more efficient, better results, more output

APPEAL TO EMOTION
Personal – job easier, look good, save face, more leisure time
Power – control, recognition, approval

FIGURE 10.2

If you are struggling in this area, let me give you three questions to ask your buyers after they have purchased your Brand. These three questions tend to get at motives and will build your data bank of reasons that people like, enjoy, or purchase your Brand.

1. "What do you think of when you think of our Brand?" or "What comes to mind when you think of our Brand?"
2. "When you (buyers) first enter the aisle (showroom, display, store, or office), what are you looking for in our product line or expecting from our Brand?"
3. "When you have purchased our Brand, what were the main reasons?"

Exercise: Think of an example where you clearly uncovered a buyer's motive(s) and were able to talk to connect that buyer to your Brand.

_____

_____

E = Educate

One of the biggest pressure valves that can be released for any salesperson is to start believing that her primary purpose in life is to educate her buyers on the Brand and the product. When you educate someone, you are making that person knowledgeable about your Brand, why it exists in the market, what it stands for, how most buyers experience it, and so on. This is a very comfortable and nonthreatening spot to sell from, especially if your buyer is not showing any willingness to migrate—such as the buyer who is stuck on the Price stair-step with a low–price point mentality and doesn't seem willing to change, or even to get into the Brand conversation. Why? Because people with strong convictions usually hate being sold, but don't mind being educated.

Exercise: Think of a time when you were able to educate a buyer and it made a difference in whether that buyer purchased the Brand, or at least in how the buyer viewed the Brand.

_____

_____

Working with TIME, Logic, and Emotion on the Staircase

Now, the neat part about the TIME migration "how-to" method is that it is flexible with regard to buyers' personalities and how buyers like to "be sold." For instance,

- Some buyers like to know that someone else has tried the Brand first and likes it. Or they like to know that other people would recommend it, or they want to hear about it from an "unbiased source" rather than from the salesperson. Use *testimonials* here.
- Some people don't care what others would recommend to them or are very independent thinkers. Instead, they have their own reasons for buying and don't have to follow the crowd. Use *investigation* or *motives* here.
- Other people process their purchases by learning all there is to know about a product or service. They won't buy until they have compared all options. Use *education* here.

No matter how you approach it with the buyer, the TIME migration method serves as a "migration magnet" to move buyers up the staircase toward Brand (see Figure 10.3).

If you examine Figure 10.3 a bit more closely, you will see a rectangular box with the words *Buyer's Focus* underneath the Brand Staircase. In teaching this concept, I have found that each step of the staircase seems to have a primary focus for the buyer, either based on logic or on emotion.

- At the Price step, buyers tend to focus mostly on *logic*. They are thinking:
  - "Can I afford it?" "Am I spending too much?" "Is it worth it?"
- At the Style step, buyers tend to focus mostly on *emotion*. They are feeling:
  - "Will I look good in this?" "How does it work?" "Does the color look good?"
- At the Quality step, buyers tend to focus mostly on *logic*. They are thinking:
  - "Will it hold up?" "Is it made of the best materials?" "What is the warranty?"
- At the Brand step, buyers tend to focus mostly on *emotion*. They are feeling:
  - "How will I experience this?" "I've always wanted this Brand." "I can't wait to try this, wear this, or drive this!"

These primary buyer mindsets and how they correlate with logic and emotion should matter to you, especially if a buyer is stuck on a certain step of the staircase. In particular, this helps the salesperson know how best to make the transition into talking about the Brand.

The reason that logic and emotion matter here is simple: There are both logical and emotional human beings. Have you ever tried to deal emotionally with a totally logical person? Or have you ever tried to deal logically with an overly emotional person? (If you have children, you are probably laughing by now, because you know how hard this can be.)

T.I.M.E. AND THE BUYER MINDSET

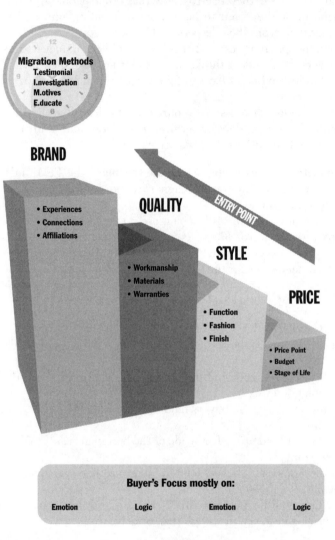

Migration Methods
T.estimonial
I.nvestigation
M.otives
E.ducate

BRAND
- Experiences
- Connections
- Affiliations

QUALITY
- Workmanship
- Materials
- Warranties

ENTRY POINT

STYLE
- Function
- Fashion
- Finish

PRICE
- Price Point
- Budget
- Stage of Life

Buyer's Focus mostly on:			
Emotion	Logic	Emotion	Logic

FIGURE 10.3

In the case of the emotional person, you probably didn't do well until you met him where he was and at least tried to understand or listen to his emotions.

In the case of the logical person, you needed to appeal to her rationality before you could possibly address the emotions behind the situation.

Now, the good news here is that emotion and logic both tie into motives, the reasons people buy. So, let logic and emotions work for you here, not against you. The best way to handle "stuck" buyers is to do a couple of things well:

- Meet them where they are at on the step.
- Match their emotion or logic factor.
- Make the transition with a tie-in transition statement.
- Put TIME on your side.

Using Brand Transitions to Start Migration

Let's take a good look at each step, making two assumptions: first, that the buyer is stuck on that step, and second, that you need some best thoughts to get the buyer to make the transition up toward the Brand.

Price Step

If a buyer is stuck on the Price step of the staircase, then the salesperson should meet him on that step and approach him based on logic until he becomes more open to the emotional side.

POSSIBLE TRANSITIONAL STATEMENTS
- "I know you are concerned about getting the best deal. I would be, too. Allow me to give you some facts about our Brand that could make this a better investment over time." *Then move to educate the buyer on the Brand.*
- "I want you to get the most for your money, so let me educate you on some options that give you more value for the money." *Then educate the buyer.*
- "I have seen other budget-minded shoppers disappointed because they bought based on price and the product didn't hold up. Unfortunately, I saw them back here in two months shopping for a replacement product. I'd like to help you avoid the same thing. Let me show you the other available Brands we carry." *Then, educate and utilize the testimonial of the other customer about the Brand.*

BEST TIPS
- Avoid using the word *price* too much. If you do, the discussion becomes too much about the almighty dollar.
- Instead, talk in terms of value for the dollar, being budget-minded, or being a shrewd buyer—not paying too much or too little for the product.
- Break the glass ceiling of price (Chapter 5) by educating, using facts, and having the buyer look at the purchase as a longer-term decision.

- Tie into the Quality step, because it also is logical and will relate to getting a good value for the dollar.

Style Step

If a buyer is stuck on the Style step of the staircase, then the salesperson should meet her on that step and approach her based on emotion until she becomes more open to the Quality or Brand story.

POSSIBLE TRANSITIONAL STATEMENTS
- "I'm glad you like the look and feel of the product, or how the product works. Let me show you another Brand that, based on our conversation, exceeds all of your fashion tastes. I believe you will be happier with it over time." *Then tie into the buyer's motives.*
- "You are very stylish in your taste—I like that. . . . Let's make sure we've covered all the possible Brands that you might find attractive, fashionable, or complementary." *Then discuss the Brand story.*
- "This has been a great conversation. Thanks. It's my job to educate you on the companies that have the best styling in this product line. Allow me to show you the other options that meet your style requirements. There may actually be some Brands that you'll like better." *Then, talk testimonials of what other customers have told you about the style options in your Brand.*

BEST TIPS
- Avoid a feature and benefit dump. The buyer will view those as logical facts that don't bring the emotions and styling of the product to life.
- Instead, use words that relate to emotions about a product—cool inside, hassle-free operation, easy operation, makes for a simple project completion, easy to install, saves you money, frees up your time for leisure activities, and so on.
- Get the buyer beyond the Style step by making the transition from the product to a discussion about emotions that directly relate to your Brand words.

Quality Step

If a buyer is stuck on the Quality step of the staircase, then the salesperson should meet him on that step and approach him based on logic until he becomes more open to the emotional side.

POSSIBLE TRANSITIONAL STATEMENTS
- "If you are looking for the best quality, let's match that up with the best Brand." *Then discuss how Quality links to Brand around the buyer's motives.*

- "I'm glad you like our Quality. We think there are things we do better than anyone we compete with. One of those things is what customers tell us about our Brand." *Then go into testimonials.*
- "One of our best quality advantages is _____. That kind of quality has gotten our Brand recognized as the safest Brand option available on the market today." *Then educate the buyer and tie into the motives you have uncovered.*

BEST TIPS

- Make sure you know what your impenetrable advantages are and take credit for them in the conversation.
- Know what awards for high quality or high standards your products have gotten and work them into your Quality story, which relates very closely to your Brand.
- Recognize the competitive situation you are selling within, and don't bash the competition or its quality. Buyers respect sellers who compete fairly.
- If you are at the Quality step, then you are not far from Brand. Make sure that the buyer knows how good your quality is (warranty, materials, workmanship), and do not be afraid to claim it.

Brand Step

If a buyer is stuck on the Brand step of the staircase, then the salesperson should meet her on that step and approach her based on emotion. Please note: if this customer is buying your Brand, then celebrate and work to keep her on this step by reminding her of the strength of your Brand. If this buyer is a strong buyer of a competitive Brand, then you need to discover why that is, and to try to get a shot at her Brand business. Note that trying to sell a competitor's Brand loyal buyer could be a long-term process.

POSSIBLE TRANSITIONAL STATEMENTS— BUYER OF YOUR BRAND

- "While I have you today, let's look at some other products within the Brand line-up." *Then use customer testimonials from the other categories.*
- "Why is it again that you like our Brand so much?" *This gets at Brand loyalty and builds your Brand words database.*

POSSIBLE TRANSITIONAL STATEMENTS— BUYER OF A COMPETITOR'S BRAND

- "It seems that you have a strong allegiance to _____ Brand. Why is that? . . . If you could get the same from our Brand, would you give us a shot?" *Then tell your Brand story.* (By the way, I am not wearing rose-colored glasses here. In some cases, I have seen buyers respond positively to this approach. In other cases, the competition has had to shoot itself in the foot before we got a shot at the business. Either way, you need to be persistent until you get your shot.)

BEST TIPS
- Don't allow hollow Brand promises to creep in (Chapter 5). That is, don't forget about the product, for it is what got you there.
- Don't take your Brand for granted. The other three steps need to remain intact, or the Brand could suffer. Such situations might occur if the quality drops, if the styling becomes old or outdated, or if the price becomes extremely unreasonable for the value and grandeur of the Brand.
- Don't believe that your Brand is bulletproof and virus-free. It takes only one big slip with the EPA, the SEC, the FDIC, or the general buying public to lead to the failure of a Brand. Look at Enron and WorldCom, to name just two.

Before we move off the staircase and focus only on the Brand step, there are a couple of things to remember. When Brand selling is done right, all of the steps will have some impact—it's just that the Brand step will be sold first. Also, my experience has been that the farther up the staircase toward Brand you go, the more loyal your buyers become and the less convincing they need in order to migrate. Why? Because they probably have purchased from you before, have a higher level of trust, or see that the Quality or Brand has served them well in the past, and thus they are willing to give you more of their business.

Practice Using Brand Language and Brand Stories

When I first started working with companies on Brand selling, I had a couple of very interesting experiences in the field.

Situation 1

One high-end Brand I was working with had a great Quality reputation, had industry-standard Style options and product listings, and was premium in its Price. Unfortunately, as in many industries, an import from China with solid quality, nice styling, good features that worked well, and a price point that was 40 percent lower to the consumer had entered the marketplace.

When the Brand salesperson approached the owner of a store to see how he could "juice up" the store's sales, he took a bit of a tongue-lashing from the owner. It went like this:

"I used to be able to sell your Brand. You've got a great name in the marketplace, and your quality is top drawer. But lately I've been trying to get my store salespeople to sell your Brand to the consumers, and, frankly, they are taking the path of least resistance and selling the imports based on price. I don't know what to do, but if you are wondering why your sales are down, that is your answer!"

The salesperson was visibly frustrated, but managed to get out a pretty good question: "How do your salespeople view our Brand?"

The owner's response was simple: "Expensive! And they can't justify the price difference to buyers."

I'll never forget the Brand salesperson's conversation with me as we left that day. "We built this marketplace with high-quality units, great fashion, and a strong Brand. Now these imports are killing us. It's like we set the table for the imports, and they pulled the tablecloth right out from under us. Now they are eating the feast that we prepared for them." Needless to say, we talked about Brand language that day.

Just how important is Brand language? Let's focus on "Expensive."

- What does that mean to the *reseller* of your Brand? Let's translate here: "_____ Brand is charging too much" or "If I can't afford it, my buyers can't afford it."
- What does that mean to the *buyer/end consumer* of your Brand? "It costs too much" or "I can't afford it" or "I wish I could afford it!"

The big turnaround for that Brand salesperson came when he created a better language set for his resellers, putting the product in a positive light. He used words like *timeless*, *craftsmanship*, *aspiring*, and *safety* to represent the Brand. He used words like *priceless* rather than *expensive* when it comes to protecting one's family. He then taught the resellers the Brand Staircase, reversed it, and sold from Brand first. The difference was phenomenal. The store owner came back to us and thanked us, because those "more expensive" sales rang through his cash register at 30 percent more profit, and his salespeople were making more money, too. He also wished that he had started teaching his sales reps the Brand selling process 15 years ago.

Situation 2

I also traveled with a sales agent who represented a high-end hardware Brand. The agent told me driving between calls, "We really have no competition within our category. Our users have grown up on our product line, and they would swear by our Brand. They recommend it to others because it has never steered them wrong. They are the word-of-mouth campaign."

He went on to say, "The people who don't do well selling this Brand haven't fallen in love with it yet. They don't know it like I do, live and breathe it like I do, trust it like I do, or understand it like I do. Worse yet, they don't talk about it like I do."

I asked, "How do you usually talk about it?"

He answered, "'Indispensable,' 'no other choice,' 'beyond imagination,' and 'prestigious.'"

His graphic descriptions show clearly that the Brand is made up of words that are true, have meaning, and are unique to your Brand and possibly your company. In Chapter 9, I discussed how to get these words from your customers because their opinion is the one that matters. Here, you will need to put the words into your Brand story.

The Art of Telling the Brand Story

Not so long ago, we used to communicate by telling stories. We would sit around as families at night and tell stories about our day at school, what our friends were up to, what the latest news was all about, and how we were going to spend our vacation. I can remember listening to my Dad read us a story each night from one of the classics: *Robin Hood, King Arthur and the Knights of the Round Table*, and *Swiss Family Robinson*. The most powerful part of that memory for me was the identity it gave me, the warmth and camaraderie I felt with friends and family. Of late, it seems as if we as people have lost our identity in the midst of the rush; we don't slow down long enough to listen to the stories and to be proud of who we are, where we work, and the Brands we represent.

We seem to have lost the art of good storytelling, as a nation to some degree and as a collective sales profession to a different degree. I am not talking about yarn spinning or fable telling. No, I'm talking about good, honest stories about how we got to where we are today as people, or as a company. Stories that knit us together as a people with similar experiences, similar backgrounds, and similar heritage—just like a family. Stories that are rich, have history, and are interesting and compelling. Stories that are attractive to others: if only they knew this story, they would understand how I think, who I am, and why it makes sense to do business with me and my company.

We need to reignite this storytelling skill, and we need to attach it to our Brand. I am about to give you some advice here about telling the Brand story that is so simple that you may need to try it out a couple of times before you believe it.

Brand stories are made up of three key parts:

1. *History:* How the Brand evolved and why
2. *Language:* Compelling and emotional words that represent the Brand well
3. *Impact:* The story's impact on you, your buyers, and the marketplace

Let me illustrate this.

I was in Ireland recently, and I visited the Guinness brewery in Dublin. I thought I was in for a nice tour, a little history, and a pint of stout beer. Instead, I was overwhelmed by the company's heritage, pride, and sense of family. What an unbelievable display of its Brand. The tour took us through every step of the brewing process. On public display was the company's Brand language, and on each step of the staircase Price, Style and Quality were in evidence. Yet, it was the Brand that stole the show. The company told the story of the Brand, what it meant to Dublin, the history of the company, and its effect on the community and its families. There were all kinds of history, language, and impact; they told the Brand story of Guinness in an unbeatable way. I was enthralled with the Brand's history, and I wanted to be part of its story. The people who worked there were also proud to be there. They shared that spirit. Guinness was not just brewing stout; it was part of the larger fabric of the society.

You see, the Brand is made up of people and how they help customers experience it, even in small ways. The Brand is made up of the collective experiences of the customers who engage it and the people who represent it every day. If it's your story, you need to make it your story, by being engaged with it and by engaging the customer. This will not happen overnight; you will need to practice it and, most importantly, live it.

What Is Your Brand Story? Let's Practice

Why practice the Brand story? Let me answer that, so that you can learn from my bad example. I had been with Black & Decker about three years and was calling on the excellent retailer Target Stores in Minneapolis for a short period of time. I was making a sales call on the power tool buyer, and when I stepped into the elevator and turned around, there stood the CEO of Target. I knew that only because I had seen his picture in the annual report. Nervously, I gestured hello and wished that someone else would hop on the elevator for the ride. No one did, and we started to ascend.

He turned to me and asked who I was with. I sputtered out Black & Decker. He immediately said, "You folks have a strong Brand; tell me, what does your Brand mean to the customers that shop in our stores?"

I had absolutely no idea how to respond, and it must have looked as if I had seen a ghost. I remember falling back on my product expertise and muttering something about our upcoming promotions. All the while, he gave me an increasingly perplexed look, as if to say, "Did you hear the question?" I never have felt more stupid during a 30-second elevator ride, nor been more relieved when the doors closed behind me than I was that day.

That is why you practice your Brand story, and that is also why you should get it down so well that you could give it in a 30-second elevator ride. To this day, the importance of knowing and articulating the Brand has been a driving factor in my career.

If you want to get to that 30-second goal, practice using the following questions, which get at the three key parts of the Brand story.

Exercise: What is the history of your Brand?

_____

_____

Exercise: What is the language of your Brand? That is, what are the compelling and emotional words that represent your Brand well?

_____

_____

Exercise: What has been the impact of your Brand on you, your buyers, or the marketplace? If the Brand is new, a better question is: what impact do you believe the Brand is destined to have on the marketplace?

_____

_____

Brand: Parting Thoughts

Notice that we have not tried to script your Brand story, to put the words in your mouth. If we did, then it wouldn't be yours—authentic, personal, and unique.

Are you ready to tell your Brand story? Are you taking credit for your history, your language, and your impact on buyers and the marketplace? Are you equipped to tell your story in a clear, concise way when it is time to talk and sell from Brand first?

You now co-own your Brand with Marketing. What will you do about it? Are you in? We hope you are, because we will next talk about your culture and the combined effort that is needed from the whole sales and marketing team to build a Branded culture. See you at Chapter 13.

Key Points

This is the chapter where the rubber meets the road in terms of applying the ideas and techniques that we have been discussing. That is, now that we understand the importance of Brand, how do we migrate the buyer toward the Brand? If the salesperson wants a successful migration process, here are the areas he should be focused on:

- The salesperson has to be able to assess buyer *mindset* at each step on the staircase. This is done through being aware of verbal clues, visual signposts, and probable outcomes (things the buyer might do).
- The salesperson has to be able to influence the buyer's level of willingness to *migrate* towards the Brand. This is done through a technique I call *TIME.* The acronym translates to *testimonials* (getting good references from satisfied users of a Brand), *investigation* (asking good lifestyle questions of the buyer), *motives* (discerning the buyer's real reasons for being interested in the Brand), and *education* (giving the buyer good information about the Brand).
- The salesperson has to be able to discern the level of *logic* and *emotion* at each step in the staircase when using the *TIME* technique. The levels of logic and emotion are important, especially if a buyer is stuck on a certain step of the staircase. In particular, this helps the salesperson by letting her know how to best make the transition into talking about the Brand.
- The salesperson should be able to enhance the migration process by being adept at using the *Brand Rules of Engagement* covered in Chapter 9—that is, having strong questioning and listening skills.
- The salesperson has a responsibility to learn how to tell the *Brand story* using intentional and accurate words that represent the Brand. The story should contain elements of the history of the company, language that represents the Brand most clearly, and a sense of the impact of the Brand on users.

PART 5

SELLING BRANDS IN THE BUSINESS-TO-BUSINESS SETTING

CHAPTER 11

DIFFERENCES IN SELLING TO THE TRADE

If you find yourself selling a trade Brand to a professional buyer, such as a purchasing manager for a plant or an industrial buyer of component parts, then you are in a business-to-business setting, where there are fundamental differences in how best to approach selling the Brand. It is important to note that all of the major principles about Brands and Brand selling that we have discussed up to now as they affect the consumer remain relevant in the business-to-business setting. There are differences, however, and the intent of this chapter is to point out the big differences in selling trade Brands and to build on what you already have learned about Brand selling to individual consumers.

This chapter and the next are especially targeted toward salespeople who call on trades like manufacturers, wholesale–distribution, plants and maintenance, or residential, commercial, or industrial construction and are not involved with the everyday consumer. This list could go on indefinitely. Suffice it to say that salespeople, leaders, and marketers who are servicing these other than retail channels will benefit greatly from this new approach to selling your Brand.

Usually these salespeople are furthest removed from the idea of Brand selling, because their Brands are not easily identifiable or visible. Also, those salespeople selling crossover Brands—to both buyers *who supply retail stores* with a consumer Brand, or resellers of a consumer Brand, and purchasing agents for wholesale distributors—will benefit greatly from this trade Brand selling discussion.

The Five Key Differences in Selling Trade Brands

Here's what is distinct about selling trade brands. We'll talk about each of these differences in detail.

1. Buyers are professionally trained and paid to buy.
2. Business is repetitious and has a regular sales-call pattern.
3. Motives can be far more production-driven.
4. Products are used within a trade, rather than within a household.
5. Purchases of goods and services have no direct impact on the buyer's lifestyle.

Buyers Are Professionally Trained and Paid to Buy

Buyers in the trades are professionals. They have been trained to purchase goods and services for companies. They have gone to school on the fundamentals of buying and negotiating with suppliers and manufacturers. Their training is usually obtained through trade schools, buying associations, professional societies, and even higher education. Often, their training is company-sponsored because their buying responsibilities and decisions have an impact on the company's profitability.

Business Is Repetitious and Has a Regular Sales-Call Pattern

Trade Brands can be bought and installed or used for installation or construction (for example, in the building trades, there is residential and commercial construction); bought and used to produce another product (chemicals, semiconductors, transmitters, fabrics, and plastics, for instance); bought and resold to distributors, who then sell to users (industrial distributors, food distributors, hardware distributors, automotive parts distributors, and aviation distributors, to name a few); in some cases, sold directly to trade users (automotive tool vans that sell directly to mechanics, route salespeople in the grocery trade); and sold directly to manufacturers of goods and services.

You can see that all of these sales interactions have two big things in common:

- The buying-and-selling process is fundamentally *repeatable.*
- The *sales-call frequency is regular in its pattern*, and there is usually some buyer–seller history.

Motives Can Be Far More Production-Driven

Professional buyers are paid based on their ability to produce the right results in their department or area of responsibility, which also helps their company financially. They normally have performance standards and metrics to hit that are focused on deliverable results. Thus, most of their visible motives tend to be very logical and could involve the following motives concerning the professional buyer's job or company:

1. Give me more output.
2. Make me more productive or efficient.
3. Save me time or money.
4. Make my job easier or hassle-free.

However, salespeople calling on the trades should not forget that trade buyers are human beings with emotions and that we should still appeal to those emotional motives (power, recognition, control). Salespeople should be conscious of the fact that in trade buyers, although these motives are often hidden, they still exist.

Products Are Used within a Trade Rather than within a Household

Trade buyers use the products they buy within their area of expertise on the job rather than at home. They are buying products to be used specifically on the job within their trade by themselves or company employees, whether they are craft workers, journeymen, carpenters, engineers, or in some other trade. Thus, trade buyers have very high performance and quality standards. They dismiss products made for homeowners as unworthy, untrustworthy, and incapable of getting the job done under the rigorous conditions found in the trade environment. Trade buyers have high expectations of the companies that they buy products and services from because they make their living using those products, as opposed to consumers, who are supporting a lifestyle with their purchases. Trade buyers cannot afford downtime. To them, time is money, and their products produce results for them within their profession or within their company.

Purchases of Goods and Services Have No Direct Impact on the Buyer's Lifestyle

Unlike consumer Brands, when trade Brands are sold to trade buyers, there is no direct link to improving the buyer's personal lifestyle. The reason for that is the broader scope and deeper level of commitment in which the goods and services are being purchased. For example:

- Trade buyers and tradespeople are buying for a company, not for their own personal use. To a great degree, this removes any direct impact on improving their lifestyle.
- Trade buyers' or tradespeople's buying patterns and behavior are influenced to a large degree by the company for which they purchase products and services. Whether the company is family owned, small, medium, or large, the buyer could come to the sales interaction with a hidden or ulterior motive: to produce a result for the company that,

over the long haul, will help him advance his career. How? By performing better, getting noticed, being viewed in a good light, getting promoted, and receiving a raise or promotion because he has performed well on the job will raise his standard of living over time, but will not have a direct impact on his lifestyle. All of these ulterior motives have an indirect effect on the buyer's lifestyle and would possibly give him more disposable income for his "home life"; however, they will not affect your ability as a trade salesperson to influence his Brand choices toward a trade Brand. Those are unrelated events.

After reviewing those five key differences in selling within the business-to-business context, it doesn't take a rocket scientist to understand the need for a broader model for selling trade Brands. One of my key customers put it best: "If you are selling to electricians, designers, or engineers, they are not going to be making a buying decision based on their own lifestyle. As a matter of fact, you will be laughed off the job site if you ask a lifestyle question. They will be far more interested in what a particular lighting system could do for them in designing a better project for their client, producing a better result for their contractor, or getting rehired next time because of their creativity and unique design. In those cases, their lifestyle doesn't enter the equation. Instead, it's the business *result* that they are looking to leverage for more work in the future. If you help them get that result, you will have a satisfied customer." I agreed with him wholeheartedly. In order to accommodate the needs of the result-driven seller, I have developed an upgraded version of the Brand Staircase for the business-to-business setting.

The Trade Buyer Stair-Step

You have studied the Brand Staircase in terms of a consumer Brand. We will now build on that foundation to construct the Trade Buyer Brand Staircase, which is relevant in the business-to-business setting. But first, think for a moment about your history as a trade salesperson. Think about

- The customers you've called on
- The relationships you've built
- The products you've sold
- The objections you've handled
- The companies you've sold for in the field

Now ask yourself, what are trade buyers looking for when considering a vendor in a business-to-business interaction? You have probably come to the same conclusion that I did. Trade buyers consider three major things when making their buying decisions:

1. The *product* you and your company have to offer
2. The *relationship* you and your company have built with them
3. The *performance* you have achieved for them

Those three elements are the main components of the Trade Buyer Stair-Step.

Now, if you remember back to the original consumer Buyer Stair-Step, you will recall that the first three steps were Price, Style, and Quality. Those three steps are the common ground for the two staircases. Let's look at the original Buyer Stair-Step that we first introduced to you when building the model (see Figure 11.1).

See how those first three steps are separate entities, each with its own set of characteristics? These steps are also important when a trade buyer is buying products for her company.

- The *Price* needs to be competitive, fair, and equitable compared to the other available product choices.

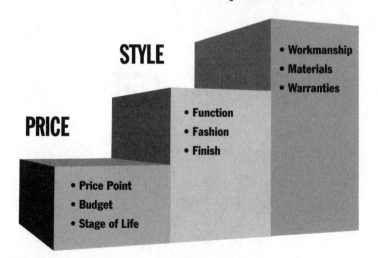

CONSUMER BUYER STAIR-STEP

QUALITY
- Workmanship
- Materials
- Warranties

STYLE
- Function
- Fashion
- Finish

PRICE
- Price Point
- Budget
- Stage of Life

FIGURE 11.1

- The *Style* needs to be functional, attractive if need be, and finished with the right surfaces for the trade application.
- The *Quality* needs to be sufficient to enable the product to meet the rigorous standards required on the job. The product needs to have a strong warranty and replacement policy and must be constructed of the best materials for the application so that it can stand up to the abuse it will be taking every day on the job.

The difference for the trade buyer is that even though all of those steps still matter, in the trade buyer's mind they are bunched together as the product offering. They essentially are the ante into the game if you are to be a player with her, and her company.

Thus, we recognize this fact when serving the trade buyer and have combined those three steps into one important step—the Product step (see Figure 11.2). The Product step is the first step of the Trade Buyer Stair-Step.

The Product Step

As previously stated, the Product step is made up of Price, Style, and Quality, but in a broader sense. Trade buyers are usually looking at your whole product offering, not just one item. (Refer again to Figure 11.2.) (*Special note to Trade salespeople selling services:* The product offering would be replaced by service offering, which would still have the same three components of Price, Style, and Quality. Accordingly, please make that mental adjustment as you navigate these questions.) They are asking questions of you and your company such as

THE PRODUCT STEP

- Price
- Style
- Quality

FIGURE 11.2

- Does the company's product offering (service offering) have quality across the board?
- Does the company have a complete and stylish product line offering?
- Are the company's pricing and terms competitive and reasonable?
- Are the warranty and service simple and easy to administer?
- Does the company stand behind its products and services?
- Do the company's products and services have a fair value for the price?
- Does the company consistently bring well-designed and innovative products to the market?
- Does the company show innovation and creativity within its category?

The interesting observation I have made over the years is that this is merely the starting point for trade buyers. Positive answers to these questions simply get you in the door. This is the ante into the buying game. This is where most companies "earn their stripes" with a buyer. It is also where most companies start doing business—on the Product step. (By the way, isn't it interesting that if most companies start doing business with you on this step, you would want to become a product expert? It is no coincidence that we give trade buyers what they want to hear about first: a good product offering based on our product expertise.)

Review your own experience on the Product step by using the following exercise.

Exercise: How strong is your company's product offering? How good are your product knowledge and your presentation of the company's product offering? How often do you enter the sales interaction by starting on the product step with your trade buyer?

The Relationship Step

Trade buyers also were described as repeat buyers who require a consistent sales-call pattern if you are to be successful in selling to them. The repeat nature of this business cycle thus builds up a history and a relationship between seller and buyer. This Relationship is the second step in the Trade Buyer Stair-Step and is grounded in three main things: trust, history, and integrity (see Figure 11.3). Here the buyer is constantly asking herself

THE RELATIONSHIP STEP

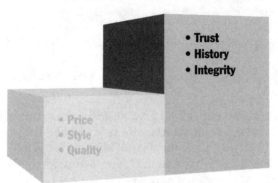

• Trust
• History
• Integrity

• Price
• Style
• Quality

FIGURE 11.3

- Can I trust the salesperson and his company?
- Have they gained my trust and confidence over time?
- Do they do business with honesty and integrity?
- Do they build relationships throughout my company?
- Do other people in our company like doing business with them?
- Is the salesperson likable and professional?
- Does he understand my business well enough to make excellent recommendations on products, applications, and services?
- Do I have easy access to the salesperson or other company personnel?

Relationships are built on trust and earned over time. Those of you who have spent your career in sales realize the immediate and long-term impact of a great relationship and the many doors it can open. You also realize how quickly a business relationship can take a turn for the worse. Relationships are indeed a double-edged sword that cuts both ways—for the good and for the bad.

For instance, how many of you trade sellers have had a relationship with one of your key trade customers that was so solid that it totally drove the business? You could have sworn that this relationship was a "business annuity" that was unchallenged and would always come your way. Maybe you couldn't even remember the last time that you lost an order to a competitor with that customer—until one fateful day when you walked out of the customer's place of business with a shocked look on your face, having just seen your annuity stop payments! Why? Because you relied on the relationship too heavily. You made too many assumptions about your "untouchable customer," and the competition found a way in. That customer went from being a "most secure" customer to an "at risk" customer, literally in the blink of an eye.

A good relationship is a tiebreaker, not a deal maker. In other words, if all else is equal, then the buyer will give the order to the salesperson with whom she has the best relationship. In summary, we cannot afford to overrely on our relationships in the trade, but relationships certainly can open many doors, so they are clearly necessary to conducting business. Review your relationships here.

Exercise: What have you done specifically to build great relationships?

Are any of your relationships at risk? Why?

The Performance Step

Trade buyers are rated largely on how well they purchase products that perform well for their company. That performance is the third thing buyers consider in looking at any supplier/vendor. They are basically asking, "How well do this salesperson and his company perform on delivering products and services?" Performance is grounded in three main items: reliability, follow-through, and problem solving (see Figure 11.4).

Here the buyer is frequently asking

- How reliable is the salesperson and her company?
- Do they have great follow-up and follow-through on any issue?
- Do they work hard to avoid problems or keep them to a minimum?
- If problems do arise, how quickly and efficiently are they handled?
- How well trained is the salesperson?
- How well do the salesperson and her company train my people to be experts on their products and services?
- Do they deliver on all commitments and promises in a timely fashion?
- Do they have on-time delivery and consistent product availability?
- Is the company's billing straightforward and accurate?
- Do the company and the salesperson consistently exceed our expectations?
- Does the salesperson perform her function well for her company?

THE PERFORMANCE STEP

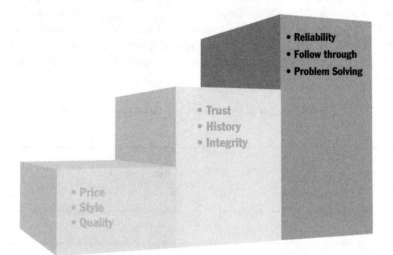

- Reliability
- Follow through
- Problem Solving

- Trust
- History
- Integrity

- Price
- Style
- Quality

FIGURE 11.4

Performance is the "what have you done for me lately" part of the stair-step. It becomes the customer's expectation as to how your company will deliver its products and services. This is where your sales promises are kept or broken, which, of course, affects the trust and credibility you have with the buyer. This is where your standards of excellence, great reliability, and follow-up should shine.

Performance can take a lot of different forms from the buyer's perspective. It can be measured in a variety of ways: delivery levels, contract specs, customer metrics, performance ratings, quality ratings, and returned goods percentages. There is also one big intangible rating, the "ease of doing business" with you and your company.

This fact is important: On the Trade Buyer Stair-Step, *performance* is different from *product* in that it relates to service after the sale. In other words, once the sale is made, performance kicks in. Once buyers have said yes to the product or service, then performance reflects how well we delivered on the promises that we made concerning that product or service. How good has your performance been on recent sales?

Exercise: Think of your personal performance and your company's collective performance. What have your customers experienced in performance from you in terms of reliability, follow-through, problem solving, training, delivery, and customer service? Has it been acceptable? Why or why not?

_____

_____

_____

_____

The Importance of Relationships

Relationships are a very strong part of doing business in the trades, and because of that they deserve special attention here. Being mindful of relationships goes beyond understanding where you sit with key buyers; it also includes knowing how deep the buyer's relationships are with the competition.

In some cases, our competition may have an "unbeatable relationship" with a customer that you have been trying to land for years. It's as if that competitor has a stranglehold on that customer and won't let go, not even for one measly sale! This could trip you up on the staircase if you're not careful.

How do we break that stranglehold on the competitor's "untouchable customer"? It's hard, isn't it? And it is hard because that loyal customer of our competitor will enter each transaction with a buyer's mindset that favors the competition. However, I have also seen cases where our perception of that relationship with a competitor is overstated and frankly incorrect. The problem is that many salespeople tend to give up on a prospect who is "owned by the competition" much too early. Remember:

- *Don't give up.* Continue to call on this noncustomer, because you never know when things will change in his or her world. The competitive salesperson may be relying solely on the relationship and nothing else, thus allowing the customer to become the "at risk" customer we talked about earlier.

- *Take a "give me a shot at earning your business" attitude to the sales call.* In other words, it doesn't hurt to find out what it would take to deliver just one piece of your product offering to this noncustomer. I have seen some great business relationships that began with one small sale within a competitor's stronghold and developed into a loyal Brand customer over time.
- *View the calls you make on this buyer as relationship-building calls.* These calls are meant to build the relationship for a future day when maybe you can earn a shot at the business. Too many salespeople don't establish a relationship with customers during the lean years, so they have nothing to draw on when the good years are at their doorstep and the opportunity to do business arises. The mere fact that you are making an attempt to build a relationship will send the buyer a trust signal about your character.

A good example of building relationships with noncustomers came for me when DeWALT was launched into the marketplace. I was leading a team of folks calling on a big customer in Alaska. It had none of our product and was quite happy with its current supplier. Regardless, it was our job to educate the company on our product line and our Brand strategy in the marketplace. We had made three trips to see their operation—in February, April, and June. At the end of the third trip, the merchandise manager pulled me aside and handed me an opening order for his stores. We had built a pretty good relationship, so I thanked him and asked him how we had been able to break through against the other supplier.

He said, "A lot of our current vendors simply won't travel to Alaska in the winter because it's too cold. However, they are more than happy to fly up in June and ask us to take them fishing. They simply use us as an excuse for a vacation getaway! When you were willing to see us in the dead of winter and come back during the fishing season but never asked to go fishing, I knew you were for real." I've never forgotten that lesson.

Awareness of the Assumption Filter

The *assumption filter* is a built-in filter and thought process that creeps into every veteran salesperson's psyche as a result of having built strong relationships with valued customers and buyers. In short, the assumption filter allows you to assume more than you should based on the strength of your relationship. It is a strength taken to a weakness. It usually manifests itself as a mental narrative that runs through the salesperson's head that acts as a filter and works against his selling efforts.

For example, because we "have developed a strong relationship over the years with the buyer," we fail to continue asking good questions because we've asked those questions before and think we know the answer, or we think that we can literally predict her behavior with regard to a certain product line. We act like mind readers. We rely on the same orders or seasonal pieces of business, and we assume that they are in the bag and don't do our homework. Before we know it, we have lost the business because of our assumption filter.

ASSUMPTION FILTER
We assume too much based on our relationship with the buyer:
We stop asking good questions.
We think we already know the answers.
We rely too heavily on long-term relationships.

We need to challenge our own thinking and stop listening through our assumption filter. Let's not stop asking good questions because we already "know the answers" based on our long-term relationship. Many a good salesperson has fallen victim to the assumption filter. Have you?

Exercise: Think of the relationships you have with your buyers. What were your most common assumptions about those relationships?

_____

_____

Now, think of a customer relationship where you felt very secure or had strong loyalty and then you experienced a lost piece of business:

What was the cause?

Why did it happen?

What were your assumptions?

_____

_____

_____

History with the Trade Buyer Stair-Step

Now let's look at the issues concerning the way we have sold in the past using Product, Relationships, and Performance (see Figure 11.5). My

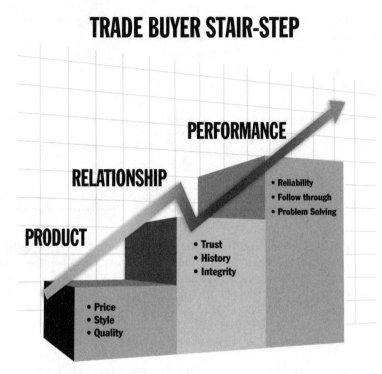

TRADE BUYER STAIR-STEP

PERFORMANCE

RELATIONSHIP

- Reliability
- Follow through
- Problem Solving

PRODUCT

- Trust
- History
- Integrity

- Price
- Style
- Quality

FIGURE 11.5

experience is that most buyers will enter the Stair-Step favoring a certain step—either Product, Relationship, or Performance. In other words, their buyer's mindset, the inclination, or the primary reason they are buying is based on a certain step. Usually the salesperson can intuitively identify which step is primary.

However, trade buyers will also look collectively at all three steps and compare suppliers or vendors. In other words, the trade buyers are comparing stair-steps to see which vendor has the *tallest stair-step* with regard to Product, Relationship, and Performance. So, as a supplier selling with this model, the only way to beat your competition in the past was to have a rock-solid stair-step and to continue to grow it taller than any of the competitors' stair-steps. There are a couple of problems with that approach.

In general, we have the same time, energy, and sales momentum issues that we had with the original Buyer Stair-Step. That is, it takes too much time to develop the right product offering, or it takes too much energy to develop and maintain relationships, or it takes too much sales momentum to continue to perform on a daily basis. In other words, we are still selling uphill with this model.

More specifically, let me highlight the issues at each step:

- *Product step.* What happens if the competition builds a better mouse-trap, or introduces new products that leapfrog your technology or specifications? How long does it take to get new product to market? Too long—ask any marketer. So much for the best product offering!
- *Relationship step:* What happens if your strong relationships go away? For instance, what if the buyer wins the lottery, gets hit by a bus, or switches companies? Or what happens if you have only that one relationship in the company and the buyer leaves—and, of course, the person you have ignored during the last five years of sales calls is now buying your product line? How long does it take to rebuild a good customer relationship from scratch? *Too long*—ask any veteran salesperson. So much for strong relationships!
- *Performance step.* What happens when you start slipping on the customer metrics, or your company has serious back-order problems, or you fail to deliver on a promise you made to the buyer? What happens when you shoot yourself in the foot on the one key performance criterion? How long does it take to prove yourself again after you have lost that piece of business? Too long—ask any senior sales leader. So much for strong performance!

The bottom line is that getting products to market, building the right relationships, and proving yourself with performance takes too much time.

THE TRUTH OF THE MATTER IS . . .
Product offerings become outdated . . .
Relationships can go awry . . .
Performance can slip in one transaction . . .
And your
Competition can duplicate all of these!

That's right—you will not always have the tallest stair-step compared with your competition. If the truth be told, we're still selling uphill—like everyone we compete against.

Selling the Brand

So, what is our remedy? The Brand and the people who represent it. We need to remember that our people are a walking billboard for the

Brand. This mentality is especially important in selling trade Brands, because they are usually less visible to the trade buyer, thus making it harder to differentiate our company and its Brand.

**The competition can't duplicate
your people and the power of your Brand.**

That is where we are headed in the next chapter—to the power of your Brand and leveraging it in the business-to-business trade Brand setting.

Key Points

Although there are some similarities, selling in a business-to-business setting is different from selling to individual consumers. These differences are:

- Buyers are professionally trained and paid to buy.
- Business is repetitious and has a regular sales-call pattern.
- Motives can be far more production-driven.
- Products are used within a trade, rather than within a household.
- Purchases of goods and services have no direct impact on the buyer's lifestyle.

Given these differences, it is obvious that a different approach to the buyer is required in the business-to-business setting. Thus, we compare the Buyer Stair-Step for the approach to the individual consumer with the Trade Buyer Stair-Step for the approach to the trade buyer. The original Buyer Stair-Step contains the steps of Price, Style, and Quality. The Trade Buyer Stair-Step contains the steps of Product, Relationship, and Performance. The first step, Product, is composed of Price, Style, and Quality.

Two things to be aware of when working with a trade buyer are the importance of relationships and avoiding a syndrome that I call applying the *assumption filter*. In terms of relationships, you should never take your buyers for granted, even though they have been customers for many years. Be forewarned about the assumption filter—it influences the salesperson to make assumptions about the buyer (which may be incorrect) based on past experience.

But there are problems with the Trade Buyer Stair-Step, just as there are with the (Consumer) Buyer Stair-Step. That is:

- It takes too much time to develop the right product offering.
- It takes too much energy to develop and maintain relationships.
- It takes too much sales momentum to continue to perform on a daily basis.
- We are still selling uphill.

However, the competition can duplicate your Product, Relationship, or Performance, but it can't duplicate you and the power of your Brand.

So, when selling to the trade buyer, you need to differentiate yourself by selling the power of your Brand.

CHAPTER 12

MIGRATING THE TRADE BUYER TOWARD THE BRAND

So how do we put the power of the Brand in play with the trade buyer? Think back to what is important to the consumer buyer:

- Mindsets
- Motives
- The focus on Price, Style, and Quality
- An identified need to migrate toward the Brand

The same needs also apply to the trade buyer. And as we began to see in Chapter 11, there is the need for a Trade Brand Staircase—one that includes a Brand step, just like the consumer Brand Staircase. Let's add that step and then make some observations and point out some differences. Look closely at Figure 12.1.

What do you notice? That's right. Trade buyers *experience* the Brand, and make *connections* to or *affiliations* with the Brand. Consumer buyers do the same thing. At least, it's the same on the surface. There is a big difference, however, in *how* trade buyers connect to, experience, or affiliate with the Brand:

That difference is that consumer buyers make lifestyle choices that are represented by the Brand. In contrast, trade buyers make choices to do business with companies and salespeople that stand for or represent certain priorities, strategies, or operating advantages—I call these *pillars*—that bring value to the trade buyer's company.

Consumer buyers connect to lifestyles represented by the Brand,
whereas
trade buyers connect to pillars that represent
(or stand for) your Brand.

THE TRADE STAIRCASE

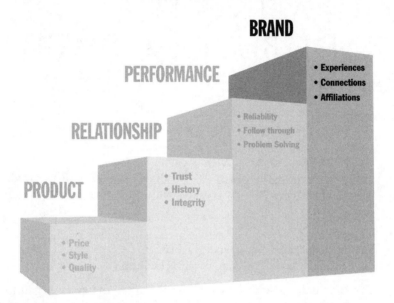

FIGURE 12.1

Both lifestyles and pillars are major drawing cards for buyers. Both bring added value for the buyers who pursue them. Importantly, both represent the primary attraction factor for their buyers. What lifestyle is to consumer buyers, pillars are to trade buyers—the primary migration magnet. If you understand this simple truth, especially if you are a salesperson who sells a crossover brand, then you will be able to mentally jump from the consumer staircase to the trade staircase at a moment's notice.

As we talk about migrating the trade buyer through the following four action steps, pillars will take a starring role as the primary migration factor for the trade salesperson.

- *Reverse the Trade Brand Staircase and sell the Brand first.*
- Identify the *Brand pillars* and show how to get them into the sales process.
- Tell *Brand stories.*
- Ask *Brand questions.*

Reverse the Trade Brand Staircase and Sell the Brand First

In a recent workshop, I was making the point about experiences, connections, and affiliations for the trade Brand and was proceeding to reverse the staircase. The top marketing executive interjected, "You know, those first three steps of the staircase put us on an even playing field with the competition. That's not where we want to play the game! By selling the Brand, we have just extended the playing field by 20 yards, and now we are constantly playing in the red zone. That's where we want to play because no one can defend against us with all of the weapons we have with the Brand."

I wholeheartedly agreed with his football analogy and added, "But wouldn't it be nice if you were always playing in the red zone by starting with the Brand first? Instead, right now you have to drive the length of the football field (figuratively going uphill) through the Product, Relationship, and Performance steps before you get to the Brand step. Instead, we need to sell the Brand first!" See Figure 12.2.

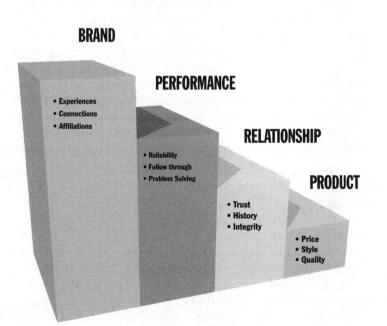

THE TRADE BRAND STAIRCASE

BRAND
- Experiences
- Connections
- Affiliations

PERFORMANCE
- Reliability
- Follow through
- Problem Solving

RELATIONSHIP
- Trust
- History
- Integrity

PRODUCT
- Price
- Style
- Quality

FIGURE 12.2

I was conducting a series of "Webex" conference calls reinforcing the Brand selling program with a key client and was asking for good examples of selling the Brand first by reversing the staircase. Three separate examples rolled out:

- A major trade buyer symposium was put together by a team of sales-people to educate the team's buyers and provide professional certification for continuing education requirements within their industry. Not only was my client servicing 80 buyers at once in this setting, but the sales team was selling the Brand simultaneously. The salespeople involved said that a number of buyers walked up to them and said, "No one else can do this," or "This is the best thing I've experienced in the last five or six years." The salespeople didn't just sell product and solidify relationships that day; they also provided a service that no one else could match. That's selling the Brand.

- Another group of salespeople described a major presentation being made to a buying committee that was to fit into a preordained agenda. The agenda was built around a certain product offering and emphasized matching the price quote. Fortunately, the salespeople chose to "extend the playing field" and sell the Brand first. The head sales team leader commented, "Instead of trying to match price and availability, we sold the company's Brand pillars from the start. We definitely opened the buyers' eyes to what we could do for them. When we left, they knew that no one else could match us."

- Another salesperson had been calling on the director of maintenance at a major university. He had been consistently losing deals based on product offerings, mostly over price issues. Following the Brand selling process, he went in selling the Brand first and selling from the strength of his company's Brand pillars. Not only did the director cancel the competitive order and reorder from our salesperson, but he also commented, "I didn't realize that you guys did all of that stuff!" (referring to the services that the salesperson was describing).

As in these examples, those of us serving the trades need to start the sales process by selling the Brand first. When that happens, the rest of the process is easier. It is easier to talk about Performance and justify the Brand's reputation. If you are doing a good job moving down the Trade Brand Staircase, then by the time you get to the Relationship step, the trade buyer understands the value that you and your company bring and gives you more credit for that value. Finally, if the Product offering lines up with the buyer's needs, then the price will become less of a determining factor. Even if price is still a big consideration in the decision process, the buyer is more focused on the "value for the dollars I'm spending" instead of thinking, "Am I getting a good deal here?" or "Does it fit into my operating budget?"

Keep in mind that these salespeople on the Webex were better equipped with the trade Brand's secret weapon—its foundation—which is having a clear understanding of your company's Brand pillars, and communicating that understanding to the trade buyer.

Brand Pillars: The Foundation of the Trade Brand

I recently visited Italy. We spent most of our time in Rome, one of the world's most famous architectural and historical cities. You can't help but fall in love with the city, its history, its art, its food, and its heritage. The architecture, ancient ruins, and artwork are astounding. Everywhere we went, we saw the history and past civilization supported by pillars and statues—places such as the Vatican, St. Peter's Square, the Sistine Chapel, the Spanish Steps, the Roman Forum, and the Coliseum. Ah, yes, the Coliseum—my favorite!

The Coliseum was built in only eight years and inaugurated in 80 A.D. Its three-story construction consisted of 80 arches and pillars on each level. The Coliseum could hold 50,000 spectators, had 76 entryways for ease of entrance, and had free admission. The builders used an earthquake-proof construction technique that consisted of placing enormous iron clamps inside the stone blocks. The structure is so solid, unshakable, and grand that almost two thousand years later, crowds from across the world still venture into the Coliseum to marvel at its architecture and the pillars and archways that hold it up. The Coliseum has become a Brand of its own. It stands for the ancient Roman Empire, and it is upheld by the pillars. The pillars are foundational to the landscape of Roman architecture.

Modern companies also have pillars that have stood the test of time. As in the Coliseum, these pillars are a foundation for the Brand and uphold the company in the midst of fierce competition. For our purposes, the pillars are the entryway for the hundreds of customers and buyers who are attracted to the Brand. The pillars honor the company's history, and its customers often speak of them with respect. Allow me to define these pillars further and give you some examples from experience.

Brand pillars are your company's impenetrable advantages. They
Are mentioned by customers
Are proven over time
Convey common sense

Let's break this definition down a bit further.

Impenetrable Advantages

These are advantages that your company has worked hard to build and has chosen to invest in over the course of its history. These strategic choices and investments are pursued with one primary purpose in mind: to provide better products or services to your key customer base. They are usually within your company's operations, approach to the marketplace, or business model. Yet they have a distinct customer focus. Their cumulative effect is to create an advantage for you as a company that is impenetrable by the competition and that is also foundational to your Brand. These impenetrable advantages differentiate your Brand from the competition and bring added value to the customer—value that the customer cannot find elsewhere among your competition, value that becomes an intangible asset for your company.

MENTIONED BY CUSTOMERS

Importantly, these pillars are generally not "birthed in the boardroom." No, they originate on the lips of the customer. The customer may mention them in an "unaided awareness" survey, or might routinely discuss aspects of them during day-to-day sales calls or on customer satisfaction surveys.

The bottom line is that these pillars are customer-driven, not company-driven. They are invested in by the company to bring noticeable value to the customers.

PROVEN OVER TIME

Pillars have history; they have been time-tested, proven over the long haul. Like the ancient pillars in the Coliseum in Rome, they represent what your company stands for. They uphold the values that your company espouses, yet they do so with the customer in mind. They are foundational to doing business with the customer, whether we know it or not. They do not have a hollow ring to them; rather, if you took them away, the customer would truly notice and probably would not be able to replace them with your competitor's offerings in the marketplace.

CONVEY COMMON SENSE

There is no huge mystery to the pillars. They have simply become so much a part of your company that they are widely seen as part of the fabric of your business. They are woven into the tapestry of your approach to the marketplace; they are like the Coliseum is to Rome. You can't imagine the skyline of your company without them solidly in place.

Let me give you a visual to solidify your learning right now. Figure 12.3 shows four generic pillars that we will use for demonstration purposes later.

BRAND PILLARS (GENERIC)

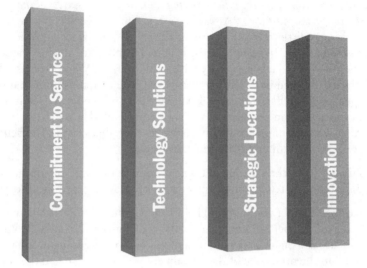

FIGURE 12.3

By the way, there is no magic to the number of pillars. I have chosen four as being a number that is very manageable for all parties. In general, I have found that companies will try to claim too many pillars, and that salespeople tend to handle four quite nicely. With that said, let's look at some examples of pillars for companies that I have been involved with while selling Brands:

- *Distribution:* "flexible and innovative solutions," "strategic locations," "quality service," "focus on technology"
- *Electrical and lighting:* "commitment to service, quality and value," "company integrity and innovation"
- *Paint and sundries:* "educators," "professional user franchise," "undisputable quality," "industry leadership"
- *Industrial products:* "end-user commitment," "guaranteed tough," "innovation and creativity," "unmatchable service"
- *Consumer packaged goods:* "category management," "national promotions," "name recognition," "product innovation"
- *Computers:* "the 'we invented it' attitude," "service expertise," "trust and security," "cutting-edge technology"

- *Hardware and fixtures:* "timeless craftsmanship," "prestige," "lifetime finish," "aspirational"

Notice that *there is very little specific description of the company's products in these pillars, yet the pillars are foundational to the success of the companies that have built them.* Also, they are unique for each company, and there is very little repetition among the pillars, among companies, or across industries. In other words, it is incredibly hard to duplicate or mimic a Brand pillar—especially within an industry. Why? Because the pillars are invested in by the company over time and, most importantly, are perceived by its customers. It is like the wind; you can't see it, but you can feel it, you perceive it, and thus you know that it exists.

Also, Brand pillars are not as visible as the pillars at the Coliseum. Instead, they are intangible assets that can be

- Hidden from the customer at worst, because of a lack of education
- Taken for granted by the customer at best, because you do them so well

An analogy that you may find helpful is to think of your Brand pillars as being hidden behind a curtain for the trade buyer. On one side of the curtain are the buyers, with their perception of your company and your Brand. On the other side of the curtain are you, the seller, and the company's Brand pillars. It is our job to draw back the curtain and unveil our pillars to the buyers in order to take credit for the Brand. I believe that your company and its salespeople need to proclaim and represent your Brand pillars in order to sell the trade Brand. Remember:

You can change the customer's perception of the company by how well you represent the Brand.

Now that we've looked at pillars in the context of company use, how do we realistically use them to make the sales interaction with the trade buyer more effective and more profitable for you?

Using the Brand Pillars to Migrate Trade Buyers

In the business-to-business setting, your pillars are the foundation of your Brand. Now, think about that for just a moment.

- What if you understood your pillars and sold them first to the customer on every call?
- What if all the people within your company who touched the customer had the same understanding of your pillars and serviced the customer based on them?

- What if your pillars could stand the test of time, even under the worst competitive pressures—even if your relationship was crumbling, or your product was becoming outdated, or your performance was slipping?

Everyone would have the same Brand language and be in sync when speaking to the trade buyers, wouldn't they? You certainly would be selling from a position of power then, wouldn't you?

I have witnessed all of the scenarios just described, and I agree with them in a perfect selling world. However, I have found a couple of inherent problems with this approach from a trade buyer's perspective. Let's take the innovation pillar as an example.

1. Trade buyers especially hate scripted salespeople who have memorized a few key words, like *innovation*, and throw them around the sales conversation as if they were magic. In short, trade buyers hate being "techniqued to death." If the trade buyer has based some of her business on the relationship that has been built over time, then it seems to me that the worst thing we can do is to send sales robots out into the field or give scripted answers to unique and sometimes complex buying situations.

2. Buyers won't necessarily respond to the word *innovation*. Let me illustrate. The consumer going to Disney World might visit the "Honey, I Shrunk the Kids" ride and be amazed by the innovation, but would call it something other than innovation. Likewise, the people at Pixar, who enjoy an excellent trade Brand, would probably view innovation in a much different light from the consumer. So salespeople will find it easier to let the customer decide what he feels is innovation.

3. Also the word *innovation*, spoken by itself, sounds like sales rhetoric, or words that would be used to "swoon the buyer." We should stay away from sales language that is off base for buyers. Instead, we need to speak in the buyers' everyday language. Conversely, the buyer would perk up immediately if the salesperson started talking in terms of "what innovation within the product offering could do for her" or "what it would mean to her or her business."

These two core thoughts—*a nonscripted sales approach* and a *"don't-put-words-in-their-mouth"* approach—have proved to be the key to unveiling Brand pillars to the trade customer. As the Brand seller, you need to find a way to think like the trade buyer. The easiest way to do this is to have salespeople answer three key questions about each Brand pillar from the customer's perspective:

- What does this pillar mean to your customer type?
- Why is this pillar important to your customers?
- How would we get this pillar into our selling process?

Notice that this type of questioning sequence gives the salesperson an opportunity to think about the different types of customers he calls on in serving his industry (distributors, fabricators, mechanics, end users, contractors, designers, plant maintenance personnel, and so on). It also digs deeply into why the pillar should even matter to the customer. Finally, it looks for natural ways for the salesperson to put the pillar into the sales process, ways that would be common sense to the trade buyer, not scripted.

To illustrate, let's again go to the innovation pillar, one of the generic pillars in Figure 12.3. Please note that this is a building process. That is, the answers to one question lead to the answers to the next.

WHAT DOES THIS PILLAR MEAN TO YOUR CUSTOMER TYPE?

Innovation could mean different things to different trade buyers:

- This particular supplier is always on the cutting edge with new products.
- It enables the trade buyer to be the first in the marketplace with new and exciting products from the supplier.
- It gives the trade customer access to better products, technology, or education, thus providing it with a competitive edge.
- It creates an opportunity for the trade company to upsell its time or premium services.
- It gives the trade buyer or company a labor advantage that differentiates it from competition, allows it to solve problems faster, or creates a better safety environment.

WHY IS THIS PILLAR IMPORTANT TO YOUR CUSTOMERS?

Why would it be important to the buyer for the supplier to have cutting-edge and exciting products and thus a competitive edge or labor advantage that differentiates it from the competition? Because:

- It makes the customer look good, like a leading-edge tradesperson, specifier, designer, craftsman, or whatever.
- It creates new selling opportunities, new customers, and new markets for the trade buyer or his company.
- It separates the customer from the pack.
- It provides the customer with higher profits, less hassle on the job, or opportunity cost over time, or it bolsters their reputation.
- It helps the trade company win more jobs, make more money, or solve its own customer problems more quickly.

By the way, the astute observer has already equated these answers to motives for the trade buyer. The reason it would be important to them is their motive, or their reason to buy.

HOW WOULD WE GET THIS PILLAR INTO OUR SELLING PROCESS?
Lastly, the salesperson needs to be thinking about how she could get this pillar into her sales process without being scripted in her approach. There are two key ways to do this: the first is to *provide evidence* of situations in which the pillar has had a positive impact on other customers, and the second is to speak to the importance of the pillar by *using the motives in her sales language.*

Here are some good examples of evidence for the innovation pillar:

• Use history and case studies, examples of past success.
• List all the Brands you sell and highlight their specific innovations.
• Get testimonials from satisfied customers.
• Show test results, show samples, and tell your story of innovation.
• Provide industry articles that highlight the innovative products.

What we have found in using this three-question approach with trade buyers is that you can now position your Brand pillars within the customer's world and get them into your Brand sales language. In short, the Brand Pillars become real very quickly, because you are thinking and talking from the customer's perspective. Now let's give you a chance to try this on for size.

Exercise, Part A: Identify a Brand pillar based on your experience with your company and its trade buyers. For the sake of this exercise, use one of these options to pick the pillar to work on:

1. This may be an intuitive process for you. If so, name the pillar and go for it.
2. If not, use one of the generic pillars from Figure 12.3.
3. If none of those pillars comes close to representing your Brand in the marketplace, then derive the pillar by asking yourself these three questions.
   • What does our product or service do for customers that no one else can duplicate? _____
   • If our company went away tomorrow, what would be missing in the marketplace? _____
   • What blockbuster product or service was a breakthrough for us in the last five to ten years? Why? _____

Our Brand pillar is _____

Exercise, Part B: Think of a customer type that you call on. Examples are distributors, retail stores, directors of maintenance, merchandise managers, purchasing agents, contractors, architects, parts buyers, specifying engineers, professional product users, and designers. (If it helps to be specific and name your customer here, feel free to do so.)

Customer type: _____

Exercise, Part C: Now, answer the three questions for that particular customer type.

1. What does this pillar mean to my customer type.

_____

_____

_____

2. Why is this pillar important to my customer?

_____

_____

_____

3. How would we get this pillar into our selling process?

_____

_____

_____

The answers derived from this exercise serve as a foundation for your Brand pillars.

The Multiplier Effect of Pillars

During Brand Selling workshops, we identify and drill down on a company's four pillars, one at a time, using this process. It is incredibly powerful to see the sales energy in the room build as we start getting to the heart of what your company does better than every other company in your industry within the marketplace. You see, the pillars are the best differentiator for your Brand, and, taken together, they have a multiplier effect. They form a rock-solid foundation for your selling efforts to the trade buyer.

Now take a look at Figure 12.4. The pillars are now stacked vertically, and they represent your Brand as columns of the Brand step of the Brand Staircase.

Taken together, these pillars create a formidable story to separate your company and its Brand from the competition. For instance, let's say for argument's sake that your four pillars were those shown in Figure 12.3 ("commitment to service," "technology solutions," "strategic locations," and "innovation").

As a salesperson, you now have choices.

You can ignore the pillars and go on selling the way you have always done; however, if you do this, what differentiates your Brand in the marketplace? You can also choose to sell from the position of only one of those pillars, and you might get a good amount of business but not drive customer loyalty. However, if you sold effectively from all of those pillars, as we have been discussing, who would want to compete against you? Not many people.

I believe that the Brand can stand on one pillar, yet it is more solid on all four. It reminds me of the stick analogy. If you try to break one stick on its own, it is not too difficult. However, if you try to break a bundle of sticks, it becomes very difficult, doesn't it? In the same way, the Brand pillars stacked together put you in a position to *sell the Brand first* and to *sell from Brand strength*.

PILLAR STACK

FIGURE 12.4

Common Debates over the Pillars

There are usually a number of questions to be answered concerning the pillars in a real-world selling situation.

WHAT HAPPENS WHEN ONE PILLAR IS CRUMBLING BEFORE YOUR EYES?

Let me answer that question with a customer story. One of my trade customers had acquired a number of small companies. The new divisions were struggling to measure up to the service-level requirements of better than 95 percent that the parent company was used to delivering in the marketplace. Interestingly, one of its pillars was "commitment to service." The sales team was struggling to believe and sell this pillar because the salespeople felt that all of the divisions should be at high service levels in order for the company to claim "commitment to service." The conversation that ensued was around the word *commitment*. That word says that we are striving to always get you product on time; it doesn't say that we are perfect and will get it right 100 percent of the time. However, if we do make a mistake, we will seek to make it right. If we don't currently live up to your shipping standards with these new additional lines, then we are committed over the long term to getting them to the same level as the parent company.

> Your Brand pillars cannot be based on couldas, shouldas, and wouldas.

In other words, as an organization of Brand salespeople, we can't get caught in the trap of saying things like

- "If only we coulda shipped that new product line with 95 percent service level like our parent company, then we coulda kept that customer."
- "If only we woulda brought that product to market sooner, we woulda taken some market share."
- "We shoulda known better than to promise innovation to the customers; we haven't had any new products for two years!"

You get the drift. Be resilient with your pillars, as Coca-Cola had to be when it changed its Coke offering (thus changing the Brand pillar "the formula") and yet was still able to bounce back, rename the product Coke Classic, and move forward. Or be like some companies that claim the pillar before they can actually deliver on the quality product.

You see, there will always be a reason for salespeople to complain that we don't have the right products to sell. Sell what you have to sell. Or, better yet, take a pillar and stand firm on it until it does become true to your customers.

WHAT ARE THE BEST TIPS ON HOW TO WORK THESE PILLARS INTO THE SALES INTERACTION?
- There is power in having all of the pillars support your selling effort.
- All the pillars together tell the Brand story.
- We purposely did not script your stories for you. You will be passionate about the stories that you have lived through and that your customers have experienced, connected to, or seen as an affiliation.
- It is important to take a long-term view of the pillars—not promising perfection, but rather making a commitment to strive to fulfill these pillars.
- Brands are becoming a key asset for companies, and that asset is best represented to the customer base by the pillars.

IF YOU HAVE NEVER IDENTIFIED THESE PILLARS BEFORE, THEN HOW DO YOU COME UP WITH THEM?
Most of the answer to this question will be saved for Chapter 13, "Building the Branded Culture," because it has implications for how the whole culture views the Brand. However, let me speak right here to the individual salesperson. In this book, you have received a bunch of sales tools and steps to help you think about and sell the Brand first. Go ask questions of your key customers to find out how they view the Brand and the things they would say that lead you to believe that they collectively have identified a Brand pillar. Use those tools tomorrow, after you are done reading. Remember that your customer's perception of the Brand is what matters the most, and that you can significantly affect that today by how you represent the Brand.

Telling Brand Stories

I'm sure you've heard the saying, "For everything there is a season. A time to sow and a time to reap. A time to laugh and a time to cry. . . ." It's the same with Brand stories. There is a time to *tell*, and a time to *ask*. The trade salesperson's challenge is knowing when to do which. We will deal with both of those here.

First and foremost, trade salespeople need to talk about the Brand and view it as an important part of their sales language. This Brand language is not just for consumer Brands. It clearly is a skill that transfers over to selling trade Brands and the solutions that you provide. You also need to talk about the trade Brand intentionally, in a way that is believable to the customer and fits in with his perception of your brand.

We spent some time in Chapter 10 on the need for storytelling in sales. That section is worth reviewing before entering into this discussion. The same skills that apply to consumer selling situations apply equally to trade selling situations when it comes to storytelling—skills like

Taking the TIME *to help customers migrate.*
- *T = testimonials*—satisfied users' statements about our Brand.
- *I = investigation*—gathering good evidence from buyers by asking Brand questions if you need to still uncover their motives.
- *M = motives*—finding out the key reasons that people buy from you in general and buy your Brand more specifically.
- *E = educate*—make someone knowledgeable about your Brand, why it exists in the market, what it stands for, how most buyers experience it, and so on.

Testimonials and education are a great example of comfortable Brand storytelling opportunities, whereas investigation and motives are great examples of Brand asking opportunities.

Overall, trade salespeople need to do a better job of communicating their company's unique Brand story. You must get comfortable with the success stories of your Brand in the marketplace, and make those stories part of your selling arsenal. This comes down to remembering good stories about your company and retelling those stories in the heat of battle. Remember that even for Trade brands,

> Everyone has a Brand story.
> The question is . . .
> Who is telling it?
> You or the competition?

You might be asking, "What happens when your Brand story isn't so rosy, when it seems that the Brand Staircase is breaking down? For instance, your company will not be launching that new product line for another year, or a key relationship has fallen apart, or your performance starts to drop?"

One of the best lessons I learned in selling was to stand by what you believe in, and continue to tell your Brand story even when your performance is falling and your world is crumbling. Such was the case when I was calling on a trade buyer for a key distributor. The company I sold for at the time was having a shipping problem on the accessories line. We were delivering at a 50 percent service level, which is unacceptable in any business, but especially in the category of product that drove the buyer's profitability, and ultimately his bonus and his paycheck.

I had already tried solving the problem by relying heavily on our good relationship and calling in "shipping favors" from our customer service team. However, our performance was becoming so bad that I was getting very concerned about losing the business. The buyer was getting particularly testy and had called me in for a line review meeting. I remember driving to see the customer and thinking, "I'm going to lose this business today!" My E^2KG was very low. Not a comfortable spot to be in.

When I arrived, the meeting started with five minutes of ranting and raving. I let the buyer vent, and when he finished, I went out on a limb and said, "Craig, our accessories probably do deserve to be kicked out today based on our shipping levels. I know our performance has been horrific on the product line, and I'm working as hard as I can to turn that around." I paused and he adamantly agreed.

"But let me tell you why you can't afford to do that. You know my company has one of the best and most promotable Brand names in the business. We are going to continue to drive demand with national advertising campaigns that will bring people into your dealers' stores. We also have the only full line of tools and accessories that will allow you to package the two together to increase your profitability in the category. We are dealing with a short-term problem here. We can and will fix it [the shipping]. I just don't want to see you make a short-term decision and suffer long-term pain by kicking us out. I am committed to making you profitable and to making you look good with this decision. Give me a shot at retaining this business and you won't regret it." I essentially had educated him on our Brand pillars, told our story, and tied into his motives of making a good decision and looking good in the long term.

I was fortunate to walk out of that distributor's office having retained the accessories business. It was one day that I intuitively got it right, told our story, and sold from Brand strength. Importantly, the lack of performance was overridden by the company's Brand pillars. I didn't know it at the time, but I had intuitively reacted to the heavy objections with the strength of the pillars and our Brand story. The pillars will stand the test of time, and they are the best place to go if one of the other steps is crumbling—be it product, relationship, or performance.

Practicing with Your Brand Stories

Now, take a moment, and go back to a situation where you succeeded in selling against another Brand. However, this time, see how many of the pillars tie directly into the story.

Exercise: Tell your Brand story using the Brand pillars you have identified for your company. They should support it nicely.

The best way of bringing the Brand story alive that I have seen is to
tie it into the pillars and use TIME to your advantage.

WHEN IS THE BEST TIME TO TELL THE BRAND STORY?

Rather than stating that there is a perfect time to tell your Brand story,
I like to say that there are proactive times and reactive times to tell the
story. My accessories Brand story came in a reactive mode during tough
objections with a developing customer. But maybe your story came during times of positive change with a loyal customer (see Table 12.1).

My general rule here on timing is this: the more loyal the customer
is, the more Brand storytelling you can do (proactive storytelling). The
more occassional or developing the customer is, the more often you
should ask Brand questions (reactive storytelling).

TABLE 12.1   Times to Tell the Trade Brand Story

Proactive	Reactive
Times of change	Heavy competition
Introduction of new products	Tough objections or problem solving
Loyal customers	Occasional or developing customers

Asking Brand Questions: When and Why

In Chapter 9, I made this statement about questions, "If there were only
one skill I could teach to salespeople (or leaders, for that matter), it would
be questioning and listening. Why? Because questions stimulate thought,
get information, and encourage people to talk. They also reveal your
curiosity, reflect that the person's opinion is important to you, and show
people that you care." This statement is equally true for trade salespeople.

As a matter of fact, questioning and listening may be even more
important for trade salespeople because of the repetitive call cycle and
the long-term relationships we have built with our trade buyers. We

lean on those relationships, we get comfortable with them, and sometimes our assumption filter kicks in and we stop asking good questions or think we already have the answers.

The best way to avoid these pitfalls is by engaging them in Brand questions. Let's define what they are first, and then discuss when and why you would use them.

Brand Questions: What They Are

As I mentioned at the beginning of this chapter, trade Brand selling differs in one very significant way from consumer Brand selling. That is, the way we get at the motives of individual consumers is through understanding their lifestyles. In contrast, the way we get to trade buyers' motives is by connecting them to your company's Brand pillars. Simply stated, Brand questions are a way to investigate the motives of a trade buyer by strategically asking a question that has two elements:

1. It includes a Brand pillar.
2. It validates a motive.

Brand questions are questions that are open-ended in format, but are targeted toward unveiling a Brand pillar, which is what differentiates you from the competition. They are also meant to bring out or validate a motive that would be helpful to the trade buyer. Your primary goal with a Brand question is to engage the buyer with the goal of migrating him toward his motive (see Figure 12.5).

For instance, when you ask the average trade salesperson what kind of questions she asks to secure business with her trade buyers, you will typically hear examples like these:

- "Tell me about your growth plans for this year."
- "What barriers, if any, are there that are preventing us from doing business together?"
- "How can we work together to develop your business?"
- "What product or SKU does best for you in this area, and why?"
- "What is it about our company that has you considering us for this opportunity?"
- "Why do you buy from the competition?"
- "What would it take to get you to switch over to our line of products?"

What's wrong with these typical questions?

1. The questions in and of themselves are not bad. Salespeople have used them in the past to open up conversation concerning the customer's goals and how they match up with the salesperson's prod-

MIGRATING TO MOTIVES

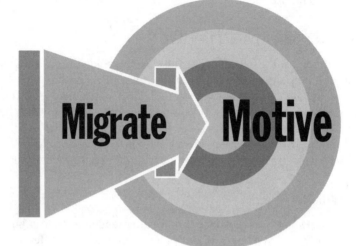

FIGURE 12.5

uct line offering. The problem is exactly that—the salesperson is generally starting at the Product line offering, which is as far away from talking about the Brand as you can be.

2. The questions are open in nature. This will allow the buyer to go in many different directions and answer what he feels like answering. The end result will be that the salesperson may get a lot of information that is irrelevant to her business or put herself in a position where she is unable to help the buyer.

3. Unfortunately, these questions are asked by almost every other salesperson on the planet. This does nothing to differentiate the salesperson from the many other competitive salespeople who call on this trade buyer on a daily basis.

Now, let's take just one of those typical questions and make it better as a Brand question. Assume in this case that our Brand pillar is "innovative solutions," and we want to validate the trade buyer's motive of "saving money" or "improving efficiency":

The Old *Question:* "How can we work together to develop your business?"

The New *Brand Question:* "How can we develop your business with our *innovative solutions* by working together to save you money or increase efficiency?"

Exercise: Compare the questions. In what ways is the second question more engaging?

_____

_____

Brand Questions: When and Why

An engaging Brand question does the following:

- It asks for information concerning the Brand pillars, which starts the conversation at the top of the Brand Staircase and sells downhill.
- It gives you relevant and pertinent information that ties specifically to one of your Brand's strengths.
- It immediately differentiates you simply by the question you asked. Also, it looks as if you put extra thought into the question (which you did) and what would be important to the buyer (motives).

Now, let's take some of those other sales questions and convert them into engaging Brand questions that specifically differentiate you from the competition. You will immediately see the difference. We will designate Brand questions as "new." It is your job to find the Brand pillar and motive in each.

Old: "Tell me about your growth plans for this year."

New: "Tell me how our excellent service could provide growth for your company, better productivity for your crews, and hassle-free delivery to all of your stores."

_____

Old: "What barriers, if any, are there that are preventing us from doing business together?"

New: "We have a strong commitment to service at our company. Based on that, how could we make your job easier with better delivery times?"

_____

Old: "What product or SKU does best for you in this area, and why?"

New: "We have excelled at innovating our products and services over the last few years. How can we work with your team to make you more profitable in your sales efforts to the end user?"

Old: "What is it about our company that has you considering us for this opportunity?"

New: "You mentioned that creativity (innovation) is important to you in considering new opportunities; in what way can we help you be creative on this current project?

Old: "Why do you buy from the competition?"

New: "Based on your past buying from the competition, I know that strategic service locations are important to you. Now that we're in place locally, where can we improve upon our service to increase your turns and ROI?"

Old: "What would it take to get you to switch over to our line of products?"

New: "Our technology (systems) allows you to order products on a 24/7 basis. How will that help you save time and money while keeping your inventory under control?"

Tips on Asking Brand Questions

1. Start with the buyer's mindset. On which step does he enter the staircase: Product, Relationship, or Performance? Remember, the further down the staircase toward product he is, the further he needs to migrate toward the Brand. Accordingly, a buyer who is far down the staircase is probably an occasional customer whom you don't know very well. This creates a strong need to ask questions that grow your knowledge of the customer, unveil your pillars to him, and at the same time speak to his motives.

2. Notice that the questions are meant to start an engaging conversation. They are meant to investigate, not interrogate. There is no need to plan for more than one or two well-placed Brand questions. Once the conversation is flowing, simply ask good follow-up questions and listen well. So "less is more" here, when it comes to the quantity of Brand questions.

3. Also, it is perfectly fine to make a statement about a Brand pillar and then follow up with a question about the trade buyer's motive(s). It is often easier for the listener to hear the fact or statement first, then listen for the accompanying question.

In summary, the benefit of asking a strong Brand question based on the pillars is that you engage the trade buyer early in a conversation that unveils what your company is best at (your Brand pillars) and is also tied into the main reasons that the buyer buys (her motives). The very fact that you are bringing those two things together is a testament to your wanting to serve the buyer with your "A" game—the best you have to offer. It also separates you from the pack.

Exercise on Migration: Putting It All Together

The case for migrating the trade buyer starts at the spot where the buyer enters the Brand Staircase—his mindset. Let's go back to what we learned in Chapter 8 when we first discussed migration for the individual consumer, but now we will tie it into the trade buyer scenario. The only difference here is that you now have new information about your trade buyer's purchase habits. That is, trade buyers buy based on Product, Relationship, and Performance.

Follow these directions:

1. Go back to the customer exercise in Table 8.1.
2. Look over your list of 15 customers. Double-check their level of business, and rerate them as necessary as loyal, developing, and occasional.
3. Now reclassify your customers' mindsets. This time write the word *Product*, *Relationship*, or *Performance* for each customer, indicating the primary step on which that customer enters the Trade Buyer Brand Staircase. You can even mark a customer as a Brand buyer if you can justify your rating.

Probable evidences of the buyer's mindset that will help you reclassify them:

Statement or action by the buyer:	*Indicates her buyer mindset*
• She lets you place the order without reviewing it.	Relationship
• "Just fax me the quote."	Product
• "If we have any problems with . . ."	Performance
• She tells others about you; she is your testimonial.	Brand
• "You've always taken care of me in the past."	Performance/ Relationship

4. Now for the challenging part. Answer these questions while looking over your newly analyzed data:

a. What trends do you find in your results?

_____

_____

b. Where do your loyal customers fall on the Trade Brand Staircase (see Figure 12.2)?

_____

_____

c. What would it take to move a customer from occasional to developing, or from developing to loyal?

_____

_____

_____

5. What customers are at risk, and why? Pick two customers that you feel may be at risk. Answer the remaining questions based on those two customers.

    a. Customer A: _____

    b. Customer B: _____

6. Ask yourself what evidence you have to justify the step that your customers are on. What have you heard them say? What have you seen them do? What might they do based on past buying behavior?

_____

_____

_____

7. Do these two customers need help migrating? Think of another time when you helped a customer migrate. What did you do that went well? Could you apply that same thinking to these customers?

_____

_____

_____

8. Pick one of the two customers to finish this exercise. Which of your company's Brand pillars are most appealing to this trade buyer? Why?

_____

_____

9. Create part of your *Brand story* to appeal to the *pillars* and the *motives* of this customer. Include testimonials, and educate the customer along the way.

_____

_____

_____

10. List two *Brand questions* that you would ask to *validate* that you have uncovered the buyer's *motives*. (This is especially important for developing or occasional customers.)

Question 1: Pillar _____ Motives _____

_____

Question 2: Pillar _____ Motives _____

_____

In my consulting, I have found that some major themes surface regarding the average trade sales territory and the collective salespeople's observations on customer loyalty and the Brand Staircase. Let me share those findings with you now. They have been summarized from actual session flipcharts following this exercise.

CUSTOMER LOYALTY OBSERVATIONS

- The majority of the customers are product-driven, and thus enter on the Product step of the staircase. In many cases they rely solely on Products.
- Occasional buyers are very product-driven, and thus are at risk. Decisions are generally based on price, exclusivity, or the "only available option."
- Relationships seem to drive loyal and developing customers; however, Performance is becoming a bigger factor in keeping loyal customers happy. Most reps feel that they have very solid Relationships.
- Loyal customers that buy based on Product were seen as heavily at risk.

- Customers are all on different steps, and they grow from Product to Performance, which takes time and energy. Product and Relationship lead to Performance; one builds on top of the other.

Now, if you are honest with yourself, as the workshop participants were, you probably have some work to do in order to migrate some key customers up toward the Brand. You also realize the importance of the other three steps in sustaining your business and putting you in a position to leverage and sell from your Brand. *In other words, we must never forget that if the first three steps—Product, Relationship, and Performance—are not kept intact, then the Brand will be seen as an empty promise.* As trade salespeople, we cannot afford to have that happen, for the Brand is indeed our great differentiator.

Key Points

Trade buyers *experience* the Brand and make *connections* to or *affiliations* with the Brand, just as consumers do with the consumer Brand Staircase. The difference is that salespeople can understand the individual consumer's Brand preferences through understanding that consumer's lifestyle choices. In contrast, salespeople can understand the trade buyer's Brand preferences and motives through communicating their company's Brand pillars.

The Brand pillars are defined as impenetrable advantages that differentiate your company from the competition. They are mentioned by customers, proven over time, convey common sense and become an intangible asset for your company. They are foundational aspects of your company that represent certain priorities, strategies, or operating advantages that bring value to the trade buyer's company. Trade buyers are most interested in vendors that supply those values. Thus, Brand pillars work for the salesperson as the main migration magnet to attract the trade buyer.

There are four action steps to selling to the trade buyer:

1. *Reverse the Trade Brand Staircase and sell the Brand first.* As in the consumer Brand Staircase, the steps on the Trade Brand Staircase need to be reversed so that the Brand is sold first.

2. *Identify the Brand pillars.* Identify them and work hard to get them into the solutions you provide and the questions you ask during the sales process.

3. *Tell Brand Stories.* Telling Brand stories is part of the Brand language of the trade salesperson. The *TIME* technique is again a

useful tool to help buyers migrate (*T = testimonials, I = investigation, M = motives, E = educate*).

4. *Ask Brand questions.* The right Brand questions get at the right Brand pillars. Ask the question so that it gets at what is important to the buyer in terms of company values, then provide a solution in your product and Brand offerings.

PART 6

IMPACT ON COMPANY CULTURE

CHAPTER 13

BUILDING THE BRANDED CULTURE

The implications of Brand selling for the culture of any organization are indeed huge. They are not taken lightly by me, my colleagues, or any of the organizations that LPD Inc. has been privileged to serve. Remember, when you start talking about the Brand, you are talking about the crown jewel of your company, the most valuable hidden asset that you can leverage. That is why this responsibility should be handled with extreme care, but not with kid gloves.

This chapter is meant to accomplish two things:

1. Discuss what the organization can do to enhance its hidden asset—the Brand.
2. Uncover how selling the Brand first should affect your organization and some internal and external moves that you can make to lay the vital groundwork for success.

Ultimately, those who have read this book will be fired up to start thinking about the changes they can implement to make their company a sell-the-Brand-first kind of place. The rewards are great for organizations that take the time and effort to instill the necessary knowledge and behaviors to make Brand selling happen.

Those of us who have worked in and around corporate cultures know that it takes time, commitment, and lots of energy to make positive and permanent changes in the culture. It could be likened to the old adage, "It's difficult to move a big ship in a small harbor." It can be cumbersome and tiring in some cases, or it can be invigorating and energizing in other cases. Here are the best tips that can be the stage setters for long-term culture change.

> ### BUILDING THE BRANDED CULTURE
> Buy-in
> Relationship
> Ambassadors
> No-nonsense approach
> Determination
> Equity
> Downhill selling

Buy-in Starts at the Top

If Brand selling is ultimately to be successful, it must start as high up in the organization as possible—hopefully at the C level (CEO, COO, CFO, president). I have been fortunate enough to work with people at all levels in firms ranging in size from small companies to members of the Fortune 500, and I have found the presence of key executives to be a tipping point for organizational buy-in.

The reason that this effort needs to start at the top is quite simple: when you mess with the firm's crown jewel—the Brand—you are bound to encounter turf wars between Sales and Marketing. This is natural and should be expected. If it happens, it is the job of senior management to intervene and be the tiebreaker, bringing the organization together around a key initiative that is critical to the long-term success of the company—that is, how it manages and articulates its Brand in the marketplace and to the customer base.

Also, the senior management team should be present and even included as guest speakers whenever the topic of the Brand is being communicated within the culture. This could be done, for instance, by inviting the CEO, the president, and/or the COO to present a short pitch at any Brand selling workshops, marketing product launches, or National sales meetings. This pitch sends a powerful message about the Brand that accomplishes three main things:

1. It welcomes the group of attendees and states the importance of the workshop or product launch from the beginning of the session. Many times the sales organization just needs to know that the top people are on board in order to start the buy-in process for itself.
2. It tells everyone present that the top people in the company are actively involved with and accountable for the Brand. Top executives "vote with their presence" when they show up and speak at a session.
3. It allows the top executives to declare their Brand and its Brand pillars, thus making a huge statement about their willingness to be

involved in the daily operations of the business. It also exposes them to the latest thinking of the field sales organization and their customer's voice. It is very similar to "management by wandering around."

Relationship between Sales and Marketing

Even when senior management has bought in, the Brand selling effort still needs to have a system in place for managing the conflicts that inevitably will arise between Sales and Marketing. There may still be an "elephant in the room" that needs to be addressed. In many organizations, Marketing and Sales are not on the same page with regard to the Brand. Often, their objectives are different, they are measured differently, and they have different views of what the Brand should do in the marketplace. To add to the complexity, the functions may be run by two different executives, one in charge of Sales and the other presiding over Marketing.

If you are a senior leader reading this, you might view getting Sales and Marketing onto the same page as a steep mountain to climb. If you find yourself at that spot, don't despair. Instead, challenge these parties to get on the same page with the Brand, and position yourself as the tiebreaker should a roadblock occur.

On the other hand, if you are fortunate enough to have a senior vice president of sales and marketing in charge of the Brand selling change effort, then it becomes an easier task because that vice president is responsible for both of these functional areas of the company's business. However, even then, management needs to be intentional about sending the "co-ownership message" early and often. At its core, that message says to the organization that these two disciplines are now going to build a different and better relationship around the Brand from the one they have had in the past. Importantly, the message needs to be clear about this new relationship and the joint ownership of the Brand.

One of my customers does this very well when the senior vice president of sales and marketing gives his pitch during the Brand Selling workshop. His main slide is simple:

- *Marketing* is the message we project to define our brand.
- *Execution* is how we perform in validating that message in the field with Sales.

He finishes by saying, "Marketing is communicating this message repetitively. Execution is performing this message consistently." He essentially has built a bridge between the two functions, with the focal point being the Brand. It is common ground that both parties can co-own, so that both are responsible for its impact in the marketplace. One big way to make it common ground is for the senior management team to proclaim it and sell it. Who owns the Brand now? Both parties!

Ambassadors within the Culture

Ambassadors constantly carry messages for the causes and the people that they represent. I was recently discussing ambassadorship and its connection between the Brand and the culture with Neil Rackham, author of *S.P.I.N. Selling*, and Sue Dunlap, a colleague who has worked diligently with me on the Business-to-Business Brand Selling workshop and process. Neil was sharing with us the work that he is currently doing at Northwestern University's Kellogg School of Business. He made an interesting comment and asked a great question about the Brand and its central position within the culture and the Sales and Marketing functions, respectively:

- "It is interesting that the Brand is clearly in a place where the sales and marketing teams can do a better job of baton passing."
- "What is the difference between representing the Brand and selling the Brand?"

He clearly hit on two of the core issues involving Brand selling that we have tried to articulate in this book. The Brand can be considered the "baton" that communicates between these two functions. The "Brand baton" needs to be passed between the functions on a regular basis, and it should become a vehicle to exchange customer feedback from the sales force with marketing communications material from the marketing team.

After one organization had identified its Brand pillars, the CEO explained that the pillars would unite the company. The pillars would be used in all of the marketing communications material: flyers, product introductions, Web site communications and structure. The company even decided to put the pillars literally on display within its show booth, using them as the actual pillars that hold up the booth! Now, when that message is coming from the top, do you believe that people come together in unity? Absolutely—by design and with intentionality.

Representing the Brand means a number of things within the culture:

- *Build ambassadors.* These are people who so represent the Brand that they live and breathe its message every day in the marketplace. Obviously your sales and marketing teams are the place to start. For instance, a $1 billion company I work with is educating both outside sales (who call directly on customers) and inside sales (who handle the phones and proactively take orders) with the same knowledge of the firm's Brand pillars and cornerstone.
- *Build brand touchpoints.* Although this language is generally overused in circles that study Brands, it is instructive when thinking about *ambassadorship.* To me, this means that anyone who touches the customer should be fully aware of and educated on the power of your Brand—the pillars, the Brand Staircase, and the relationship that the customers have with the sales team and the company. One of my customers, a division of a Fortune 100 company in the lighting and electrical products business, is educating all employees who touch the customer with a four-hour module on the Brand Staircase and the company's pillars. Many of these people are in functions other than Sales, yet they have a sufficient impact on the customer such that senior management saw immersing them in the fundamentals of understanding the Brand to be a wise choice.
- *Inoculate the culture.* The company culture needs to be immersed in this approach in order to build accountability. Also, reinforcement tools should be built into the process to keep the key concepts fresh and at the top of people's mind. In the lighting, aviation, and consumer goods businesses, LPD Inc. has educated and reinforced the initial learning with Webex reminders of key concepts. This serves to reacquaint the participants with key ideas and best practices and also acts as a "booster shot" for their learning. We also accumulate in-the-field success stories, great Brand questions, and customers' perception of the pillars. In all cases, these are hosted on the companies' intranet sites and serve as a constant reminder for veterans that the story of the Brand needs to continue to be reinforced and told within the culture.

No-Nonsense Approach

Throughout this book, we have talked about how Brands have penetrated our society and become a part of our daily living. For the average consumer buyer or trade buyer, Brands are now commonsense choices. They stand for your company's position in the marketplace and differentiate you from the competition. That said, this commonsense approach with the buyer should become a no-nonsense approach within the BRANDED culture.

That means that when companies are launching new products, they should intentionally include the Brand. When they are making choices that will affect the marketplace—such as price increases, line extensions, customer add-ons, end-user strategies, and consumer and trade advertising—they should be thinking about the Brand and how it will be affected in a no-nonsense way. This approach should even spill over to how the sales team is equipped to talk about the Brand.

For instance, LPD Inc. recently launched the Brand selling program with a top customer. The senior managers in this organization agreed to put every salesperson through the Brand selling workshop—all 120 of them—within a one-month period. The reason was to send a no-nonsense statement to the organization that basically said, "You can't afford to miss this; overnight we are going to create a Brand selling organization that will take the market by storm." Interestingly enough, this was the first time in their company's history that people within the company could remember being equipped so quickly to put into practice the skills they had learned at a workshop and thus create an immediate common language around the Brand. In the past, it would have taken a minimum of one year to get everyone on the same page.

Another example of a no-nonsense approach involved a company's mission statement. Let me ask, how many of you know your company's mission statement? I routinely ask participants in programs to tell me what their company's mission statement is without looking at the plaque in the conference room. As you can probably guess, no one gets it right. The reason is that most companies have mission statements that are a paragraph long and read something like this:

Our mission is to blah, blah, blah, focus on the customer, blah, blah, blah, blah, while improving market share, blah, blah, blah, investing in dynamic products, blah, blah, blah, servicing the industry, blah, blah, blah, blah, delivering shareholder value, blah, blah, blah, while valuing employees.

Now, please don't get me wrong; I believe in mission statements and company visions. They set the values for the company and set the direction in which it is headed. They also are very meaningful for the people who participated in building them in the first place and in articulating them within the culture. Unfortunately, not enough people participate in the building process.

However, I also believe that mission statements should be memorable and repeatable so that they really come alive in a culture. Unfortunately, most of them are neither. To battle this mission statement syndrome, one of my customer's key sales leaders stated this concerning the Brand pillars, "Aren't these Brand pillars really what our mission statement is all about? However, they are much easier to remember, focused on the customer, and really represent who we are, don't they?" The key points here are simple:

- Whenever possible, salespeople should be involved in the building of the Brand pillars from a customer perspective in order to understand their meaning and articulate them in the marketplace.
- If the Brand pillars could be more *visible* within all functions of your organization, then wouldn't it be easier to *visualize* what your company really stands for and communicate that to the customer.

Let's see, plaques or pillars? Which would be the best no-nonsense approach? Food for thought.

Determination to Include the Customer

By now you have a sense for my strong tendency to focus on the buyers/customers and their perceptions of the Brand, for those perceptions are the ones that really matter. A recent article in the *Harvard Business Review* by Ronald Rust and colleagues entitled "Customer-Centered Brand Management" puts it this way:

> *Brands exist to serve customers. But you'd never know that from the way Brands are managed. The problem is, for all that managers buy into this long-term customer focus, most have not bought into its logical implications. Listen to them talk, and you may hear customer, customer, customer. But watch them act, and you'll see the truth: It's all about the Brand. Brand management still trumps customer management in most large companies, and that focus is increasingly incompatible with growth" (p. 1).*

As leaders in the culture, you must be determined to help Brand management and customer management coexist. The challenge here is to help the Brand represent your company and align with the customer's perceptions at the same time. How do we do this?

- By building on the company's history and identifying your Brand pillars.
- By being persistent in the message about the Brand that you send to both sets of customers—internal and external.
- By encouraging storytelling around the Brand.
- By continually asking for customer input in a variety of ways: key user groups, distributors' councils, user focus groups, customer surveys, and customers speaking at sales meetings on how they would like to be sold. These customer forums are also a great place to clearly understand the customer's perception of your Brand pillars.

These things don't just happen by themselves. Senior management needs to show determination and resilience when it comes to connecting the customer intentionally to the Brand.

Tracy Bilbrough, president and CEO of Juno Lighting Group, a division of the Schneider Electric/Square D company, put the customer perspective very well in his presentation that opened the company's Brand Selling workshops. "We want to grab a piece of that customer's heart; no one else has captured that space, no one has positioned themselves yet. We have an opportunity to grab it first, to have the first mover advantage, like Volvo has become associated with Safety." He went on to conclude, "Product will always be king, so we need to continue to provide new and innovative products to the marketplace. However, the sales force will become our best marketing weapon. They will tell the customer what our Brand stands for . . . so they need to be equipped with what they should say consistently, day after day!"

Equity: Brand as the Hidden Asset

We have discussed how the Brand is becoming the one great differentiator that the competition cannot duplicate. We have also discussed how your Brand pillars remain hidden behind the sales curtain until you as salespeople are able to unveil them to the buyer. Until lately, the marketplace has not been bold enough to place a value on this hidden asset.

Today, the marketplace is beginning to recognize the Brand as a key asset, and it now attaches a value to how much a Brand delivers to a company's bottom line. Two of the world's most prominent business magazines have made bold statements about Brands and their equity potential. *Fortune* magazine said:

> "In the 21st Century, Branding ultimately will
> be the only unique differentiator between companies.
> Brand equity is now a key asset."

Fortune then reinforced its position with a recent article called *Breakaway Brands*. Partnering with Landor Associates, a Brand and design consulting firm in association with Brand Economics they asked 9,000 consumers what they thought of 2,500 Brands.

Landor mined a huge database of brand perceptions called the Brand Asset Valuator, *or* BAV, *to identify ten products that scored the largest increases in Brand strength from 2001–2004 . . . then calculated the pop in economic value each of these breakaway brands gave their parent companies. They looked at two major factors: Brand strength and Brand stature.*

- Brand strength—this is a combination of two properties:
  - *Differentiation* is the degree to which a Brand stands out.
  - *Relevance* is the degree to which consumers believe a Brand meets their needs

- Brand stature—again this is a combination of two properties:
  - *Esteem* is how well regarded the Brand is
  - *Knowledge* refers to whether the consumer understands it

The combination of these four factors led to identifying 10 Brands that broke away from the rest of the pack. The Brands included iPod, Leapfrog, Subway, DeWALT, Gerber, BP, Eggo, Sony, Sierra Mist and Google. The article then projected the value the company gained economically resulting from its BAV measure. It concluded

> *. . . BrandEconomics analysis found that companies with strong, well-regarded Brands had an intangible value of 250 percent of annual sales; companies with listless Brands had one of only 70 percent. In important ways, though, the value of a Brand is incalculable. A rising Brand secures more customer loyalty, higher margins, greater pricing flexibility, and new opportunities for growth.*

Suffice it to say, there is value in the hidden asset—the Brand.

Then *Forbes* came out with a study in conjunction with New York–based marketing consultants Vivaldi Partners. The study, part of its *Beyond the Balance Sheet: Brand Value* series,

> *began by surveying chief marketing officers and consumers, asking them to identify brands they felt were both growing fast and being innovative. Next they screened brand-owning companies that beat their peers in earnings growth. They then valued the remaining forty companies using a discounted cash flow model that also factored in the percentage of the business being driven by the brand.*

Instead of re-creating *Forbes*'s chart and unveiling the top 20 brands, I thought it might be more interesting to call out the subtleties behind this finding that point to the Brand equity trend I am talking about:

- How many times have you seen anyone try to measure the value of a Brand using a discounted cash flow model? In other words, when has the Brand ever had a true financial measurement attached to it within our business community? Based on what I've witnessed, not very often. You see, that's a big step, when we start applying some major accounting logic to what has been considered to be an emotional and largely intangible subject in the past.

- Would *Forbes and Fortune* magazines be investing in studies to determine the asset value (or contribution to cash flow) of a Brand if companies didn't have this squarely on their radar? No, they wouldn't. Brands are now being recognized as adding clear value as an asset. In your company's Brand(s), you now have a key asset that is just becoming visible in the marketplace. You should treat it like any other key asset, as a valuable part of your business and your future.

Downhill Selling

I will end this challenge to become a BRANDED culture by going back to the reversed Brand Staircase and the theme of this book—sell the Brand first. By now, whether you are primarily a consumer, trade, crossover, or service Brand seller, I hope that you are grounded in the vision of the Brand Staircase—that it has been fully implanted in your subconscious. Momentum is created when you sell the Brand first and start selling downhill. You can leverage your time, energy, and sales momentum until by the time you get to the bottom of the Staircase, the Price objection has nearly gone away or become a "value for the money" consideration, rather than a "your product is too expensive" buyer mentality.

I leave you with one question that you must now deal with if you are to individually contribute to the BRANDED culture:

If you only had 10 minutes to sell, what would you sell first?

Key Points

What does it take to bring about cultural change within an organization so that it is able to absorb the ideas and practices of Brand selling? This chapter provides tips for organizational decision makers who have bought into the concepts of Brand selling and want to integrate a Brand selling program in their company.

The stage setters for building the BRANDED culture:

- *Buy-in* means that the impetus for culture change has to start at the top, with the COO, the CEO, the CFO, and other senior executives endorsing and talking up the Brand advantage.
- *Relationship* means that both Sales and Marketing in your organization have to put aside their turf wars and jointly own and be responsible for the success of a Brand selling program.
- *Ambassadors* should be everyone who represents your Brand in the marketplace. This should include your salespeople, your resellers,

and your senior management, who should live and breathe the Brand and be able to discuss its virtues at a moment's notice.

- *No-nonsense approach* means that you take a commonsense approach to the Brand. Companies should intentionally include Brand. When marketplace choices are being made, Brand should be a major consideration. The sales team should always be equipped to talk about the Brand.

- *Determination* means that you should be singly focused on being able to manage Brand and customers at the same time. The challenge here is to help the Brand represent your company and align with the customers' perceptions at the same time.

- *Equity* means that Brand is becoming a key intangible asset in more and more companies and is gaining parity with other key assets. Soon it may no longer be considered a hidden asset.

- *Downhill selling* is the focus of this book. Sell the Brand first and watch the momentum pick up. You will not be pushing the ball uphill any longer. Instead, the ball will roll downhill—another way of saying your sales will be easier and more successful.

REFERENCES

CHAPTER 1

Davis, S. M., and Dunn, M.: *Building the Brand-Driven Business: Operationalize Your Brand to Drive Profitable Growth* (San Francisco: Jossey-Bass, 2002).

Silverstein, M. J., and Fiske, N.: *Trading Up: The New American Luxury* (New York: Portfolio, 2003).

Stobart, P. (ed.): *Brand Power* (New York: New York University Press, 1994).

CHAPTER 2

Davis, S. M., and Dunn, M.: *Building the Brand-Driven Business: Operationalize Your Brand to Drive Profitable Growth* (San Francisco: Jossey-Bass, 2002).

Gobé, M.: *Emotional Branding* (New York: Allworth Press, 2001).

Schultz, D., and Schultz, H.: *Brand Babble: Sense and Nonsense about Branding* (Mason, Ohio: South-Western Educational Publishers, 2003).

CHAPTER 3

Harkavy, M. D.: *100 Best Companies to Sell For* (New York: John Wiley, 1989).

Silverstein, M. J., and Fiske, N.: *Trading Up: The New American Luxury* (New York: Portfolio, 2003).

CHAPTER 4

Schultz, D., and Schultz, H.: *Brand Babble: Sense and Nonsense about Branding* (Mason, Ohio: South-Western Educational Publishers, 2003).

CHAPTER 5

Morrison, A., White, R. A., and Van Velsor, E.: *Breaking the Glass Ceiling: Can Women Reach the Top of America's Largest Corporations?* (Reading, Mass.: Addison-Wesley, 1994).

CHAPTER 8

Atkin, D.: *The Culting of Brands: When Customers Become True Believers* (New York: Portfolio, 2004).

Dolan, Robert J.: "The Black and Decker Corporation-Power Tools Division" (Harvard Business Case: field study #9-595-057, March 30, 1995).

Dolan, Robert J.: "Operation Sudden Impact" (Harvard Business Case: field study # 9-595-060, June 20, 1995).

CHAPTER 13

Badenhausen, K.: "Beyond the Balance Sheet: Brand Values," *Forbes*, June 20, 2005, pp. 115–119.

Ehrbar, A.: "Breakaway Brands: How to Build a Breakaway Brand," *Fortune*, October 31, 2005, pp. 153–170.

Rackham, N. *S.P.I.N. Selling: Situation. Problem. Implication. Need-Payoff* (New York: McGraw-Hill, 1988).

Rust, R. T., Zeithaml, V. A., and Lemon, K. L.: "Customer-Centered Brand Management," *Harvard Business Review*, September 2004.

INDEX

ABOUT THE AUTHOR

Dan Stiff has been successful within the profession of selling for close to 30 years. Currently, he operates his own training and consulting company called LPD Inc.—Leadership Performance Development, Inc.—which develops, conducts, and certifies training programs for executives, leaders, experienced sales professionals, and college graduates. Previous to this, Dan built his career around various sales and leadership roles at NCR, Black & Decker and its subsidiary DeWALT. He then led the training organization at Black & Decker / DeWALT, where developing leaders and coaching salespeople were the key focus areas. Dan is an experienced salesperson, leader, and practitioner who understands the issues and problems facing salespeople and their leaders today.

LPD Inc., founded in 1999, develops and delivers customized workshops to thousands of participants on the topics of leadership, sales performance, and development of people. Dan has trained over 12,000 business executives as a consultant, director, leader, and sales trainer. He also operates in collaboration with other sales and training professionals in conducting small to large-scale workshops, tailored to the client's needs. He personally covers a customer base of over 600 attendees a year, and LPD Inc. facilitators have engaged customers in widely dispersed industries including:

Chemicals	Industrial distribution / MRO	Energy
Aviation parts	Retail stores	Entertainment
Technical temp. services	Electrical lighting	Computers
Decorative hardware	Windows / coverings	Insurance
Industrial tools	Pharmaceuticals	Medical
Food service	Professional paint / sundry	Accounting
Hardware / tools	Telecommunications	Banking

LDP's Brand Selling workshop and the ideas associated with *Selling the Brand First*, were created after witnessing many salespeople struggle with conventional sales methods that did not work. Dan engages the customers with a specialized approach to their issues and shows how the Brand affects their culture.

Additionally, he has mentored and counseled sales leaders and executives throughout his career. Dan has recruited on major college campuses to hire job candidates into top companies. He has taught salespeople—rookies, veterans, and masters alike—to challenge, motivate, and improve their sales mindsets and skill sets.

He is an independent contractor for the Ken Blanchard Companies and is certified in several major leadership training and development programs, including Situational Leadership. He also enjoys a strong working relationship with the Center for Creative Leadership, rated number one by Business Week for the last six years for its Leadership Development Program.

Dan holds an undergraduate degree in Business Marketing / Education from Montana State University. He is a twelve-year member and past Director of the Sales and Marketing Trainers Association. He is a member of the Strategic Accounts Management Association (SAMA). Additionally, Dan actively contributes to his community by assisting in the Sandtown Habitat for Humanity and in leadership roles within his local church. He, his wife, and two sons reside in Baltimore, Maryland.

Should you desire more information on these business applications please contact:

LPD Inc.
Dan Stiff, President
10 Farm Ridge Ct.
Baldwin, MD. 21013
dstiff@lpdinc.com